POC

WILD FLOWERS
OF THE
MEDITERRANEAN

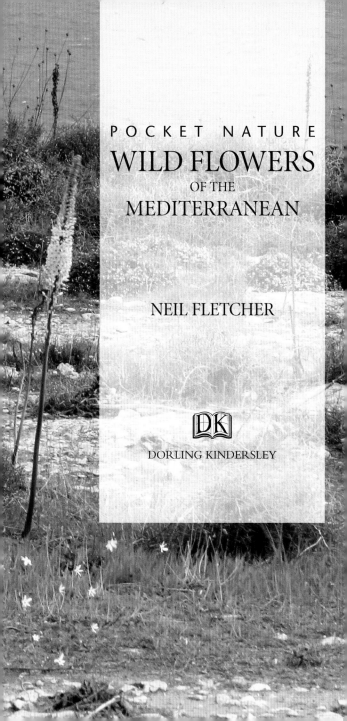

POCKET NATURE
WILD FLOWERS
OF THE
MEDITERRANEAN

NEIL FLETCHER

DK

DORLING KINDERSLEY

LONDON, NEW YORK, MUNICH,
MELBOURNE, AND DELHI

DK DELHI
Project Editor Glenda Fernandes
Senior Editor Dipali Singh
Editors Saloni Talwar, Ankush Saikia,
Rohan Sinha
Project Designer Kavita Dutta
Designers Enosh Francis, Neerja Rawat
DTP Coordinator Pankaj Sharma
DTP Designers Govind Mittal,
Pushpak Tyagi, Harish Aggarwal
Head of Publishing Aparna Sharma

DK LONDON
Senior Art Editor Ina Stradins
Senior Editor Angeles Gavira Guerrero
Project Editor Rebecca Warren
DTP Designer Laragh Kedwell
Picture Editor Neil Fletcher
Illustrator Gill Tomblin
Production Controller Inderjit Bhullar
Managing Art Editor Phil Ormerod
Managing Editor Sarah Larter
Art Director Bryn Walls
Reference Publisher Jonathan Metcalf

First published in Great Britain in 2007 by
Dorling Kindersley Limited
80 Strand, London WC2R 0RL

A Penguin Company

Copyright © 2007
Dorling Kindersley Limited

ISBN 978-1-4053-1813-6

Reproduced by Colourscan, Singapore
Printed and bound in China by Sheck Wah Tong
Printing Press Ltd.

Disclaimer Culinary, herbal, or medicinal uses
mentioned in the book are purely anecdotal.
They are not recommendations of the author or
the publisher and should not be undertaken.

see our complete catalogue at
www.dk.com

CONTENTS

How this book works

This guide covers the 307 most commonly seen wild flower species in the Mediterranean region. At the beginning of the book is a short introduction which focuses on the process of identification in the field. For ease of access, the species are then organized into five chapters based on flower colour: White, Pink-Red, Purple-Blue, Green-Brown, and Yellow. Within these colour groups the flowers are broadly organized by family, so that similar plants are kept together for ease of comparison.

SCIENTIFIC NAME

▽ GROUP
INTRODUCTIONS
Each of the five chapters opens with an introductory page describing the group's shared characteristics. Photographs of representative species show the diversity in the group.

HABITAT PICTURE
Shows the species in its natural habitat.

HABITAT CAPTION
Describes the habitat or range of habitats in which you are likely to find the plant.

INHABITS *dry grassland, roadsides, garigue, pastures, and open woodland, particularly on limestone soil.*

SCALE DRAWING
To give an indication of the plant's height, a drawing of the plant is set next to an illustration that represents this guide. See panel top right.

DETAIL PICTURES
These tinted boxes show individual parts of the plant in greater detail, and may include leaves, flowers, or fruit.

White

In spring, white is one of the most common flower colours: the comparatively few insect pollinators that are in flight at this time are attracted to the striking contrast of the flower against the foliage. Pale flower colour can also help moths to locate flowers at night. This chapter also incorporates flowers that have other colours mixed with white, such as pink in Starry Clover, yellow in Crown Daisy, or purple in the Riviera Crocus.

138

Cu
Cata

Cupid
its bri
dry gr
Chico
the de
the fl
dark e

leaf with
narrow
lobes

dark cen
flowerhe

PLANT HEIGHT 40–80cm.
FLOWER SIZE Up to 6cm wide
FLOWERING TIME June–Sept
LEAVES Almost linear, with sm
FRUIT Achene with narrow sca
DISTRIBUTION W. Mediterrane
SIMILAR SPECIES Chicory (p.
Lettuce (below); C. lutea has y

Blu
Lactu

The b
for th
often

FOUND *on rocky or stony ground, alongside old walls, and other dry habitats, on limestone.*

▷ SINGLE-PAGE
ENTRIES
Species that exhibit greater or more complex features, or are of special interest, are given a full page.

NOTES
Describe striking or unique features that will aid identification, or provide interesting background information. **Please note:** *Culinary, herbal, or medicinal uses mentioned are purely anecdotal. They are not recommendations of the author or the publisher and should not be undertaken.*

Hoary Stock
Matthiola incana (BRASSICACEAE)

This is a robust plant with a branched and woody base, and with a similar habit to the yellow-flowered Wallflower (p.176). Like the Wallflower it has been cultivated for use as a garden plant, though its strikingly coloured flowers occur quite freely in wild plants. They may be pure white, bright purple, or the petals may be streaked with both colours, often with all three colour forms growing together. The leaves are densely covered with very fine hairs which give them a frosted appearance, the name *incana* comes from the Latin *incanus*, meaning hoary, or hairy.

purple or white flowers

compact, bushy habit

grey, narrow leaf-foil

PLANT HEIGHT 30–80cm.
FLOWER SIZE 3cm wide.
FLOWERING TIME February–May.
LEAVES Oblong, hairy, narrow and usually untoothed.
FRUIT Narrow, curved siliqua, up to 12cm long.
DISTRIBUTION Throughout the region.
SIMILAR SPECIES Sea Stock (M. sinuata), which has leaves that are lobed or toothed.

▽ SPECIES ENTRIES

The typical page describes two wild flower species. Each entry follows the same easy-to-access structure. All have one main photograph of the species, which is taken in the plant's natural setting in the wild. This is supported by one or more detail pictures that show the individual parts of the plant in close-up. Annotations, scale artworks, and a data box add key information and complete the entry.

SCALE MEASUREMENTS
Two small scale drawings are placed next to each other in every entry as a rough indication of plant size. The drawing of the book represents this guide, which is 19cm high. The plant illustration is an accurate drawing of the species featured in the entry. The scale represents average height.

Book height
19cm

Average plant height
20cm

CHAPTER HEADING

E-BLUE

one

caerulea (Asteraceae)

n eye-catching plant of late summer, when flowers shine out among the surrounding a much neater plant than the similar), but may always be identified by ass-like translucent bracts below , each with a ein.

papery, translucent bracts

lue ray orets

COMMON NAME

FAMILY NAME

DESCRIPTION
Conveys the main features and distinguishing characteristics of the species.

PHOTOGRAPHS
Illustrate the plant in its natural setting.

ANNOTATION
Characteristic features of the species are picked out in the annotation.

COLOUR BANDS
Bands are colour-coded, with a different colour for each of the five chapters.

SCALE LABEL
The label under the scale artwork indicates the growth habit or life cycle of the plant.
ANNUAL *The plant completes its life cycle in a single year and then dies.*
BIENNIAL *The plant germinates in the first year, then flowers, fruits, and dies in the second year.*
PERENNIAL *The plant survives and flowers year after year, over-wintering above or below ground.*

ettuce

anis (Asteraceae)

: flowers of this plant may easily go unseen, en only during the early morning and are to two or three hours before midday in sunny weather. It is a rather weak, straggly plant, with mostly basal leaves that are finely divided into narrow, toothed lobes, and which exude a milky latex when cut.

strap-shaped ray florets

owerheads branched usters

long, narrow buds

narrow, toothed leaflets

PERENNIAL

flowerhead of 12–20 florets

PLANT HEIGHT *30–80cm.*
FLOWER SIZE *Up to 3cm wide.*
FLOWERING TIME *April–July.*
LEAVES *Pinnate, grey-green with a pale midrib.*
FRUIT *Achene with a pappus of rough hair.*
DISTRIBUTION *Throughout W. Mediterranean.*
SIMILAR SPECIES *Cupidone (above); Salsify (p.99) with pinker flowers; and Chicory (p.137).*

OTHER KEY INFORMATION
These coloured panels provide consistent information on the following points:
PLANT HEIGHT: *the plant's height range.*
FLOWER SIZE: *the length or width of the flowers or flowerheads.*
FLOWERING TIME: *the months during which the plant produces flowers.*
LEAVES: *a brief description of the leaves, giving leaf arrangement, shape, surface or margin features, and, where of interest, colour.*
FRUIT: *a brief description of the fruit, giving fruit type and, where of note, colour, and size.*
DISTRIBUTION: *a brief description of where the plant occurs within the Western Mediterranean region.*
SIMILAR SPECIES: *lists plant that look similar to the featured species, often describing a distinguishing feature.*

Anatomy

Flowering plants have evolved in different ways to cope with a wide variety of local conditions, adopting different lifestyles and developing different physical characteristics in order to compete for resources. Some plants, for example, are annuals, others perennials or biennials; most get their energy from photosynthesis, but some parasitize other plants or adopt a carnivorous lifestyle; some use tendrils to climb up towards the light, others develop tall stems to rise above surrounding vegetation. Each plant part has a specific function. For the vast majority, the leaves are the food factories that enable the plant to store energy; the roots provide anchorage and absorb water and essential minerals; and the flowers are the plant's reproductive parts. Using the correct terms will add precision to your descriptions and help identification.

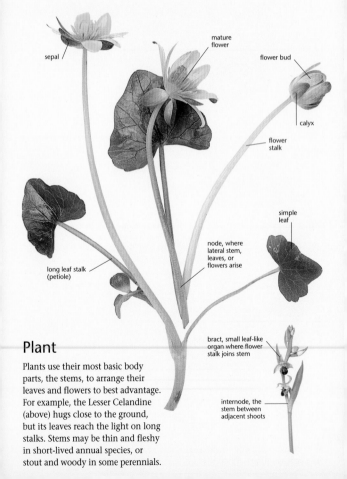

sepal

mature flower

flower bud

calyx

flower stalk

simple leaf

node, where lateral stem, leaves, or flowers arise

long leaf stalk (petiole)

bract, small leaf-like organ where flower stalk joins stem

internode, the stem between adjacent shoots

Plant

Plants use their most basic body parts, the stems, to arrange their leaves and flowers to best advantage. For example, the Lesser Celandine (above) hugs close to the ground, but its leaves reach the light on long stalks. Stems may be thin and fleshy in short-lived annual species, or stout and woody in some perennials.

Flower

All parts of the flower work together to promote fertilization. The female ovary, found at the base of the style and stigma, is fertilized by the pollen, which is produced by the male anthers. The sepals, collectively known as the calyx, and petals surround and protect the reproductive parts. Flowerheads are made up of small flowers called florets. Insects pick up pollen and distribute it to the stigmas of other flowers.

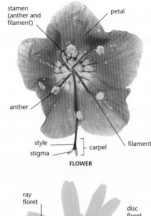

stamen (anther and filament)
petal
anther
style
stigma
carpel
filament

FLOWER

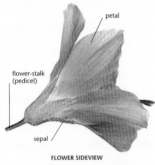

petal
flower-stalk (pedicel)
sepal

FLOWER SIDEVIEW

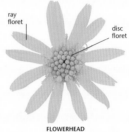

ray floret
disc floret

FLOWERHEAD

midrib (central vein)
leaf stalk (petiole)
veins

LEAF

Leaf

Green chlorophyll in the leaves harnesses the sun's energy to manufacture sugars and sustain growth. Leaf shape and stem arrangement evolve to maximize available light, and reduce water loss. For example, lower leaves often have a long stalk, while leaves higher up the plant may be smaller and stalkless, so as not to shade those below.

Fruit and Seed

Once the ovary has been fertilized, a fruit forms around one or many of the developing seeds. The fruit covering protects the seed as it develops, and often plays a role in its effective dispersal. For instance, an achene may have feathered hair to aid wind dispersal, pods and capsules split open when the seeds are ripe, and fleshy fruit such as berries attract animals to eat them as a dispersal strategy.

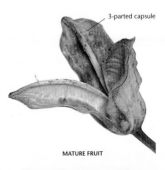

3-parted capsule

MATURE FRUIT

Identification

The flower form or the leaf type alone may be enough to pinpoint a species but, generally, this kind of identification comes with experience. As a beginner, it is important to note all features, including habitat or flowering season, before deciding upon a precise identification.

Growth

Habit is a term used to describe a plant's overall form or mode of growth. The height of individual plants may be affected by such factors as grazing or mowing, but the habit will usually remain the same throughout the species.

STEMLESS

TUFTED

PROSTRATE

TRAILING

CLIMBING

SPREADING

ERECT

SHRUB

TREE

Flowers

Flowers are an obvious plant feature, and their colour can assist identification, but be aware of those species that exist in several colour forms. Also note how the flowers are clustered, and the form and number of petals and sepals.

FLOWER ARRANGEMENT

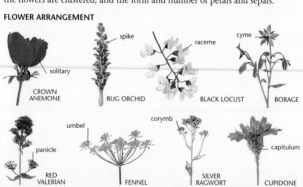

spike

raceme

cyme

solitary

CROWN ANEMONE

BUG ORCHID

BLACK LOCUST

BORAGE

panicle

umbel

corymb

capitulum

RED VALERIAN

FENNEL

SILVER RAGWORT

CUPIDONE

FLOWER FEATURES

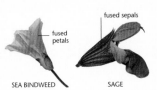

ST. JOHN'S WORT

SEA BINDWEED

SAGE

YELLOW BEE ORCHID

Leaves

Assess the colour, texture, and shape of the leaves, how they are divided, whether they have toothed margins, and how they are arranged on the stem. Remember that lower leaves may differ from those above.

LEAF SHAPES

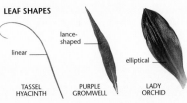

TASSEL HYACINTH

PURPLE GROMWELL

LADY ORCHID

RED VALERIAN

SEA BINDWEED

SMILAX

ARISTOLOCHIA PISTOLOCHIA

JUDAS TREE

DISC MEDICK

CASTOR OIL PLANT

CROWN VETCH

RED STAR THISTLE

WILD CARROT

CLARY

ROMAN NETTLE

LEAF ARRANGEMENT

TUBEROUS COMFREY

GREATER PERIWINKLE

LONICERA IMPLEXA

Fruit

Fruit occur in a huge variety of forms. Closely-related species often develop fruit of a similar type, thus the slight differences between them may be key identification characters. Fruit may also be a useful diagnostic feature if the plant is discovered after the flowers have faded and disappeared.

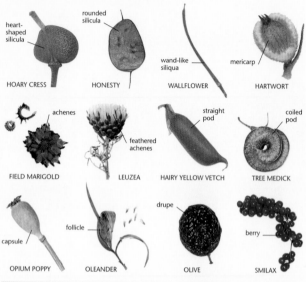

heart-shaped silicula

HOARY CRESS

rounded silicula

HONESTY

wand-like siliqua

WALLFLOWER

mericarp

HARTWORT

achenes

FIELD MARIGOLD

feathered achenes

LEUZEA

straight pod

HAIRY YELLOW VETCH

coiled pod

TREE MEDICK

capsule

OPIUM POPPY

follicle

OLEANDER

drupe

OLIVE

berry

SMILAX

Seasons

Even though the green parts of the plant are visible for a much longer period than the flowers, the time of flowering can still provide major clues to a species' identity. In general, plants will flower earlier in warm, sheltered locations, or later at higher altitudes.

SIMILAR FLOWERS
Galactites (left) flowers earlier than the late summer Red Star Thistle (right), but their seasons can overlap.

Distribution

It may be useful to take account of where a species normally occurs, as this can often eliminate potential mis-identification. However, note that sometimes a species may be found outside its normal range, as a vagrant or garden escape, although not usually in large quantities.

THYMUS CAPITATUS
Found throughout the Western Mediterranean region, except that it is absent from France.

THYMUS VULGARIS
Occurs in Spain, S. France and Italy, but not in Portugal. It is naturalized in the Balearic Islands.

Habitat

Habitat categories can be defined by: land-forms, such as mountains, coast or lowlands; vegetation, such as grassland or woodland; and human management, such as past or present grazing, farming, or forestry practices.

CONIFEROUS WOODLAND
Luezea can tolerate the semi-shade of pine woods.

BROAD LEAVED WOODLAND
Tuberous Comfrey prefers damp and shady areas.

SALT MARSHES
Sea Purslane is able to tolerate the salt-laden inundation of these sites.

CULTIVATED GROUND
The tenacious Bermuda Buttercup proliferates in ploughed soil.

SANDY AND ROCKY SHORES
Sea Rocket thrives on dry, coastal sands.

MAQUIS
Myrtle is one of the trees that characterizes this dense, shrubby habitat.

GARIGUE
Globe Thistle is one of the many grazing-resistant plants to thrive here.

GRASSY GROUND AND WAYSIDES
Red Vetchling requires the support of grasses to grow.

Soil

Soil types are crucial in determining which plant species can grow where. Basic – lime-rich or chalky – soils generally support a greater diversity of species than other soils: their alkaline chemistry provides more nutrients.

WELL-DRAINED
Felty Germander is one of the plant species that has adapted to dry, sandy soil with poor water-retention.

POORLY DRAINED
Birthwort prefers the moist, sheltered conditions of drainage ditches or alongside old walls.

ACID
French Lavender is able to tolerate the low nutrient levels of acidic, sandy soil.

NEUTRAL
Spotted Deadnettle prefers neutral pH soil conditions that are neither too acidic nor too alkaline.

BASIC
Common Lavender is one of the many flowers that grow abundantly on calcium-rich chalk or limestone soil.

White

In spring, white is one of the most common flower colours; the comparatively few insect pollinators that are in flight at this time are attracted to the striking contrast of the flower against the foliage. Pale flower colour can also help moths to locate flowers at night. This chapter also incorporates flowers that have other colours mixed with white, such as pink in Starry Clover, yellow in Crown Daisy, or purple in the Riviera Crocus.

JUPITER'S BEARD   WHITE ROCK-ROSE   WHITE GERMAN IRIS   GUM CISTUS

American Pokeweed

Phytolacca americana (Phytolaccaceae)

Originally, a native of North America, this vigorous and robust weed has become established in waste places throughout the Mediterranean. It produces spiked racemes of flowers, with five small white petals and a green ovary in the centre that enlarges and becomes dark purple as the fruit matures.

OCCURS *in waste places, rubbish tips, in gardens or near cemeteries, often where there is rubble.*

large leaves

green and white flowers

leaf with toothed margin

reddish stems

PERENNIAL

PLANT HEIGHT *1–2.5m.*
FLOWER SIZE *5–6mm wide.*
FLOWERING TIME *June–October.*
LEAVES *Elliptical, 1–2.5cm long, untoothed, ripening from green to purple.*
FRUIT *Slightly ribbed berry, 1cm wide.*
DISTRIBUTION *Throughout the region.*
SIMILAR SPECIES *None.*

Paronychia argentea

Paronychia argentea (Caryophyllaceae)

This is a mat-forming plant with small, pointed leaves in opposite pairs on trailing stems. The papery-looking flowers have five tiny, bristly pointed sepals and no petals. They are easily recognized by the large silvery, translucent bracts, which look a little like crumpled cellophane. The name *argentea* comes from the Latin word for silver, referring to the bracts.

FORMS *mats in dry, sandy places such as dunes or along the edges of coastal tracks.*

yellow-centred flower

PERENNIAL

silvery bracts around flower

small, simple leaf

PLANT HEIGHT *5–10cm.*
FLOWER SIZE *0.8–1cm wide.*
FLOWERING TIME *March–June.*
LEAVES *Oblong, grey-green turning reddish.*
FRUIT *Simple achene.*
DISTRIBUTION *Throughout the region.*
SIMILAR SPECIES *P. capitata, which has hairier leaves but is very difficult to separate.*

Fragrant Clematis

Clematis flammula (Ranunculaceae)

This deciduous, woody climber is equally at home scrambling over the ground and low vegetation as it is climbing up a tree. The ribbed stems and leaf stalks are sensitive to touch and quickly wrap themselves around any object for support. The creamy white flowers grow in loose clusters and are highly fragrant. They are more delicate than the flowers of Traveller's Joy (*C. vitalba*), which is also common in the region, and retain their narrow white sepals for longer.

SPRAWLS *over ground and over hedges and bushes, or climbs up walls and trees, in semi-shaded places and open woods.*

leaflets in groups of 3

4 or 5 white sepals

PERENNIAL

flowers in clusters

numerous stamens

NOTE

The word Clematis comes originally from the Greek word klema, *meaning tendril; the Latin word* flammula *means little flame, referring to the flowers with several upright stamens.*

PLANT HEIGHT *Up to 4m.*
FLOWER SIZE *3cm wide.*
FLOWERING TIME *May–August.*
LEAVES *Groups of three spear-shaped, twice-divided leaflets.*
FRUIT *Flattened achene with very feathery plume.*
DISTRIBUTION *Throughout the region.*
SIMILAR SPECIES *Traveller's Joy* (C. vitalba), *which is unscented, with slightly toothed, once-divided leaves.*

Caper

Capparis spinosa (Capparidaceae)

A sprawling shrub, Caper is woody at the base but has
weak, floppy stems that trail over the ground. It is also
somewhat spiny, though not on all the shoots. As the
spines makes picking the caper buds rather difficult, a
spineless variety is grown commercially for harvesting.
The leaves are very distinctive: dark green and leathery,
they are round or paddle-shaped. The flowers are
equally characteristic, with four white petals
and four reddish or greenish sepals, and
long red or purple stamens arranged like
a brush. They open early in the
morning but often fade by midday.

OCCURS *as isolated
bushes on rocky places,
at the foot of old walls
and cliffs, usually
close to the sea.*

PERENNIAL

protruding style

numerous red-
tipped stamens

leaf with
rounded tip

dark red
bud

PLANT HEIGHT *30–100cm.*
FLOWER SIZE *5–7cm wide.*
FLOWERING TIME *May–July.*
LEAVES *Alternate, rounded, leathery, with a short stalk.*
FRUIT *Green or yellow berry, up to 5cm long.*
DISTRIBUTION *Throughout the region.*
SIMILAR SPECIES *C. ovata, which has narrower, spear-shaped leaves
that are spine-tipped.*

NOTE

*The unopened buds
(capers) of this plant
are not only pickled
in oil, brine, or
vinegar and used as
a condiment, but
have also been
effective as a
treatment to prevent
cataracts of the eye.*

Italian Catchfly

Silene italica (Caryophyllaceae)

The petals of this plant are usually tightly in-rolled during the daytime, so that only the red-veined sepals and petal undersides are visible, and the plant may easily go unnoticed. However, the petals unfurl fully in the evening and are faintly scented to attract pollinating moths. They remain open until the early morning, but furl up again when the sun shines directly upon them. The stems of this plant are covered with short, sticky hair.

FLOURISHES *on roadsides, cultivated or fallow land, rocky slopes, and crevices, on dry or chalky soil. Usually close to light shade.*

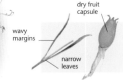

dry fruit capsule

wavy margins

narrow leaves

calyx-tube with red veins

deeply lobed petals

PERENNIAL

PLANT HEIGHT *Up to 60cm.*
FLOWER SIZE *1.4–2cm wide.*
FLOWERING TIME *April–July.*
LEAVES *Opposite pairs, lance-shaped, hairy.*
FRUIT *Capsule split by six teeth.*
DISTRIBUTION *Throughout the region.*
SIMILAR SPECIES *Bladder Campion (S. vulgaris), which has grossly inflated sepals.*

Ramping Fumitory

Fumaria capreolata (Papaveraceae)

This scrambling and climbing plant has dense spikes of creamy white flowers with reddish purple tips. Each flower is a complex shape made up of four petals forming two lips, with a pouch or spur at the base, and two almost transparent sepals on either side. The plant is rarely visited by insects and the flowers are usually self-pollinated. Despite appearances, fumitories are closely related to poppies.

CLIMBS *on old walls or hedges on cultivated or waste ground, often in the semi-shade.*

wedge-shaped leaf lobes

ANNUAL

dark-tipped flowers

flowers curve downwards as they mature

PLANT HEIGHT *20–100cm.*
FLOWER SIZE *1–1.4cm long.*
FLOWERING TIME *March–June.*
LEAVES *Alternate; pale greyish green lobes.*
FRUIT *Smooth capsule, 2.5mm wide.*
DISTRIBUTION *Throughout the region.*
SIMILAR SPECIES *Common Fumitory (p.64), which has more erect, deep pink flowers.*

Sweet Alison

Lobularia maritima (Brassicaceae)

This spreading plant is often cultivated in gardens as an annual bedding plant, where it forms rounded cushions of white, pink, or purple flowers. In the wild however, the flowers, which are sweetly scented, are always white with a pink-tinged centre, and the plant tends to grow rather more upright and straggly. The leaves often have a greyish look, due to a fine covering of hair.

SPREADS *over dry ground in sandy or rocky places on hillsides or waste ground, often close to the sea.*

flowers in tight clusters

pinkish centre to flowers

untoothed leaves

PERENNIAL

stems branch at base

PLANT HEIGHT *10–30cm.*
FLOWER SIZE *4–5mm wide.*
FLOWERING TIME *April–September.*
LEAVES *Alternate, linear to lance-shaped.*
FRUIT *Egg-shaped silicula, 3.5mm long.*
DISTRIBUTION *Throughout the region.*
SIMILAR SPECIES *Wild Candytuft (Iberis amara), which has unequal petals.*

Annual Candytuft

Iberis pinnata (Brassicaceae)

Candytufts (*Iberis* species) are easily recognized by the outer petals of each flower, which are longer than the inner ones, giving them a "rabbit-eared" look. Annual Candytuft, however, may be identified by its white or pink round-topped flower clusters, and very narrow, oblong leaves which are pinnately divided, unlike the unlobed leaves of the other candytufts.

GROWS *in fields and on dry, rocky hillsides; where the ground is disturbed or cultivated. Prefers limestone or chalky soil.*

unequal-sized petals

ANNUAL

flowers in dense clusters

pink-tinged white flowers

PLANT HEIGHT *10–40cm.*
FLOWER SIZE *6–8mm wide.*
FLOWERING TIME *April–July.*
LEAVES *Alternate, with 2–6 linear segments.*
FRUIT *Almost square silicula, 5–6mm long.*
DISTRIBUTION *Throughout the region.*
SIMILAR SPECIES *Other species have unlobed leaves.*

Hoary Cress

Cardaria draba (Brassicaceae)

GROWS *in drifts along roadways, trackways, and on cultivated and disturbed ground, on chalky or neutral soil, and often on the coast.*

NOTE

This species belongs to a group of plants known as pepperworts – the leaves were used for flavouring food before the discovery of pepper.

The foaming mass of tiny creamy white flowers borne on many-branched stems, gives Hoary Cress a frosted appearance. It often forms attractive drifts, particularly along roadsides. Each tiny flower has four white petals, and eventually develops into a heart-shaped fruit, but has the rather unpleasant odour of cabbages. The toothed, greyish leaves are slightly succulent in texture, and clasp the stem with downward-pointing lobes. In recent years it has become an increasingly common plant in regions outside of its southern European home, spread initially by the movement of troops in the early nineteenth century.

PERENNIAL

flowers in clusters

unstalked stem leaves

white petals

heart-shaped fruit

PLANT HEIGHT *30–80cm.*
FLOWER SIZE *5–6mm wide.*
FLOWERING TIME *February–June.*
LEAVES *Alternate, oval, coarsely toothed; basal leaves may be untoothed.*
FRUIT *Heart-shaped silicula, 3–4mm long.*
DISTRIBUTION *Throughout the region.*
SIMILAR SPECIES *Dittander (Lepidium latifolium), which is taller with leathery, finely-toothed leaves, and grows on marshy ground.*

Corn Mignonette

Reseda phyteuma (Resedaceae)

A low-growing plant, Corn Mignonette is rather inconspicuous, but nevertheless common and widespread, especially on cultivated land. The tiny flowers have six white petals, each of which is finely divided into narrow, "frilly" lobes. The six green sepals form a star-shaped backdrop to the flower, and each has a whitish margin created by a covering of very fine hair. The unripe stamens droop downwards, with the large pale brown anthers creating a "beard" effect, but as they ripen, the stamens swing upwards to bring the pollen within reach of visiting insects.

FLOURISHES *on cultivated, disturbed, and waste ground, on roadsides and field margins, and in olive groves and vineyards. Prefers open, sunny areas and bare soil.*

NOTE

The leaves are edible, and may be used as a pot-herb, but the yield is very poor for the effort involved in plucking them.

six green sepals

ANNUAL

drooping unripe anthers

frilly tufts to petals

leaf usually unlobed

persistent calyx

pendant fruit capsule

wavy leaf margin

PLANT HEIGHT *10–40cm.*
FLOWER SIZE *6–10mm wide.*
FLOWERING TIME *April–July.*
LEAVES *Oblong, mostly unlobed or with one or two lobes near the base.*
FRUIT *Nodding, oblong capsule with three points at apex.*
DISTRIBUTION *Throughout the region.*
SIMILAR SPECIES *Mignonette (R. odorata), which has sweetly scented flowers and occurs in the eastern Mediterranean region.*

White Mignonette

Reseda alba (Resedaceae)

FOUND *on disturbed and waste ground, waysides, and dry, rocky places inland or near the coast.*

White Mignonette is a much taller, bushier plant than Corn Mignonette (p.21). The white, lobed petals curl around the unopened flower-buds like fingers, and unfurl to reveal about 20 prominent stamens. The leaves are shiny dark green and much divided, with 10 to 15 pairs of wavy lobes and a prominent midrib. The oblong fruit capsules remain erect on the tall stems after flowering.

lance-shaped lobes

pale green midrib

ANNUAL/PERENNIAL

prominent creamy stamens

erect fruit

PLANT HEIGHT *30–80cm.*
FLOWER SIZE *8–9mm wide.*
FLOWERING TIME *March–September.*
LEAVES *Alternate, pinnately cut.*
FRUIT *Erect, elliptical four-angled capsule.*
DISTRIBUTION *Throughout the region.*
SIMILAR SPECIES *Wild Mignonette (p.175), which has yellow flowers.*

Navelwort

Umbilicus rupestris (Crassulaceae)

GROWS *on cliffs, rocky outcrops, old walls, and stony banks, from sea-level up to 2,500m.*

The coin-shaped leaves of this plant are very characteristic, being fleshy and circular, with a dimple in the centre of each leaf where the stem joins underneath. The tall flowering spikes are also disctinctive, with many drooping flowers, each with a five-parted tube. The colour of the flowers varies from cream or green to deep pink.

long, tapered spike

dimple in centre

shallowly lobed leaf margin

PERENNIAL

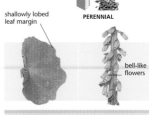

bell-like flowers

PLANT HEIGHT *15–40cm.*
FLOWER SIZE *8–10mm long.*
FLOWERING TIME *June–August.*
LEAVES *Basal rosettes, circular, fleshy.*
FRUIT *Group of follicles with tiny seeds.*
DISTRIBUTION *Throughout the region.*
SIMILAR SPECIES *U. horizontalis, which has leafier stems and smaller stalkless leaves.*

Dog Rose

Rosa canina (Rosaceae)

Perhaps one of the prettiest wildflowers to grace the countryside in early summer, the Dog Rose has long, arching, thorn-covered stems; it clambers over bushes and hedges or occasionally forms free-standing bushes. The stems and leaves are free from any hair or glands, and the thorns are hooked at the end like an eagle's beak. The scentless flowers have five white petals that are usually flushed with pale pink, setting off the numerous yellow stamens. The styles form a small dome, rather than a column, in the centre of the flower.

SCRAMBLES *over hedges and bushes, along woodland margins, and in rough, scrubby, grassy places.*

PERENNIAL

pink-flushed petals

numerous yellow stamens

coarsely toothed margins

pinnately divided leaflets

oval red rosehip

NOTE

The hips have long been used in commercial preparations to ease coughs and sore throats; they may also be fermented to make wine.

PLANT HEIGHT *1–2.5cm.*
FLOWER SIZE *4–5cm wide.*
FLOWERING TIME *June–July.*
LEAVES *Alternate, with long stipules attached to the leaf stalk.*
FRUIT *Oval to round red hips.*
DISTRIBUTION *Throughout the region.*
SIMILAR SPECIES *R. sempervirens (p.24), which has a column-shaped style.*

Rosa sempervirens

Rosa sempervirens (Rosaceae)

FOUND *in hedges, open woods, roadsides, waste ground, and scrub, and often near the coast.*

This evergreen, wild rose species has a bushy habit with long, clambering stems that are only sparsely spined. The leaves are divided into three to seven leaflets, with a slightly leathery texture and glossy surface. Each white flower has a column-shaped style in the centre.

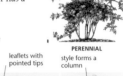

PERENNIAL

glossy leaflets

flowers in loose clusters

leaflets with pointed tips

style forms a column

PLANT HEIGHT *1–5m.*
FLOWER SIZE *2.5–4cm wide.*
FLOWERING TIME *March–July.*
LEAVES *Pinnate, leathery, and shiny.*
FRUIT *Egg-shaped red hip, 1cm long.*
DISTRIBUTUION *Throughout the region.*
SIMILAR SPECIES *Dog Rose (p.23); other roses do not have columnar styles.*

Azarole

Crataegus azarolus (Rosaceae)

OCCURS *in a variety of wooded or scrubby habitats, roadsides, and hillsides.*

A native to the Mediterranean, this small tree or shrub has spiny shoots that are hairy when young. The white or faintly pink-tinged flowers are found in loose, rounded clusters scattered over the branches. The leaves are glossy green above and downy when young. The leaf lobes are narrow at the base and large-toothed at the tips.

narrow leaf lobes

spines on older twigs

PERENNIAL

5 rounded petals

flowers in small clusters

PLANT HEIGHT *3–10m.*
FLOWER SIZE *1.5–2cm.*
FLOWERING TIME *March–May.*
LEAVES *Oval, divided into 3–5 narrow lobes.*
FRUIT *Oval berry, orange-red or yellow.*
DISTRIBUTION *Throughout the region.*
SIMILAR SPECIES *Hawthorn (C. monogyna), which has broader leaflets and smaller flowers.*

Black Locust

Robinia pseudacacia (Fabaceae)

Although originating from North America, Black Locust is so widely planted in the Mediterranean region that this large tree with abundant hanging flower racemes is a common sight in spring. The pea-like flowers are scented and have white petals and reddish sepals. The pinnate leaves are divided into regular oval leaflets. The spine-like stipules at the base of the leaves have given rise to its alternative name of False Acacia. The fruit of this tree is a flattened pod.

PLANTED on roadsides to stabilize light, sandy soil, but naturalized in woods and abandoned, scrubby places.

oval leaflets

PERENNIAL

pendant racemes of flowers

NOTE

The wood of Black Locust is close-grained, dense, and hard. It is used for fence-posts and floors, and for ship-building as it has a considerable resistance to decay.

pairs of leaflets

red calyx

PLANT HEIGHT *Up to 25m.*
FLOWER SIZE *1.5–2cm.*
FLOWERING TIME *April–June.*
LEAVES *Pinnate, with 4–10 pairs of oval leaflets.*
FRUIT *Brown, flattened pod up to 10cm long.*
DISTRIBUTION *Throughout the region.*
SIMILAR SPECIES *Robinia viscosa, which has pink flowers, and is occasionally planted in the region.*

White Melilot

Melilotus alba (Fabaceae)

PROLIFERATES *in open fields, uncultivated and waste land, and roadsides; also thrives in vineyards and olive groves.*

Straggly and rather untidy looking, White Melilot is a very common plant in the region. It is sometimes grown as a fodder crop and it acts as an excellent green manure, improving the nitrogen content of the soil. Its white pea-flowers are clustered into long spikes at the tips of the stems, which are slender and hairless. The spikes nearly always contain unopened buds as well as those that have gone to seed. The scattered leaves are alternately arranged and each leaf is divided into three rather long, toothed leaflets. The leaves smell of newly mown hay.

unopened buds at tip

untidy flower-spikes

ANNUAL/BIENNIAL

small flowers

oval leaflet

NOTE

The fresh leaves and young shoots may be eaten, raw or cooked, but the presence of coumarin in the dried leaves, which gives them their pleasant smell, makes them toxic.

PLANT HEIGHT *0.5–1.5m.*
FLOWER SIZE *4mm long.*
FLOWERING TIME *May–August.*
LEAVES *Alternate, with narrow, gently toothed margins.*
FRUIT *Small grey-brown pod, containing one seed.*
DISTRIBUTION *Throughout the region.*
SIMILAR SPECIES *Ribbed Melilot (M. officinalis), which has yellow flowers; however, it is not common in the region.*

Star Clover

Trifolium stellatum (Fabaceae)

When in flower and seen en masse, this low, spreading plant appears like mist lying over the ground. Each tiny flower is partially hidden by the long calyx-teeth of the sepals, and is pink in bud, maturing to white as it opens. When in fruit, each calyx opens out completely making the flowerhead look like a crimson, starry ball. The stems and leaves are covered with soft hair, each leaf in the typical clover shape, but with a silvery, dark-veined stipule at the base.

FORMS *carpets in grassy cultivated and waste land, fields, roadsides, and stony ground, avoiding very dry areas.*

ANNUAL

flowerheads mature from pink to white

trifoliate leaf

starry calyx in fruit

rounded flowerhead

veined stipules

NOTE

This Mediterranean plant occurs in just one site in Great Britain – Shoreham in Sussex, where it has been since 1804, when it was accidentally carried in ballast from a ship visiting the harbour.

PLANT HEIGHT *8–20cm.*
FLOWER SIZE *Flowerhead 2.5cm wide.*
FLOWERING TIME *March–July.*
LEAVES *Divided into three heart-shaped leaflets.*
FRUIT *Pod hidden within the star-shaped calyx.*
DISTRIBUTION *Throughout the region.*
SIMILAR SPECIES *T. cherleri, which is rather similar in flower, but without the starry calyx in fruit.*

Dorycnium

Dorycnium hirsutum (Fabaceae)

INHABITS *rocky, grassy or sandy places, maquis, and garigue. Occurs in the open or in light woodland, where it may grow taller.*

A spreading plant, Dorycnium often forms small, shrubby mounds, which appear grey-green, due to the dense covering of hair on the leaves and stems. Each leaf is divided into five elliptical leaflets, but with the basal leaflets flanking the stem, much like stipules. Borne in tight clusters at the end of the stems, the flowers are white but the red-tipped hairy sepals give them a pinkish hue.

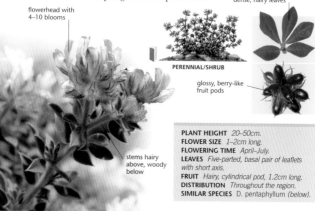

flowerhead with 4–10 blooms

dense, hairy leaves

PERENNIAL/SHRUB

glossy, berry-like fruit pods

stems hairy above, woody below

PLANT HEIGHT	20–50cm.
FLOWER SIZE	1–2cm long.
FLOWERING TIME	April–July.
LEAVES	Five-parted, basal pair of leaflets with short axis.
FRUIT	Hairy, cylindrical pod, 1.2cm long.
DISTRIBUTION	Throughout the region.
SIMILAR SPECIES	D. pentaphyllum (below).

Dorycnium pentaphyllum

Dorycnium pentaphyllum (Fabaceae)

FORMS *in dry, rocky places, maquis, or garigue; often where there is light shade.*

This plant is similar in form to Dorycnium, but has a finer and more graceful habit. The leaves are also five-parted, but the leaflets all arise from the same point and are much more slender, like five fingers. The flowers are smaller, born from a hairy calyx which is less strongly marked. The berry-like pods are also smaller, clustered together and turning brown when ripe.

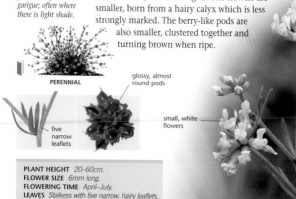

PERENNIAL

glossy, almost round pods

five narrow leaflets

small, white flowers

PLANT HEIGHT	20–60cm.
FLOWER SIZE	6mm long.
FLOWERING TIME	April–July.
LEAVES	Stalkless with five narrow, hairy leaflets.
FRUIT	Egg-shaped pod, glossy green ripening brown.
DISTRIBUTION	Throughout the region.
SIMILAR SPECIES	D. hirsutum (above).

stalkless leaves

Jupiter's Beard

Anthyllis barba-jovis (Fabaceae)

A striking and unmistakable shrub of coastal regions, Jupiter's Beard is tall and often rather straggly, with a coarse and woody stem that branches towards the top of the plant. The leaves are pinnate with several pairs of fairly narrow leaflets, densely covered on their undersides with silvery hair, which gives the margins of the uppersides a halo effect. The upper stems are also felted with silver hair. The creamy white flowers are clustered together as they are in the Clover *(Trifolium)* species, but with a ruff of narrow bracts beneath them. The plant's frothy, silvery appearance is said to resemble the beard of Jupiter.

GROWS *in cultivated areas or rocky cliffs and roadsides next to the coast, often in association with* Smilax aspera *(p.159).*

PERENNIAL

NOTE

Most members of the pea family produce large seed pods of characteristic shapes, but Anthyllis *produces a tiny pod which remains hidden within the hairy calyx.*

round clusters of flowers

silver-haired stems

numerous pairs of small leaflets

narrow bracts

PLANT HEIGHT 0.8–1.8m.
FLOWER SIZE 9–11mm long.
FLOWERING TIME April–June.
LEAVES Pinnately divided, silvery below.
FRUIT Pod enclosed within calyx.
DISTRIBUTION Throughout the region.
SIMILAR SPECIES A. cytisoides, which has trifoliate leaves, from Southern France westwards.

Orange

Citrus sinensis (Rutaceae)

Many *Citrus* species are cultivated in the Mediterranean, having originated in Asia, but the common, unmistakable Orange is perhaps the most widespread. The fragrant, pinkish white flowers hang in small clusters and have five petals and up to 20 stamens. The flowers are often present at the same time as the ripening fruit.

FOUND *in orchards, gardens, abandoned settlements, and small village squares.*

hanging flower clusters

ripened fruit

elliptical leaves

PERENNIAL

rounded fruit

PLANT HEIGHT *Up to 10m.*
FLOWER SIZE *1–1.5cm wide.*
FLOWERING TIME *January–December.*
LEAVES *Elliptical, rounded base, winged stalk.*
FRUIT *Orange berry, 7–12cm wide.*
DISTRIBUTION *Throughout the region.*
SIMILAR SPECIES *Seville Orange (C. aurantium), which has a rough skin.*

Daphne gnidium

Daphne gnidium (Thymelaeaceae)

This evergreen shrub has erect stems branched only at the base, and dense foliage. At first sight, the smooth leaves and upswept appearance give the impression of the Large Mediterranean Spurge (p.150), but this plant produces small white, four-petalled flowers followed by red to black berries. The whole plant is extremely poisonous.

OCCURS *in rocky places such as garigue, maquis, open woods, and scrub, often as widely scattered bushes.*

stalkless leaves

flower clusters at stem-tips

PERENNIAL

4 white petals

large red berry

PLANT HEIGHT *0.5–2m.*
FLOWER SIZE *4–6mm wide.*
FLOWERING TIME *March–October.*
LEAVES *Narrow, leathery, and bluish green.*
FRUIT *Red berry, 1–1.5cm wide.*
DISTRIBUTION *Throughout the region.*
SIMILAR SPECIES *Spurge Laurel (p.156), which has drooping green flowers.*

Gum Cistus

Cistus ladanifer (Cistaceae)

This shrub is one of the largest and most impressive types of *Cistus* growing in the Mediterranean. It has long, narrow leaves, which are pale grey-green and delicately veined beneath, but are dark, glossy green on top, with a very sticky surface that often becomes dulled with trapped dust. They give off a strong but pleasant fragrance if crushed. The flowers are large and very distinctive, with five tissuepaper-like white petals, each with a conspicuous purple blotch at the base, and numerous yellow stamens in the centre. Sometimes a completely unspotted form of this plant may be found, and both forms may be seen growing together.

GROWS *in maquis, garigue, open pine woods, and dry hillsides, avoiding limestone and preferring sandier soil.*

PERENNIAL

purple blotch

yellow stamens

lance-shaped leaves

central vein

crumpled white petals

NOTE

In hot weather the sticky hair on the leaf surface produce a highly scented oily resin called Ladanum (not to be confused with the opium-distillate Laudanum), which is used in perfumery.

PLANT HEIGHT *Up to 2.5m.*
FLOWER SIZE *7–10cm wide.*
FLOWERING TIME *April–June.*
LEAVES *Narrow, lance-shaped, sticky and glossy above.*
FRUIT *Capsule with 10 chambers.*
DISTRIBUTION *Portugal, Spain, S. France, and N.W. Africa.*
SIMILAR SPECIES *Narrow-leaved Cistus (p.32) and C. clusii, which have flowers that are only 3cm wide.*

Narrow-leaved Cistus

Cistus monspeliensis (Cistaceae)

GROWS *in scrubby, rocky places, open maquis, and typically in garigue; prefers acid soil.*

At first sight, this plant is similar to the unspotted form of Gum Cistus (p.31), but the flowers are considerably smaller, and produced in clusters of up to eight. The leaves, reddish stems, and flower buds are covered in glandular hair that produce a sticky resin, which is very difficult to remove from the fingers.

pure white petals

narrow, glossy green leaves

PERENNIAL

flowers in clusters

yellow stamens

PLANT HEIGHT	*40–100cm.*
FLOWER SIZE	*2–3cm wide.*
FLOWERING TIME	*April–June.*
LEAVES	*Opposite, lance-shaped.*
FRUIT	*Ten-chambered capsule.*
DISTRIBUTION	*Throughout the region.*
SIMILAR SPECIES	*Gum Cistus (p.31), which has flowers up to 10cm wide.*

Sage-leaved Cistus

Cistus salvifolius (Cistaceae)

OCCURS *in garigue, rocky places, stony dry hillsides, open maquis, and woodland clearings, especially of pine.*

This shrub is one of the most common *Cistus* species in the region, and has a very faint aroma. Like Narrow-leaved Cistus (above, the white flowers are borne in clusters, but the leaves are quite different, being oval with undulating edges and a hairy surface.

white petals

wrinkled leaf

PERENNIAL

numerous yellow stamens

flowers in clusters

PLANT HEIGHT	*30–100cm.*
FLOWER SIZE	*Up to 5cm wide.*
FLOWERING TIME	*April–June.*
LEAVES	*Hairy on both sides, with wavy edges.*
FRUIT	*Hairy capsule, 8mm long.*
DISTRIBUTION	*Throughout the region.*
SIMILAR SPECIES	*C. populifolius, which has hairless leaves with a heart-shaped base.*

White Rock-rose

Helianthemum apenninum (Cistaceae)

A much smaller and more delicate plant than the *Cistus* species, White Rock-rose often forms spreading colonies. It has thin, wiry stems that are covered with fine white hair. The stalked flowers have five strongly veined flower sepals, three of which are large and two very small.

THRIVES *in grassy and rocky habitats, either as single plants or forming a large colony, usually in the open.*

rounded petals

drooping flower buds

5 sepals

inrolled margins

PERENNIAL

PLANT HEIGHT *15–30cm.*
FLOWER SIZE *1.5–2.5cm.*
FLOWERING TIME *May–July.*
LEAVES *Opposite, linear to lance-shaped.*
FRUIT *Three-chambered capsule.*
DISTRIBUTION *Throughout the region.*
SIMILAR SPECIES *A form with pink petals grows in the Balearic Islands and N.W. Italy.*

Myrtle

Myrtus communis (Myrtaceae)

This medium-sized evergreen shrub is highly valued for its fragrant leaves and flowers, and its oil is used in perfumery. Its stalkless, dark green leaves are glossy above and duller below, with an inset central vein. The flowers, borne on long stalks, have five white, rounded white petals and numerous brush-like stamens, which are also white in colour.

GROWS *in damp spots in maquis, open woods, roadsides, or near the coast.*

leathery leaf

numerous white stamens

PERENNIAL

rounded petals

globular buds

PLANT HEIGHT *1–4m.*
FLOWER SIZE *2–3cm wide.*
FLOWERING TIME *May–August.*
LEAVES *Opposite, oval, and pointed.*
FRUIT *Oblong blue-black berry.*
DISTRIBUTION *Throughout the region.*
SIMILAR SPECIES *M. communis subsp. tarentina, which has narrower leaves.*

Wild Carrot

Daucus carota (Apiaceae)

This is one of the easiest members of the carrot family to identify, even though it is highly variable and there are many subspecies. The umbels of flowers are domed at first, then flatten out, but there is almost always a single dark purple flower in the centre of the umbel. In fruit, the umbel closes up into a ball, resembling a bird's nest.

INHABITS *grassy and waste places, roadsides, dry cliffs, and field margins. Prefers dry, open situations, often near the coast.*

finely divided leaves

lace-like umbels fan out

dense fruit clusters

ANNUAL/BIENNIAL

PLANT HEIGHT *30–100cm.*
FLOWER SIZE *Umbels 5–10cm wide.*
FLOWERING TIME *March–September.*
LEAVES *Alternate, finely divided, fern-like.*
FRUIT *Two-parted mericarp, 2–4mm long.*
DISTRIBUTION *Throughout the region.*
SIMILAR SPECIES *D. muricatus, which has fruit with rows of silvery spines.*

Hartwort

Tordylium maximum (Apiaceae)

A common and widespread member of the carrot family, Hartwort is not very notable for its flowers, which are in small, flat-topped umbels. The fruit however, is rather more noticeable. Each mericarp is a bristly, flattened green disc with a white, thickened ridge, so that it resembles a miniature tart. The umbel curves inward as the fruit matures. The lower leaves have oval, toothed segments, while the upper have narrower segments.

INHABITS *cultivated, fallow, and waste ground, along roadsides, seashores, and occasionally rocky ground; in full sun.*

upper leaf with narrow segments

ANNUAL

ridged stems

mericarp with thickened margin

small flowerhead with unequal petals

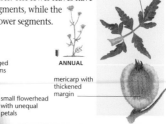

PLANT HEIGHT *40–100cm.*
FLOWER SIZE *Umbels 2–4cm wide.*
FLOWERING TIME *April–July.*
LEAVES *Pinnate, bristly hairy.*
FRUIT *Disc-shaped mericarp, 5–8mm long.*
DISTRIBUTION *Throughout the region.*
SIMILAR SPECIES *T. apulum, which has larger flowers.*

Tree Heath

Erica arborea (Ericaceae)

This evergreen tree, with an upright to spreading head, usually has several main stems and is often shrubby. It has a rather upswept appearance, with woody older stems, and younger stems covered in woolly hair. The slender, needle-like, bright green leaves are densely arranged in whorls of three or four on the upright, hairy shoots. Carried on the short side shoots, the small, short-stalked, honey-scented flowers are white, fading to brown. The fruit is small, brown, and dry, containing many tiny seeds. Several forms are cultivated in gardens; a shrubby form, *E. arborea* var. *alpina*, is grown in gardens for its ability to withstand hard frost.

OCCURS *in maquis, evergreen woods, rocky hillsides, and embankments, usually close to other trees, on acid soil.*

pyramidal spikes

tiny white flowers

PERENNIAL

shrubby, spreading habit

NOTE
Traditionally, wood from the roots of this tree was used to make briar pipes in S. Europe; "briar" comes from bruyère, French for heather.

PLANT HEIGHT *1–4m.*
FLOWER SIZE *2.5–4mm long.*
FLOWERING TIME *February–June.*
LEAVES *Needle-like, 5mm long, in whorls of three or four.*
FRUIT *Small brown capsule containing many seeds.*
DISTRIBUTION *Throughout the region.*
SIMILAR SPECIES *Spanish Heath (E. australis), which has purple flowers; Portuguese Heath (E. lusitanica), which has larger, pink-tinged flowers.*

Strawberry Tree

Arbutus unedo (Ericaceae)

OCCURS *in maquis, rocky slopes, evergreen scrub, and woodland margins; generally on acid soil.*

This small tree or shrub is very characteristic of Mediterranean maquis woodland. A member of the heather family, it has clusters of drooping urn- or bell-shaped flowers, typical of the family. The fissured, flaking bark is dull red-brown in colour. The delicious-looking fruit resembles a strawberry or, more closely, a lychee fruit, but they are poor in taste – as indicated by its name *unedo,* which means "I eat only one".

PERENNIAL

bell-like flowers

toothed leaf margins

fruit with pimpled surface

glossy leaves

drooping flower clusters

NOTE

The fruit may be insipid, but contains a high percentage of sugar, and may be used to make jams or preserves. The wood is very hard and used for turning or for making good-quality charcoal.

PLANT HEIGHT *2–10m.*
FLOWER SIZE *8mm long.*
FLOWERING TIME *October–March.*
LEAVES *Alternate, elliptical, glossy with serrated margins.*
FRUIT *Rounded berry, ripening from yellow to scarlet.*
DISTRIBUTION *Throughout the region.*
SIMILAR SPECIES *Greek Strawberry Tree (A. andrachne), of the E. Mediterranean region, which has brightly coloured bark.*

Bristly-fruited Silkweed

Gomphocarpus fruticosus (Asclepiadaceae)

Introduced to the region from southern Africa, this plant is now widely cultivated for its ornamental value. The long, narrow leaves sweep upwards, with clusters of creamy white flowers drooping down from their axils. Each flower has five white petals and a cluster of pinkish scales in the centre. The bristle-covered fruit turn orange-yellow in late summer.

GROWS *in damp waste ground, rocky water-courses, and riverbanks; often near to the coast.*

PERENNIAL

narrow leaves

reddish stems

umbels of white flowers

bristly fruit

PLANT HEIGHT *1–2m.*
FLOWER SIZE *1.5cm wide.*
FLOWERING TIME *May–August.*
LEAVES *Lance-shaped leaves, in whorls of 3.*
FRUIT *Egg or boat-shaped, 4–6cm long.*
DISTRIBUTION *Throughout the region.*
SIMILAR SPECIES *Swallow-wort (Vincetoxicum hirundinaria), which has smaller flowers.*

Heliotrope

Heliotropium europaeum (Boraginaceae)

A rather diminutive arable weed, Heliotrope produces flowers in a long coil, which gradually unfurls as the flowers open. The tiny five-petalled flowers have a faint blue or creamy tinge to the white petals, and a yellow centre. The long-stalked leaves are covered with soft hair.

FOUND *in waste places, fields, roadsides, and olive groves; usually where there is plenty of bare soil.*

spear-shaped leaf

blue-tinged petals

unwinding flowerheads

flowers in tight coil

ANNUAL

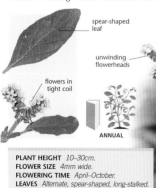

PLANT HEIGHT *10–30cm.*
FLOWER SIZE *4mm wide.*
FLOWERING TIME *April–October.*
LEAVES *Alternate, spear-shaped, long-stalked.*
FRUIT *Cluster of four nutlets.*
DISTRIBUTION *Throughout the region.*
SIMILAR SPECIES *H. supinum, which is a sprawling plant with a single nutlet.*

Tuberous Comfrey

Symphytum tuberosum (Boraginaceae)

A low-growing, creeping plant with tuberous roots, Tuberous Comfrey has short, bristly stems that have few or no branches. The lowest leaves are often withered by flowering time so that only the stem leaves remain. The creamy white flowers droop downwards like little bells or miniature trumpets and are borne in coiled clusters. The name *Symphytum* comes from the Greek *symphyo*, meaning "unite", and refers to the ancient belief that related plants were a useful remedy for treating broken bones. The leaves however, do make an effective treatment for bruises.

FOUND in damp habitats, woods, and stream banks, and alongside ditches, in shady places.

drooping flower cluster

stalkless stem leaf

bell-like white flowers

bristly, slightly winged stems

PERENNIAL

NOTE

When roasted until brown and brittle, and then finely ground, the roots are reputed to make an unusually smooth coffee substitute.

PLANT HEIGHT *15–40cm.*
FLOWER SIZE *1.4–1.9cm long.*
FLOWERING TIME *April–June.*
LEAVES *Alternate, oval to lance-shaped, roughly hairy.*
FRUIT *Oval nutlet.*
DISTRIBUTION *Throughout the region.*
SIMILAR SPECIES *S. officinale, which is taller with white or blue flowers, sporadic in the region.*

Felty Germander

Teucrium polium (Lamiaceae)

This is a low-growing, upright plant with a woody base, and is easily recognized by its thick covering of white or golden hairs. The flowers themselves are very small, with a single lip, and may be white, pinkish, or occasionally red. The leaves are adapted to the dry, hot conditions of the plant's environment, being rather thick and covered with down to retain moisture. There are several subspecies: subsp. *capitatum* has flowers in broadly-domed compound heads and stems covered with grey hair; subsp. *polium* (pictured here) is similar but has flowers in simple heads; subsp. *aureum* is covered in golden hair, has pale yellow flowers, and is found in mountainous areas.

FORMS *cushions on dry, rocky or sandy ground, and garigue in exposed places, often near the coast or on mountains.*

PERENNIAL

tiny single-lipped flowers

grey felty hair on stem

NOTE

The bruised leaves release a pleasant aromatic scent, and may be used in a steam bath for colds and fevers, or as a refreshing herbal tea.

erect stems

lobed leaf margin

compound heads

ssp. *capitatum*

PLANT HEIGHT *20–40cm.*
FLOWER SIZE *5mm long.*
FLOWERING TIME *April–July.*
LEAVES *Opposite pairs, oblong, up to 2.5cm long, with lobed margins.*
FRUIT *Four single-seeded nutlets.*
DISTRIBUTION *Throughout the region.*
SIMILAR SPECIES *White Horehound (Marrubium vulgare), which is a white-felted species with two-lipped flowers in the leaf axils.*

Winter Savory

Satureja montana (Lamiaceae)

OCCURS *on rocky slopes, at the base of inland cliffs, and on stony pasture; often in mountainous areas.*

Reminiscent of a small Rosemary, this small aromatic shrub is often woody at the base. It has narrow, opposite leaves, which are simple, almost linear or lance-shaped, and end in a sharp point. The two-lipped flowers, borne in loose clusters, are three-lobed in the lower part and are most often white, but may also be pink or purple.

flowers white, pink, or purple

narrow leaves

flowers in loose clusters

3-lobed lower lip

PERENNIAL

PLANT HEIGHT *10–40cm.*
FLOWER SIZE *0.6–1.2cm long.*
FLOWERING TIME *July–September.*
LEAVES *Opposite, narrow, pointed.*
FRUIT *Four nutlets remaining in the calyx.*
DISTRIBUTION *Throughout, except islands.*
SIMILAR SPECIES *Summer Savory (S. hortensis), which has smaller flowers.*

Bellardia

Bellardia trixago (Scrophulariaceae)

FOUND *on open ground on cultivated or waste places, stony ground, roadsides, pastures, and olive groves.*

Commonly mistaken as a member of the Mint family, Bellardia has toothed, opposite leaves and two-lipped flowers. It has a four-sided, pyramid-shaped head of flowers, partially concealed by large toothed bracts. Some plants form side branches.

"orderly" appearance

ANNUAL

pyramid of bracts

narrow, lance-shaped leaves

pink and white flowers

PLANT HEIGHT *20–70cm.*
FLOWER SIZE *2–2.5cm long.*
FLOWERING TIME *April–June.*
LEAVES *Opposite, lance-shaped, toothed.*
FRUIT *Rounded capsule, ripening in autumn.*
DISTRIBUTION *Throughout the region.*
SIMILAR SPECIES *Yellow Bartsia (Parentucellia viscosa), which has yellow flowers.*

Bear's Breech

Acanthus mollis (Acanthaceae)

This handsome herbaceous plant has come to be adopted as a common garden plant. Usually hairless, the long-stalked leaves are mostly basal, forming large and very glossy blades which are deeply divided into toothed lobes, almost to the midrib, and are soft to the touch. The flowers are arranged in a tall, cylindrical spike, each flower with a visible three-lobed white lip and a tough, hooded calyx, which is greenish purple and strongly veined. Very spiny, large oval bracts sit below each flower.

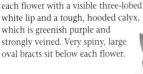

GROWS *in shady places in woods, scrub, and roadsides, though found mainly in the hills; also cultivated in gardens.*

PERENNIAL

NOTE

The Acanthus *leaf inspired a popular design in classical architecture, especially on the capitals of Greek Corinthian columns, and was also adopted by the Romans.*

calyx forms a hood

white lower lip

sharp, spiny bracts

deeply divided leaves

PLANT HEIGHT *0.5–1m.*
FLOWER SIZE *3.5–5cm long.*
FLOWERING TIME *May–July.*
LEAVES *Oval, divided almost to the midrib, not spiny, dark green.*
FRUIT *Explosive capsule containing large black seeds.*
DISTRIBUTION *Throughout the region.*
SIMILAR SPECIES *Spiny Bear's Breech (A. spinosus) of E. Mediterranean, which has doubly-divided, spiny, thistle-like leaves.*

Bean Broomrape

Orobanche crenata (Orobanchaceae)

OCCURS *on roadsides, fields, gardens, alongside ditches, and particularly in plots of broad beans and peas.*

Like all broomrapes, Bean Broomrape is a plant totally lacking in chlorophyll. It receives all its nutrients by parasitizing the roots of other plants, such as various members of the pea family, especially cultivated beans. It has a single stem with a few brown, leaf-like scales at the bottom, and a spike of two-lipped, pink or lilac-veined white flowers.

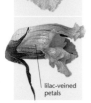

yellowish stigma inside flower

lilac-veined petals

dense flower spike

ANNUAL/PERENNIAL

small scales on stem

PLANT HEIGHT *Up to 70cm.*
FLOWER SIZE *2–3cm long.*
FLOWERING TIME *March–July.*
LEAVES *Leaf-like brown scales, 2.5cm long.*
FRUIT *Many-seeded capsule.*
DISTRIBUTION *Throughout the region.*
SIMILAR SPECIES *Common Broomrape* (O. minor), *which has smaller flowers.*

Lauristinus

Viburnum tinus (Caprifoliaceae)

GROWS *in maquis, among scrub, in gardens, and in open woods on hillsides.*

In spring, this attractive shrub produces heads of tightly clustered white flowers on downy, reddish young stems. The older bark is grey in colour. The blue-black, metallic-looking fruits are often seen on the plant at the same time as the flowers. The oval, leathery leaves are in opposite pairs.

domed flowerhead

PERENNIAL

fruit cluster

dark green leaves

oval leaf

PLANT HEIGHT *Up to 6m.*
FLOWER SIZE *6–9mm wide.*
FLOWERING TIME *January–June.*
LEAVES *Opposite, untoothed, and dark green.*
FRUIT *Egg-shaped dark blue berry, 6–8mm long.*
DISTRIBUTION *Throughout the region.*
SIMILAR SPECIES *None.*

Dwarf Elder

Sambucus ebulus (Caprifoliaceae)

This strong-smelling plant often grows in large patches, and is hard to miss. Even when not in flower, the plant may be identified by its characteristic leaves, strongly divided into long, narrow, slightly toothed leaflets. The abundant flowers are produced in domed clusters, each with five white petals and a ring of purple anthers. In late summer, clusters of glossy purple-black berries are produced, which although edible if cooked, are best avoided as they can cause digestive upset.
The leaves and stems are poisonous.

FORMS *large patches or colonies on damp, disturbed ground, roadsides, woodland margins, and hedgerows.*

PERENNIAL

toothed leaflets

tightly clustered
white flowers

purple
anthers

purple-black
berries

PLANT HEIGHT *0.8–1.5m.*
FLOWER SIZE *Clusters 7–14cm wide.*
FLOWERING TIME *May–July.*
LEAVES *Opposite, pinnate, finely toothed.*
FRUIT *Small, fleshy berries.*
DISTRIBUTION *Throughout the region.*
SIMILAR SPECIES *Common Elder (S. nigra), which is a shrub with woody stems and edible berries.*

NOTE

The bark and the leaves of this plant have an unpleasant smell, much like wet fur or stale perspiration, and is said to repel mice. A blue dye or ink can be made from the berries.

Leuzea

Leuzea conifera (Asteraceae)

Instantly identified though difficult to spot, this plant produces a single flowerhead, which has silvery brown bracts and looks similar to a pine cone. The flowers consist of short white or pink florets, emerging from the bracts like a short brush, which fan out in a fruit. The leaves are divided into very narrow lobes, and are dark green above and silvery below.

OCCURS *as sporadic plants in scrub, garigue, rocky ground, and open pine woods.*

head fans out in a fruit

short, unbranched stems

papery brown bracts

narrow lobes

PERENNIAL

PLANT HEIGHT *10–30cm.*
FLOWER SIZE *About 5cm long.*
FLOWERING TIME *May–August.*
LEAVES *Pinnate with narrow lobes, silvery below and dark green above.*
FRUIT *Long-haired black achene.*
DISTRIBUTION *Throughout the region.*
SIMILAR SPECIES *None.*

Southern Daisy

Bellis sylvestris (Asteraceae)

Although very similar to Common Daisy *(Bellis perennis)*, Southern Daisy has a longer flower-stalk and larger flowers, each with white ray florets that are often tinged red below. It is most likely to be seen flowering in late autumn or early spring.

GROWS *in sheltered, shady places such as woods and thickets, or in open garigue and roadsides.*

pink-tinged petals

strap-shaped ray florets

central yellow disc

spoon-shaped leaf

PERENNIAL

PLANT HEIGHT *10–30cm.*
FLOWER SIZE *2–4cm wide.*
FLOWERING TIME *September–May.*
LEAVES *Basal, spoon-shaped, three-veined.*
FRUIT *Hairless achene.*
DISTRIBUTION *Throughout the region.*
SIMILAR SPECIES *Annual Daisy* (B. annua), *which has smaller flowers and few stem leaves.*

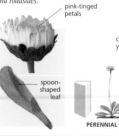

Crown Daisy

Chrysanthnemum coronarium (Asteraceae)

An attractive plant, Crown Daisy frequently grows in abundance creating a mass of colour in spring. The leaves are deeply divided into feathery fronds, which provide a backdrop to the showy flowers. The thickened stems support flowers that always have yellow disc florets, but the ray florets may be yellow, or white with yellow at the base, and often both are found growing together.

FORMS *extensive colonies in fields, olive groves, cultivated and fallow ground, also along roadsides, and seashores.*

broad ray florets

finely divided leaves

white and yellow form

NOTE

Although an ornamental plant in the West, it is grown as a vegetable in the Orient. The young shoots and leaves are regularly harvested as they become bitter if allowed to grow.

all-yellow form

ANNUAL

bushy habit

PLANT HEIGHT *30–75cm.*
FLOWER SIZE *3–6cm wide.*
FLOWERING TIME *March–September.*
LEAVES *Finely divided with toothed, lance-shaped lobes.*
FRUIT *Achene without a tuft of hair.*
DISTRIBUTION *Throughout the region.*
SIMILAR SPECIES *Corn Marigold (C. segetum), which has all-yellow flowers and non-feathery, lobed fleshy leaves.*

Common Asphodel

Asphodelus aestivus (Liliaceae)

This sturdy, hairless, and robust plant grows from thickened roots. Common Asphodel can be easily identified by its height and its long stem that is branched at the top. The arching leaves arise from the plant's base. They are grey-green and V-shaped in section so that they have a slight fold running along their length. The white flowers open from branched clusters of red and white-striped buds.

OCCURS *in dry areas on bare rocky ground, garigue, hillsides, roadsides, olive groves, open woodland, and pastures; occasionally by the coast.*

flowerheads on branched stems

clusters of buds

PERENNIAL

NOTE

The tubers contain a great deal of starch and have been used to make a strong glue used in bookbinding. They are also edible, but must be boiled first to remove any bitterness.

solitary main stem

pointed, V-shaped leaves

orange anthers

PLANT HEIGHT *0.6–1.5m.*
FLOWER SIZE *2–3.5cm wide.*
FLOWERING TIME *February–June.*
LEAVES *Basal, strap-shaped, up to 50cm long, with a keel beneath.*
FRUIT *Rounded capsule, about 7mm wide.*
DISTRIBUTION *Throughout the region.*
SIMILAR SPECIES *White Asphodel (A. albus), which has all its flowers in a single spike on an unbranched stem, and larger fruit capsules.*

Hollow-stemmed Asphodel

Asphodelus fistulosus (Liliaceae)

A smaller, more delicate plant than Common Asphodel, this species has hollow stems that are branched at the base as well as above, arising from a clump of hollow, rush-like leaves that remain upright. The white flowers have a dark central vein on each petal.

GROWS *in dry rocky and waste places, garigue, olive groves, and pastures, sometimes forming extensive colonies.*

PERENNIAL

slender stems

striped buds

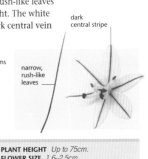

dark central stripe

narrow, rush-like leaves

PLANT HEIGHT *Up to 75cm.*	

PLANT HEIGHT *Up to 75cm.*
FLOWER SIZE *1.6–2.5cm.*
FLOWERING TIME *February–June.*
LEAVES *Cylindrical, not more than 5mm wide.*
FRUIT *Round capsule, about 5mm wide.*
DISTRIBUTION *Throughout the region.*
SIMILAR SPECIES *Yellow Asphodel (Asphodeline lutea), which has yellow flowers.*

Sea Squill

Urginea maritima (Liliaceae)

Also known as *Drimia maritima*, this plant produces tall spikes of white flowers in late summer, long after its leaves have died away. A half-buried bulb throws up glossy leaves in spring, followed by a tall, naked stem topped by several hundred star-shaped flowers.

FOUND *on open sandy or rocky ground, fallow fields, and hillsides; usually near the coast.*

strap-shaped leaves

cylindrical flowerhead

short-stalked flowers

thick root

PERENNIAL

PLANT HEIGHT *Up to 1.5m.*
FLOWER SIZE *1–1.6cm wide.*
FLOWERING TIME *July–October.*
LEAVES *Up to 1m long and 10cm wide.*
FRUIT *Three-sided capsule with winged seeds.*
DISTRIBUTION *Throughout the region.*
SIMILAR SPECIES *U. undulata is shorter, has linear leaves and few greyish pink flowers.*

Ornithogalum narbonense

Ornithogalum narbonense (Liliaceae)

GROWS *in a variety of grassy habitats, such as olive groves, vineyards, cultivated fields, and hillsides.*

This attractive and widespread plant is one of the most common *Ornithogalum* species in the region. It has a triangular raceme of spirally arranged flowers, opening at the bottom first and then towards the top, the flowers closing up against the stem once more as the fruit develop. The flowers have six petals, each with a broad green stripe.

narrow leaf

green-striped petals

green band on outside

wide-based anthers

PLANT HEIGHT	*30–50cm.*
FLOWER SIZE	*2.5cm wide.*
FLOWERING TIME	*May–July.*
LEAVES	*Four to six, linear, at flowering time.*
FRUIT	*Three-chambered capsule.*
DISTRIBUTION	*Throughout the region.*
SIMILAR SPECIES	*St. Bernards Lily (Anthericum liliago), has long, curved styles.*

PERENNIAL

Star of Bethlehem

Ornithogalum umbellatum (Liliaceae)

The six-petalled, star-shaped flowers borne by this plant appear together to form a flat-topped cluster, like an umbel. Each petal has a broad green stripe on the outside, which is visible whenever the flower is less than fully open.

OCCURS *in grassy places, woodland glades, meadows, roadsides, scrub, and waste land.*

long, narrow leaves

yellow anthers

PERENNIAL

grass-like leaf

green stripe on petal

PLANT HEIGHT	*15–30cm.*
FLOWER SIZE	*3–4cm wide.*
FLOWERING TIME	*March–May.*
LEAVES	*Basal, linear, with pale stripe.*
FRUIT	*Three-parted capsule with many seeds.*
DISTRIBUTION	*Throughout most of Europe.*
SIMILAR SPECIES	*O. collinum, which has a very short flowering stem.*

Naples Garlic

Allium neapolitanum (Liliaceae)

This species produces an abundance of star-shaped flowers from within a papery, green spathe. The flowers are fairly long-stalked, and spread apart to form a rather untidy umbel. The leaves are few in number, each leaf tapering to a fine point, with a flat surface and a prominent keel on the underside. The plant has a very mild smell of garlic.

FOUND *in dry grassy habitats, roadsides, fields, and open woodland; widely grown in gardens.*

spathe surrounds buds

flat leaf

star-shaped flowers

PERENNIAL

loose umbel

plain white petals

PLANT HEIGHT *20–50cm.*
FLOWER SIZE *2cm wide.*
FLOWERING TIME *February–May.*
LEAVES *Narrow, tapering, with keel on back.*
FRUIT *Capsule, persisting for many months.*
DISTRIBUTION *Throughout the region.*
SIMILAR SPECIES *A. subhirsutum, which has leaves with a hairy margin.*

Three-cornered Leek

Allium triquetrum (Liliaceae)

One of the most distinctive of the *Allium* species, this plant is easily recognized by its nodding head of bell-like flowers all facing in one direction. The petals of each flower overlap for much of their length, never opening out fully, and each has a narrow green stripe, visible on both the inside and the outside of the flower. The stems are markedly triangular in cross-section, with sharp edges. The leaves have a prominent keel so they too are somewhat triangular in cross-section. When crushed, they produce a strong garlic smell.

SEEN *in damp, semi-shaded spots such as woodland clearings, grassy places, and road verges; often cultivated.*

spathe encloses young flowers

narrow green stripe

strongly angled stem

drooping head of flowers

PERENNIAL

PLANT HEIGHT *20–45cm*
FLOWER SIZE *1.8cm long.*
FLOWERING TIME *March–May.*
LEAVES *Narrow, tapering, with keel on back.*
FRUIT *Three-parted capsule with many seeds.*
DISTRIBUTION *Throughout W. Europe.*
SIMILAR SPECIES *A. pendulinum, which has much smaller flowers.*

Poet's Narcissus

Narcissus poeticus (Amaryllidaceae)

FORMS *clumps in meadows, pastures, and along woodland margins; often grows at altitude.*

This attractive daffodil is often cultivated in gardens, and comes into flower later than many other varieties. The flowers are always solitary on each stem and the six pure white tepals are often backswept. The corona is yellow, often, but not always, with a red ring. Its flowering stem has two ridges bearing three to five flat leaves. The fruit is a three-chambered capsule.

backswept tepals

twisted leaves

red-ringed, shallow corona

PERENNIAL

ringless form

PLANT HEIGHT 30–60cm.
FLOWER SIZE Up to 6cm wide.
FLOWERING TIME April–June.
LEAVES Narrow, flat, grey-green.
FRUIT Capsule with three compartments.
DISTRIBUTION Throughout the region, except for most islands.
SIMILAR SPECIES N. serotinus, which is smaller.

Polyanthus Narcissus

Narcissus tazetta (Amaryllidaceae)

FOUND *in meadows, grassy ground, field margins, and cultivated ground such as olive groves.*

One of the most eye-catching flowers of early spring with its bicoloured flowers of white tepals and yellow coronas, Polyanthus Narcissus is also exquisitely scented. Between 3–12 flowers are produced from the papery spathe, each with different stalk lengths so that the blooms more or less face the same direction.

cup-shaped corona

broad white tepals

vertically clustered flowers

PERENNIAL

flat leaves

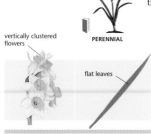

PLANT HEIGHT 25–60cm.
FLOWER SIZE 2.5–4cm wide.
FLOWERING TIME February–May.
LEAVES 3–6 blue-green leaves, keeled below.
FRUIT Three-parted capsule.
DISTRIBUTION Throughout except Italy, Sicily.
SIMILAR SPECIES Paperwhite Narcissus (N. papyraceus), which has all-white flowers.

Sea Daffodil

Pancratium maritimum (Amaryllidaceae)

Producing brilliant white flowers out of the sand in the hottest part of the year, the Sea Daffodil is one of the most attractive plants of the Mediterranean. It grows from a bulb, which is buried deeply and produces narrow, slightly twisted leaves in the winter or early spring, though these often start to die by flowering time. The single stem bears a cluster of 3–14 white, daffodil-like flowers, each with six tepals and a central corona that is almost as long as the tepals, and divided at the mouth into 12 broad teeth.

OCCURS *only in sandy coastal habitats and sand dunes, though the plant does well in gardens where there is no frost.*

green-striped bud

PERENNIAL

long tepals

long, toothed corona

twisted leaf

narrow white tepals

strap-shaped blade

NOTE

The name Pancratium comes from Greek meaning "strength", as the plant is able to flower in extremely hot, dry conditions, due to the deeply buried bulb which can reach fertile soil.

PLANT HEIGHT *Up to 50cm.*
FLOWER SIZE *10–15cm long.*
FLOWERING TIME *July–October.*
LEAVES *Narrow, strap-shaped, blue-green 1–2cm wide.*
FRUIT *Large, three-sided, rounded capsule containing large black seeds.*
DISTRIBUTION *Throughout the region.*
SIMILAR SPECIES *Illyrian Sea Lily (P. illyricum) of Corsica and Sardinia, which has a very short corona and much wider leaves.*

White German Iris

Iris germanica ssp. *florentina* (Iridaceae)

OCCURS *along roadsides, field margins, olive groves, abandoned vineyards, and other cultivated sites.*

PERENNIAL

This subspecies of the German Iris (p.143), which usually bears blue flowers, has been cultivated for centuries for its scented roots, and is usually seen growing close to human habitation. Both the "standard" and "fall" petals of the flowers are pure white with a faint bluish tinge, and a yellow "beard" running down the centre of each fall petal. The spathe is always pale brown and papery by flowering time. The plant grows from thick rhizomes, which also form a dense mat of fibrous roots, often crowding out other plants.

bluish white petals

raised central "beard"

flat leaves

standard petal

NOTE

The dried root is the source of Orris powder, which smells like violets. It is used in perfumery and for toothpaste, as well as medicinally for treating wounds and chest infections.

PLANT HEIGHT 50–90cm.
FLOWER SIZE 9–11cm long.
FLOWERING TIME April–June.
LEAVES Broad, sword-shaped, up to 4cm wide.
FRUIT Capsule containing pear-shaped seeds.
DISTRIBUTION Throughout the region.
SIMILAR SPECIES Iris albicans, which is shorter, with spathes that remain green at flowering time.

Riviera Crocus

Crocus versicolor (Iridaceae)

There are many *Crocus* species in the region, but each usually only grows in a relatively small area, and location is often the best guide to identification. Riviera Crocus is very variable in colour, ranging from white to purple, but always with conspicuous feather-edged stripes on the outside petals.

GROWS *in rocky or grassy places, meadows, and clearings in deciduous woodland; also frequently cultivated.*

grey-green leaves

exterior purple stripes

plain inner petals

yellow stamens

PERENNIAL

PLANT HEIGHT	Up to 20cm.
FLOWER SIZE	Petals 3cm long.
FLOWERING TIME	January–May.
LEAVES	Linear, appearing before flowers.
FRUIT	Capsule at or below ground level.
DISTRIBUTION	S.E. France and N.W. Italy.
SIMILAR SPECIES	C. corsica – only in Corsica; C. cambessedessii – only in Balearic Islands.

Romulea bulbocodium

Romulea bulbocodium (Iridaceae)

Although crocus-like, the *Romulea* species differ from the *Crocus* species in that they have a true stem – the *Crocus* flowers appear directly from the ground. The stem of *Romulea bulbocodium* carries up to six flowers, which vary in colour from white to violet. It has long, very narrow leaves with four grooves along their length.

FOUND *in grassy, rocky, and sandy places, in lowlands or mountains.*

prominent stamens

short petals open wide

linear leaf

faint stripes

PERENNIAL

PLANT HEIGHT	Up to 10cm.
FLOWER SIZE	2.5cm wide.
FLOWERING TIME	February–May.
LEAVES	Linear, four-grooved, dark green.
FRUIT	Capsule containing many brown seeds.
DISTRIBUTION	Throughout except Balearic Is.
SIMILAR SPECIES	Sand Crocus (R. columnae), which has purple flowers with dark stripes.

Narrow-leaved Helleborine

Cephalanthera longifolia (Orchidaceae)

The large, pure white flowers of this orchid show up brightly in the dim light of woodland shade, though they may also occur in damp or sheltered meadows out in the open. The flowers are borne in slender racemes, often rather loosely arranged on short, horizontal stalks. Both the sepals and petals are fairly long and pointed, although the lower lip is shorter and bears orange markings. This is a particularly leafy orchid, with eight to twenty, alternately arranged leaves that are held upright on the stem. They are exceptionally long and narrow, and taper towards the tip.

FOUND *in woods, scrub, shady embankments, and sheltered meadows, sometimes forming a loose colony.*

flower buds held vertically

sepals and petals similar

PERENNIAL

long, tapered leaf

orange inside lip

NOTE

In Cephalanthera *orchids the sepals and petals are similar in shape, size, and colour, while the petals and sepals of other orchids are totally different, with an extended lower lip.*

PLANT HEIGHT *40–60cm.*
FLOWER SIZE *Lower lip 1–1.6cm long.*
FLOWERING TIME *April–June.*
LEAVES *Alternate, lance-shaped to linear and tapered, dark green.*
FRUIT *Capsule containing many tiny seeds.*
DISTRIBUTION *Throughout the region.*
SIMILAR SPECIES *White Helleborine (C. damasonium), which has broader leaves and creamy white flowers, often only partly opening.*

Pink-Red

Red flowers bloom almost exclusively in high summer, when most insects are in flight. Curiously, the colour red is invisible to most insect species, but red flowers may contrast greatly against their background of leaves or soil. The white element in a pink flower is much more reflective, and may also reflect ultraviolet, which is visible to bees and other insects. In some plants, such as in the Bougainvillea below, modified leaves or bracts are brilliantly coloured to attract insects towards the less obvious, true flowers.

SPOTTED
DEADNETTLE

OLEANDER

RED VETCHLING

TREE MALLOW

Bougainvillea

Bougainvillea glabra (Nyctaginaceae)

A native of Brazil, Bougainvillea is so widely planted in the Mediterranean region that it has become characteristic of the area. The strikingly colored flowers, which range from pink to purple, are in fact bracts – modified leaves below the true flowers. Flowering almost all the year round, Bougainvillea has flowers which are small creamy, white trumpets with a frilly margin.

GROWS *in gardens or along walls and fences. It does not occur in wild areas outside the tropics.*

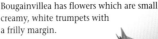

glossy oval leaves

3 pink bracts

true flowers

small, tubular flowers

PERENNIAL

PLANT HEIGHT *Up to 10m.*
FLOWER SIZE *True flowers 1.5–2.5cm long.*
FLOWERING TIME *February–October.*
LEAVES *Alternate, oval, glossy dark green.*
FRUIT *Cultivated plant is sterile.*
DISTRIBUTION *Throughout the region.*
SIMILAR SPECIES *B. spectabilis, which has hairy leaves.*

Hottentot Fig

Carpobrotus edulis (Aizoaceae)

Originally from South Africa, Hottentot Fig has become widely naturalized in the region. Impossible to ignore, the large, showy flowers have yellow or pinkish red petals – both forms often seen growing together – and a large central disc of many yellow stamens. The succulent leaves are triangular in cross-section, and widest towards their bases. Though edible, the ripe fruit are not very fleshy or tasty.

FORMS *a low, creeping carpet of leaves and flowers over sandy ground or cliffs at the coast, often planted.*

large flowers

curved, fleshy leaf

central disc of stamens

numerous linear petals

PERENNIAL

PLANT HEIGHT *Up to 25cm.*
FLOWER SIZE *7–9cm wide.*
FLOWERING TIME *April–July.*
LEAVES *Opposite, triangular in section.*
FRUIT *Fleshy and fig-like with many seeds.*
DISTRIBUTION *Throughout the region.*
SIMILAR SPECIES *C. acinaciformis, which has larger, brighter purple flowers.*

Lesser Sea-spurrey

Spergularia marina (Caryophyllaceae)

A low-growing plant of coastal habitats, Lesser Sea-spurrey produces diminutive pink flowers which quickly close in dull weather. The five petals each have a whitish base, and the sepals, which are longer than the petals, are clearly visible in-between. The stems are slender, with linear, fleshy leaves that form a mat over the ground, the flowers always on top facing upwards.

SPREADS *over the ground in sandy grassland, salt marshes, or salt pans; occasionally seen inland.*

5 pink petals

hairy flower-buds

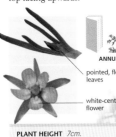

ANNUAL/BIENNIAL

pointed, fleshy leaves

white-centred flower

PLANT HEIGHT *7cm.*
FLOWER SIZE *5–8mm wide.*
FLOWERING TIME *April–August.*
LEAVES *Opposite or whorled, linear, fleshy.*
FRUIT *Capsule containing seeds.*
DISTRIBUTION *Throughout the region.*
SIMILAR SPECIES *S. rubra, which has non-fleshy leaves; S. media, which has larger flowers.*

Soapwort

Saponaria officinalis (Caryophyllaceae)

A robust plant that spreads by underground runners, Soapwort has fleshy, veined leaves, which were once gathered and boiled to make a soapy lather for washing. The flowers are in tight clusters, each of the petals broadening towards the tip like an aeroplane propeller, and are notable for their very long, pale green sepal tubes.

FOUND *in grassy places, hedgerows, and roadsides; on waste, fallow, and cultivated land.*

oval to elliptic leaves

pale pink flowers

PERENNIAL

leafy stem

long sepal tube

PLANT HEIGHT *60–90cm.*
FLOWER SIZE *2.5–2.8cm wide.*
FLOWERING TIME *June–September.*
LEAVES *Opposite, veined.*
FRUIT *Many-sided capsule with four teeth.*
DISTRIBUTION *Throughout the region.*
SIMILAR SPECIES *Rock Soapwort (S. ocymoides), which has dark pink flowers.*

Corncockle

Agrostemma githago (Caryophyllaceae)

With modern farming practices, this plant has gone from being a familiar cornfield weed to a rare wildflower, both in farmlands and in the wild. The five broadly overlapping petals are deep pink, paler towards the centre, and open into a shallow saucer-shape. The long, hairy sepals taper to a fine point, projecting beyond the petals like a star. The hairy leaves are long and narrow, and somewhat greyish. The large black seeds are finely sculpted, resembling a drill-bit.

OCCURS *sporadically in "unimproved" cornfields or other cultivated land where cereal crops grow, sometimes escaping.*

ANNUAL

overlapping petals

sepals joined below

untoothed leaf margins

narrow leaf

pale flower centre

NOTE

The Corncockle's poisonous seeds may contaminate flour, which is why farmers have, over the years, worked to eradicate the plant.

PLANT HEIGHT *60–100cm.*
FLOWER SIZE *3–5cm wide.*
FLOWERING TIME *May–August.*
LEAVES *Opposite, well-spaced along the stem.*
FRUIT *Capsule, 1–2.2cm long, containing large black seeds.*
DISTRIBUTION *Throughout the region.*
SIMILAR SPECIES *None, the size and shape of the flowers are unique in the region.*

Small-flowered Catchfly

Silene gallica (Caryophyllaceae)

The flowers of this short, sticky plant have five twisted petals which occur in a range of colours. They may be white, pink, or white with pink or crimson blotches on them and are produced from a strongly veined and hairy calyx which swells as the fruit develops. The leaves are opposite, stalkless, and untoothed.

FOUND *in dry cultivated places, waste ground, or close to seashores, often on sandy soil.*

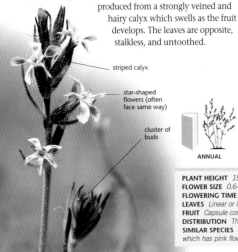

simple upper leaves

striped calyx

star-shaped flowers (often face same way)

cluster of buds

twisted petals

ANNUAL

PLANT HEIGHT *15–40cm.*
FLOWER SIZE *0.6–1cm wide.*
FLOWERING TIME *March–June.*
LEAVES *Linear or lance-shaped.*
FRUIT *Capsule containing brown seeds.*
DISTRIBUTION *Throughout the region.*
SIMILAR SPECIES *Sand Catchfly (S. conica), which has pink flowers, 5mm wide.*

Kohlrauschia

Petrorhagia velutina (Caryophyllaceae)

One of several small-flowered "pinks" in the region, this plant has comparatively large flowers with five bright pink, slightly cleft petals which emerge from brown papery bracts. Only one flower opens from the bracts at a time. The linear leaves are in opposite pairs or crowded at the base.

GROWS *in grassy or rocky ground, hillslopes, garigue, and sandy places.*

solitary flower

notched petals

brown papery bracts

linear basal leaf

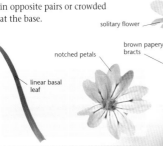

ANNUAL

PLANT HEIGHT *10–40cm.*
FLOWER SIZE *7–9mm wide.*
FLOWERING TIME *March–May.*
LEAVES *Opposite, meeting to form a sheath.*
FRUIT *Capsule with four teeth.*
DISTRIBUTION *Throughout the region.*
SIMILAR SPECIES *P. prolifera, which produces several flowers from the bracts at a time.*

Crown Anemone

Anemone coronaria (Ranunculaceae)

Like many other members of the buttercup family, Anemones never have a fixed number of "petals" (actually sepals). Crown Anemone has sepals that are distinctly showy, creating huge splashes of colour in the early spring. The flowers may be red, violet, blue, or white, often with one colour predominating in a particular area, and there is a ruff of finely divided, feathery bracts just below each flower. The leaves are divided into three delicately lobed segments.

FORMS *extensive colonies in pastures, olive-groves, grassy fields, vineyards, and on hillslopes; also grown in gardens.*

finely lobed basal leaf

feathery bracts

dark stamens in centre

5–8 sepals

PERENNIAL

NOTE

Also known as Poppy Anemone, this plant is widely grown in temperate regions as an ornamental plant. Many cultivars exist, including "double" forms with multiple sepals.

violet flowers

PLANT HEIGHT *15–40cm.*
FLOWER SIZE *3.5–6.5cm wide.*
FLOWERING TIME *January–April.*
LEAVES *Basal, lobed, and toothed.*
FRUIT *Cluster of woolly achenes.*
DISTRIBUTION *Throughout the region.*
SIMILAR SPECIES *A. pavonina, which has bracts lower down the stem, less divided leaves, and a white ring in the centre of the flower.*

Anemone hortensis

Anemone hortensis (Ranunculaceae)

Another species widely grown in gardens, (the name *hortensis* means "of gardens") this plant usually flowers much later than Crown Anemone. It has 12–19 narrow, petal-like sepals, usually pale purple in colour, with much less variation than in many other species, and dark blue or purple anthers. There is a ruff of simply divided bracts about halfway along the flower stem. The leaves, which are all basal, are on short stems. They are three-lobed, but divided into very narrow segments that are difficult to distinguish.

OCCURS in small colonies in fields, olive groves, and grassy places in woodland; usually found in semi-shade.

up to 19 petals

numerous dark anthers

PERENNIAL

NOTE

At times, Anemone x fulgens, *a hybrid of this species and* Anemone pavonina *is found where they grow together.* A. heldreichii – *a form with white petals, is now considered a separate species.*

segmented leaves

narrow, pink-purple sepals

PLANT HEIGHT 20–45cm.
FLOWER SIZE 5cm wide.
FLOWERING TIME February–May.
LEAVES Basal, lobed, divided into very narrow segments.
FRUIT Woolly achene.
DISTRIBUTION France, Italy, and Sicily.
SIMILAR SPECIES A. pavonina, which has fewer petals in red, pink, or purple, and less finely lobed leaves.

Common Peony

Paeonia officinalis (Paeoniaceae)

OCCURS *in meadows, grassy and bushy places where it is not too dry; also grown in gardens.*

Peonies are bushy, showy plants with 5–10 petals and three green sepals beneath them. This species has brilliant red petals, and numerous yellow anthers supported by red filaments. The long-stalked leaves are divided into 17–30 narrow segments, and are hairy below. Three large follicles form the fruit.

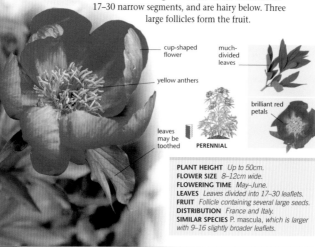

cup-shaped flower

much-divided leaves

yellow anthers

brilliant red petals

leaves may be toothed

PERENNIAL

PLANT HEIGHT Up to 50cm.
FLOWER SIZE 8–12cm wide.
FLOWERING TIME May–June.
LEAVES Leaves divided into 17–30 leaflets.
FRUIT Follicle containing several large seeds.
DISTRIBUTION France and Italy.
SIMILAR SPECIES P. mascula, which is larger with 9–16 slightly broader leaflets.

Opium Poppy

Papaver somniferum (Papaveraceae)

FOUND *on disturbed ground of all kinds, fields, roadsides, olive groves, vineyards, and wasteland.*

Grown in the region since ancient times, the Opium Poppy is very variable in size. It has four pink, or occasionally white petals which have a dark crimson blotch at the base. Tissue-like in texture, the petals curve to form a bowl. The grey-green leaves are fleshy or waxy, and are toothed. The large seed capsule is oval or rounded.

yellow anthers

wavy margins

dark-centred flowers

ANNUAL

PLANT HEIGHT 20–100cm.
FLOWER SIZE 4–9cm wide.
FLOWERING TIME April–August.
LEAVES Fleshy, toothed, clasping the stem.
FRUIT Globose capsule, 2–3cm wide.
DISTRIBUTION Throughout the region.
SIMILAR SPECIES No other poppies have pink flowers.

Common Poppy

Papaver rhoeas (Papaveraceae)

Common Poppies often appear in great profusion in cultivated fields or land that has been disturbed after a long period of neglect. They have pinnately divided leaves and four red petals with or without black blotches. The best clue to identification is the seed capsule, which in this case is smooth, with holes near the flattened top.

FLOURISHES *in arable fields and field margins, disturbed and waste ground, and on roadsides.*

pinnately divided leaves

black-centred flower

ANNUAL

brilliant red petals

oval fruit capsule

PLANT HEIGHT *30–60cm.*
FLOWER SIZE *7.5–10cm wide.*
FLOWERING TIME *June–September.*
LEAVES *Alternate and toothed.*
FRUIT *Capsule with hundreds of tiny seeds.*
DISTRIBUTION *Throughout the region.*
SIMILAR SPECIES *P. hybridum, which has a bristly, rounded capsule.*

Red Horned Poppy

Glaucium corniculatum (Papaveraceae)

This species has elongated fruit similar to the Yellow Horned Poppy (p.171), but is a smaller annual plant. The flowers are orange-red with black blotches at the base. The basal leaves are oblong and lobed and the stem leaves are oval with wavy margins.

INHABITS *waste ground, fields, and margins of cultivated areas; usually found on sandy soil near the coast.*

lobed lower leaf

ANNUAL

black blotches at base

yellow anthers

4 orange-red petals

PLANT HEIGHT *30–40cm.*
FLOWER SIZE *3–5cm wide.*
FLOWERING TIME *April–July.*
LEAVES *Waxy, lobed or rounded, and wavy.*
FRUIT *Pod-like capsule, 10–15cm long.*
DISTRIBUTION *Throughout the region.*
SIMILAR SPECIES *Yellow Horned Poppy (p.171) has yellow flowers without blotches.*

Common Fumitory

Fumaria officinalis (Papaveraceae)

SPRAWLS *over bare ground or grassy places in cultivated fields, wasteland, pastures, and along roadsides.*

This is a common and widespread weed found throughout most of Europe. It has rather weak stems and often grows partly supported by other plants. It produces upright racemes of flowers, each flower with a pouched spur at the back, and two crimson-tipped lips at the front. The straggly stems bear finely divided leaves, each leaflet on its own stalk. The name *Fumaria* refers to smoke, perhaps due to an ancient belief that the plant rose spontaneously from vapours in the ground, or conversely that the leaves have a smoke-like appearance.

ANNUAL

feathery, divided leaves

dark-tipped flowers

thin leaf stalk

flowers in racemes

pouched spur

NOTE

The plant has been held in high esteem since Roman times for its medicinal properties, particular for skin treatments. The flowers yield a yellow dye which has been used for colouring wool.

PLANT HEIGHT *10–30cm.*
FLOWER SIZE *7–9mm long.*
FLOWERING TIME *May-October.*
LEAVES *Alternate, pinnately divided into lobed, stalked leaflets.*
FRUIT *Single-seeded, round capsule.*
DISTRIBUTION *Throughout the region.*
SIMILAR SPECIES *There are several other pink-flowered fumitories in the region, usually with smaller flowers.*

Hoary Stock

Matthiola incana (Brassicaceae)

This is a robust plant with a branched and woody base, and with a similar habit to the yellow-flowered Wallflower (p.173). Like the Wallflower it has been cultivated for use as a garden plant, though its strikingly coloured flowers occur quite freely in wild plants. They may be pure white, bright purple, or the petals may be streaked with both colours, often with all three colour forms growing together. The leaves are densely covered with very fine hairs which give them a frosted appearance, the name *incana* comes from the Latin *incanus*, meaning hoary, or hairy.

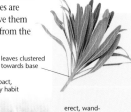

GROWS *on cliffs and other coastal habitats including roadsides, though often cultivated elsewhere; usually on limestone.*

leaves clustered towards base

PERENNIAL

purple or white flowers

compact, bushy habit

erect, wand-like fruit

NOTE

The sweetly scented flowers may be used as an attractive garnish for salads and desserts. The coloured variety of flowers also yield a dark blue or purple dye.

PLANT HEIGHT *20–80cm.*
FLOWER SIZE *3cm wide.*
FLOWERING TIME *February–May.*
LEAVES *Oblong, fairly narrow and usually untoothed.*
FRUIT *Narrow, curved siliqua, up to 16cm long.*
DISTRIBUTION *Throughout the region.*
SIMILAR SPECIES *Sea Stock (M.sinuata), which has toothed or lobed leaves.*

Honesty

Lunaria annua (Brassicaceae)

OCCURS *on roadsides, banks, wasteland, rubbish tips, and cultivated land.*

This attractive plant, which originates from the Mediterranean region, has been cultivated as a garden plant and is now established throughout much of Europe. The flowers may be purple or occasionally white, but the fruits are particularly distinctive. The rounded silicula splits to reveal a persistent silvery membrane, like a full moon, to which the seeds are attached.

coarsely toothed leaf

rounded fruit

BIENNIAL

flowers in clusters

deep green foliage

4-petalled flowers

PLANT HEIGHT	*50–100cm.*
FLOWER SIZE	*2.5–3cm wide.*
FLOWERING TIME	*April–June.*
LEAVES	*Alternate, heart-shaped, coarsely toothed, dark green.*
FRUIT	*Round, flat silicula, 3–5cm wide.*
DISTRIBUTION	*Throughout the region.*
SIMILAR SPECIES	*None.*

Sea Rocket

Cakile maritima (Brassicaceae)

FOUND *in open, sandy areas, dunes, and shingle beaches on coastal sites.*

In common with many coastal plants living in dry soil, the Sea Rocket has fleshy leaves that retain moisture. They are oblong, bright green, and deeply lobed into rounded "fingers". The pale pink flowers are clustered at the top of the stems, and the fleshy, bullet-shaped fruit has two shoulder-like projections at the base.

clusters of flowers

ANNUAL

long, rounded segments

pale midrib

4 petals

PLANT HEIGHT	*Up to 30cm.*
FLOWER SIZE	*0.6–1.2cm wide.*
FLOWERING TIME	*June–September.*
LEAVES	*Alternate, pinnately lobed, fleshy.*
FRUIT	*Siliqua, 2cm long, with two segments.*
DISTRIBUTION	*Throughout the region.*
SIMILAR SPECIES	*Three-horned Stock (Matthiola tricuspidata), which has longer fruit.*

Judas Tree

Cercis siliquastrum (Fabaceae)

This small tree is impossible to miss when the pea-type flowers burst open in spring, punctuating the countryside with colour. Appearing before the leaves, the flowers grow directly from the trunk and branches. The leaves themselves are a yellowish green, often suffused with red at first, and are almost round or kidney shaped. The flat seed-pods are pale green at first, ripening to a rich tobacco brown by midsummer. There is a tradition that this was the tree on which Judas Iscariot hanged himself, and that the flowers blush with shame.

FOUND *on rocky hills, maquis, woods, and gardens. Often cultivated for its ornamental value and widely naturalized.*

PERENNIAL

lime green rounded leaves

abundant pink flowers

leaves appear at flowering time

standard and wing petals are erect

NOTE

The flowers of the Judas Tree have a sweetish-acid taste and may be added to salads, and the buds are used in place of capers. The wood is very fine-grained and polishes extremely well.

PLANT HEIGHT *Up to 10m.*
FLOWER SIZE *2cm long.*
FLOWERING TIME *March–April.*
LEAVES *Yellow-green, rounded or slightly heart-shaped, shiny when young.*
FRUIT *Flattened pod, 6–10cm long.*
DISTRIBUTION *Throughout the region.*
SIMILAR SPECIES *Apricot, Almond, and Peach (Prunus sp.) trees, which also have pink flowers in early spring.*

Montpelier Milk-vetch

Astragalus monspessulanus (Fabaceae)

RADIATES *from one spot over dry, stony ground, grassy banks, and rocky places.*

The leaves and flower stalks of this species spread out directly from the roots. The ladder-like leaves are pinnately divided into 10–20 pairs of tiny, oval, dark green leaflets. The flower stalks are longer than the leaves, terminating in an untidy cluster of red to purplish peaflowers.

sprawling habit

tiny paired leaflets

long, narrow, standard petal

long flower stalks

PLANT HEIGHT *10–30cm.*
FLOWER SIZE *About 1.5cm long.*
FLOWERING TIME *April–August.*
LEAVES *Pinnate, numerous tiny leaflets.*
FRUIT *Cylindrical pod, up to 4.5cm long.*
DISTRIBUTION *Throughout, except islands.*
SIMILAR SPECIES *A. purpureus, which has branching stems and small, oval, hairy pods.*

PERENNIAL

Vicia narbonensis

Vicia narbonensis (Fabaceae)

GROWS *on grassy banks, roadsides, waste places, garigue, and bushy areas.*

The leaves of this rather inconspicuous species have only two or three pairs of large leaflets, unlike most vetches which have many more. The stalkless flowers tend to be half-hidden within the leaflets, and are white veined with red or purple streaks or all purple. The straight seed pod turns black or brown when ripe.

white with red-purple streaks

large oval leaflets

hairless seed pod

ANNUAL

flowers in leaf axils

PLANT HEIGHT *20–60cm.*
FLOWER SIZE *2–3cm long.*
FLOWERING TIME *March–June.*
LEAVES *Divided into rounded or oval leaflets.*
FRUIT *Straight pod, 3–7cm long.*
DISTRIBUTION *Throughout the region.*
SIMILAR SPECIES *The large leaflets and stalkless flowers of this plant are unique.*

Fodder Vetch

Vicia villosus (Fabaceae)

This is a variable plant that may grow as high as two metres given enough supporting vegetation. The flowers grow in tall, dense clusters, and are a mixture of reddish violet and blue, often with whitish wings. The leaves have up to 12 pairs of almost linear leaflets, ending in a branched tendril. The hairless fruit pod is slender and brown, with a netted surface.

OCCURS *in cultivated land, grassy and waste places, and along roadsides. Sometimes grown as a fodder crop.*

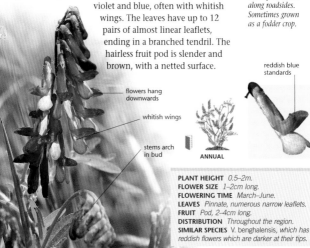

flowers hang downwards

whitish wings

stems arch in bud

ANNUAL

reddish blue standards

PLANT HEIGHT	0.5–2m.
FLOWER SIZE	1–2cm long.
FLOWERING TIME	March–June.
LEAVES	Pinnate, numerous narrow leaflets.
FRUIT	Pod, 2–4cm long.
DISTRIBUTION	Throughout the region.
SIMILAR SPECIES	V. benghalensis, which has reddish flowers which are darker at their tips.

Common Vetch

Vicia sativa (Fabaceae)

This widespread species is native to the region, but now occurs all over Europe. Although it is very variable in terms of leaf-shape, in the Mediterranean the leaflets are commonly heart-shaped with blunt or notched tips. Tiny stipules at the base have a black spot, often visited by ants. The flowers are usually in pairs, with pink-red standards and often have darker wings.

CLIMBS *over grasses and other vegetation in cultivated fields, wasteland, roadsides, banks, and scrub.*

3–8 pairs of leaflets

pink-red standard petal

notched tips

PLANT HEIGHT	50–120cm.
FLOWER SIZE	1.8–2.5cm long.
FLOWERING TIME	February–June.
LEAVES	Alternate, pinnately divided.
FRUIT	Hairy pod, 2.5–6cm long.
DISTRIBUTION	Throughout the region.
SIMILAR SPECIES	V. lathyroides, which has smaller flowers and unspotted stipules.

PERENNIAL

single or paired flowers

Red Vetchling

Lathyrus cicera (Fabaceae)

OCCURS *on waste and cultivated ground, or in olive groves and orchards in sunny areas.*

The leaves of this clambering plant are scarcely noticeable among long grasses. The leaves are divided into long, simple paired leaflets, with tendrils between them that are often branched. At their base are a pair of arrow-shaped stipules attached to the slightly winged stems. The flowers, however, are easy to spot due to their brilliant scarlet coloration, even though they are rather small.

long, lance-shaped leaves

branched tendril

PERENNIAL

bright scarlet pea-flower

pod has double ridge

PLANT HEIGHT *20–80cm.*
FLOWER SIZE *1–1.5cm long.*
FLOWERING TIME *March–May.*
LEAVES *Pair of narrow, lance-shaped leaflets.*
FRUIT *Hairless, rounded pod, 2–4cm long.*
DISTRIBUTION *Throughout the area.*
SIMILAR SPECIES *Annual Yellow Vetchling (L. annus), which has red-veined yellow flowers.*

Broad-leaved Everlasting Pea

Lathyrus latifolius (Fabaceae)

CLAMBERS *over vegetation on rough grassy and bushy sites, roadsides, wasteland, and woodland margins.*

A vigorous climber, this plant has been introduced throughout Europe where cultivated forms have become naturalized and flower even more freely. The stems and leaf stalks have very broad wings. The leaflets are prominently veined with a pair of stipules at the base.

long branching tendril

lance-shaped leaflets

slender fruit pod

PERENNIAL

flower clusters on erect stalks

PLANT HEIGHT *1–3m.*
FLOWER SIZE *2–3cm long.*
FLOWERING TIME *May–July.*
LEAVES *Broad leaflets with branching tendril.*
FRUIT *Pod, 5–10cm long, ripening to brown.*
DISTRIBUTION *Throughout the region.*
SIMILAR SPECIES *L. sylvestris, which has narrower leaflets and shorter pods.*

Wild Pea

Pisum sativum (Fabaceae)

The flowers of this climbing plant are large and distinctive. The upper petals (or standards) are deep pink, often with dark veins. The lower side petals (or wings) are fused to the keel underneath, and are usually a deep purple colour. The flowers of cultivated garden peas, which are ultimately derived from the wild plant, are usually white in coloration. The leaves are divided into oval leaflets and terminate in a branched tendril, with a pair of heart-shaped stipules, which have toothed margins, at the base.

SPRAWLS *and climbs over rocks and low vegetation in bushy places and woodland edges or on cultivated land, usually in the semi-shade.*

ANNUAL

oval leaflets

dark purple wing petals

toothed stipules

pink standards

NOTE

The plant has a history of cultivation for its edible seeds since prehistoric times. There is some evidence from India and China that the oil from the seeds of the wild plant have a contraceptive effect in both men and women.

PLANT HEIGHT 0.6–2m.
FLOWER SIZE 2–3.5cm wide.
FLOWERING TIME April–June.
LEAVES Pinnately divided into 1–3 pairs of oval leaflets and a tendril.
FRUIT Net-veined pod ripening yellow-brown, 3–12cm long.
DISTRIBUTION Throughout the region.
SIMILAR SPECIES Plants with much paler flowers may be the true species, those with dark petals are sometimes considered to be P. elatius.

Narrow-leaved Crimson Clover

OCCURS in dry places, usually on disturbed acid soil, such as vineyards, waste or cultivated land, and olive groves.

Trifolium angustifolium (Fabaceae)

This distinctive member of the pea family has stems that branch at the base before ascending, and are topped with long, conical flowerheads. The small pink flowers remain half-hidden within the hairy sepals. The distinctive leaves are divided into three very long, pointed leaflets.

ANNUAL

brush-like flowerhead

winged stipules at leaf base

3 narrow leaflets

tiny pink flowers

PLANT HEIGHT *10–40cm.*
FLOWER SIZE *Flowerhead up to 8cm long.*
FLOWERING TIME *April–July.*
LEAVES *Trifoliate, with pointed leaflets.*
FRUIT *Pod hidden inside calyx.*
DISTRIBUTION *Throughout the region.*
SIMILAR SPECIES *Crimson Clover (T. incarnatum), which has heart-shaped leaflets.*

Winged Pea

GROWS over disturbed, cultivated, or waste land in olive groves, vineyards, fields, and roadsides.

Tetragonolobus purpureus (Fabaceae)

The leaves of this usually sprawling plant are divided into three fairly large (up to 4cm) leaflets, each shaped like a rounded kite but with a pointed tip, and with two broad stipules at the base. The brightly-coloured flowers are borne singly or in pairs.

ANNUAL

pod with 4 wavy wings

dark blotch on wing petals

blood-red flowers

hairy leaves and stems

PLANT HEIGHT *10–30cm.*
FLOWER SIZE *1.5–2.2cm long.*
FLOWERING TIME *February–May.*
LEAVES *Three rounded leaflets.*
FRUIT *Edible pod, 3–8cm long.*
DISTRIBUTION *Throughout the region, but absent from Portugal and Corsica.*
SIMILAR SPECIES *None.*

Spiny Rest-harrow

Ononis spinosa (Fabaceae)

Although the shape of its leaflets and size of its flowers vary, this small shrub is always recognizable. The Spiny Rest-harrow flower has a broad, erect standard petal and a narrow, upwardly curved keel, flanked by pale pink or white wing petals. The stems are sparsely covered with sharp, woody spines.

FOUND *in dry, bushy places such as roadsides, rocky ground, waste places, and occasionally on seashores.*

pink standard petal

sharply curved keel

PERENNIAL

3 toothed leaflets

woody spine

PLANT HEIGHT *20–60cm.*
FLOWER SIZE *1–2cm.*
FLOWERING TIME *April–July.*
LEAVES *Trifoliate, narrow to oval leaflets.*
FRUIT *Single-seeded pod, up to 1cm long.*
DISTRIBUTION *Throughout the region.*
SIMILAR SPECIES *O. diffusa, which has more rounded leaflets and is spineless.*

Sainfoin

Onobrychis viciifolia (Fabaceae)

A tall, attractive plant, Sainfoin is sometimes grown for cattle fodder or as a "green manure". The long-stalked flowers are clustered in spikes; each petal with crimson stripes on a pink background. The leaves are pinnately divided with very slender, ladder-like leaflets. The unusual, rounded seed pods have coarse, toothed ridges.

FORMS *clumps or small colonies on roadsides, waste ground, grassy places, and in cultivated fields.*

PERENNIAL

dense spike of flowers

crimson striped petals

narrow leaflets

developing fruit at base of flowerhead

PLANT HEIGHT *20–80cm.*
FLOWER SIZE *1–1.4cm long.*
FLOWERING TIME *March–July.*
LEAVES *Pinnate, up to 14 pairs of leaflets.*
FRUIT *Flattened pod with toothed ridges.*
DISTRIBUTION *Throughout the region.*
SIMILAR SPECIES *Italian Sainfoin (p.74); many few-flowered species with spiny fruit pods.*

Italian Sainfoin

Hedysarum coronarium (Fabaceae)

GROWS *in fields as a fodder crop but often escaping to roadsides, cultivated and fallow land, or waste ground.*

This brilliantly-coloured plant is often grown as a fodder crop or to improve the soil. The leaves have 3–5 pairs of oval, slightly hairy leaflets. Up to 35 flowers are produced in tidy, pyramid-shaped clusters. Each bright reddish purple flower has a few white streaks on the standard petal. The fruit pod is divided into 2–4 bristly disc-shaped segments.

pyramid-shaped flower cluster

red-crimson flowers

PERENNIAL

white-streaked standard

oval leaflets

PLANT HEIGHT *Up to 1m.*
FLOWER SIZE *1.2–1.5cm long.*
FLOWERING TIME *April–June.*
LEAVES *Pinnate, grey-green, hairy leaflets.*
FRUIT *Pod with bristly, disc-shaped segments.*
DISTRIBUTION *Throughout the region.*
SIMILAR SPECIES *Onobrychis species (p.73), which have narrower leaves and toothed pods.*

Crown Vetch

Coronilla varia (Fabaceae)

INHABITS *grassy places such as meadows, roadsides, wasteland, and open scrub, or along ditches.*

This attractive plant has flowers that may be pink, lilac, or more often bicolored. They are arranged in a ring or crown of 20 or so short-stalked flowers at the top of a leafless, hairless stalk. The leaves are pinnate with small, well-separated leaflets that often end in a tiny point. The narrow seed pods are produced in a ring, each with 3–8 segments, and break easily into single-seeded sections.

oblong leaflets

pink and white petals

10–20 flowers per head

PERENNIAL

ring-shaped flowerhead

PLANT HEIGHT *30–100cm.*
FLOWER SIZE *1–1.5cm long.*
FLOWERING TIME *March–July.*
LEAVES *Alternate, pinnate with oval leaflets.*
FRUIT *Slender pod, 2–6cm long.*
DISTRIBUTION *Throughout the region except for many islands.*
SIMILAR SPECIES *None.*

Pink Oxalis

Oxalis articulata (Oxalidaceae)

Originally from South America, this colorful little plant has now become widely established. The bright pink flowers open only in strong light, unfurling like an umbrella and facing the sun, and are borne in long-stalked clusters on long stems. The leaves are divided into three distinctly heart-shaped leaflets, which also fold down at night.

OCCURS in grassy areas of roadsides, waste ground, gardens, olive groves, and other cultivated land.

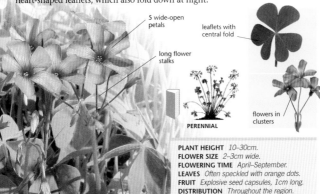

5 wide-open petals

leaflets with central fold

long flower stalks

flowers in clusters

PERENNIAL

PLANT HEIGHT *10–30cm.*
FLOWER SIZE *2–3cm wide.*
FLOWERING TIME *April–September.*
LEAVES *Often speckled with orange dots.*
FRUIT *Explosive seed capsules, 1cm long.*
DISTRIBUTION *Throughout the region.*
SIMILAR SPECIES *O. purpurea, which has solitary flowers with a white centre.*

Mallow-leaved Storksbill

Erodium malacoides (Geraniaceae)

One of the most common storksbills in the Mediterranean region, this plant gets its name from the softly hairy leaves that are lobed and toothed like those of those of the *Malvaceae* family. The small pink flowers are never produced in abundance at any one time. The tiny pointed sepals are visible between each of the petals.

INHABITS dry open places, roadsides, waste or cultivated land; prefers stony, arid soil.

flowers in umbel

toothed leaves

ANNUAL/BIENNIAL

heart-shaped leaf base

pointed sepals

PLANT HEIGHT *20–60cm.*
FLOWER SIZE *1.2–1.8cm long.*
FLOWERING TIME *February–May.*
LEAVES *Oblong, lobed, and toothed.*
FRUIT *Five-seeded fruit with 3.5cm-long beak.*
DISTRIBUTION *Throughout the region.*
SIMILAR SPECIES *Erodium chium, which has more deeply lobed leaves.*

Castor Oil Plant

Ricinus communis (Euphorbiaceae)

OCCURS *on disturbed ground of cultivated fields, waste ground, roadsides, and often by the banks of rivers or streams.*

Native to tropical Africa, Castor Oil Plant is a fast-growing shrub that survives well in more temperate climates. It has large, palmate leaves that have a shiny surface often flushed with bronze or purple. Though separate, the male and female flowers are borne together in large, upright clusters. The female flowers are at the top of the panicle with many red stigmas, giving them a spiky appearance. The male flowers are below and have numerous yellow anthers. The fruit is a capsule and usually with a spiny surface.

palmate leaf

developing red female flowers

yellow male flowers

ANNUAL/PERENNIAL

NOTE

The oil extracted from the seeds of the plant is an efficient laxative. Cultivated for over 2,000 years, this plant also contains the water-soluble poison Ricin, which is not present in the oil.

palmate leaf on red stem

"spiky" female flowers

PLANT HEIGHT *Up to 4m.*
FLOWER SIZE *Panicle 10–30cm long.*
FLOWERING TIME *February–September.*
LEAVES *Up to 60cm wide, with lance-shaped lobes, often red or purple.*
FRUIT *Capsule, 1.5–2cm wide, covered with spines and containing three shiny, reddish beans.*
DISTRIBUTION *Throughout the region.*
SIMILAR SPECIES *None.*

Lentisc

Pistacia lentiscus (Anacardiaceae)

Belonging to the cashew nut family, this evergreen shrub produces a sticky resin called mastic which has numerous applications. The male and female flowers are borne on different plants: the red male flowers being more easily noticed than the greenish female ones. The leaf-stalks are clearly winged, and there is no terminal leaflet.

INHABITS *dry, rocky places, garigue, and maquis. Occasionally found on sand dunes.*

PERENNIAL

clusters of male flowers

pair of leaflets

winged leaf-stalk

dark red male flowers

PLANT HEIGHT *1–3m.*
FLOWER SIZE *Up to 3cm long.*
FLOWERING TIME *March–June.*
LEAVES *Pinnate, leathery, winged stalks, no terminal leaflet.*
FRUIT *Red-black berry, 4-5mm wide.*
DISTRIBUTION *Throughout the region.*
SIMILAR SPECIES *Turpentine Tree (below).*

Turpentine Tree

Pistachia terebinthus (Anacardiaceae)

This small tree is deciduous with aromatic leaves that have a resinous smell. The leaves are pinnate, with leathery lobes and a terminal leaflet. Unlike Lentisc (above) , its leaf-stalks are not winged. The flowers are in long-branched clusters, with the male and female flowers on separate trees. The plant is most distinctive when the bright red fruit have developed.

GROWS *in open woods, maquis, pine forest, and rocky gullies; especially on limestone.*

leaves have terminal leaflet

PERENNIAL

flower cluster

numerous red berries

PLANT HEIGHT *2–5m.*
FLOWER SIZE *Clusters up to 15cm long.*
FLOWERING TIME *April–June.*
LEAVES *Pinnate, with terminal leaflet.*
FRUIT *Red berry ripens brown, 5–7mm long.*
DISTRIBUTION *Throughout the region*
SIMILAR SPECIES *Lentisc (above); Pistachio (P. vera), which has larger, three-lobed leaves.*

Common Mallow

Malva sylvestris (Malvaceae)

This is a robust, hairy-stemmed plant frequently found on wasteland throughout Europe. In the Mediterranean region, it often grows in a prostrate form, sprawling over the ground. The flowers are distinctive with five notched, pink to purple petals, with darker veins along their length, and a long column of pale pink stamens. Borne separately on long stalks, the flowers grow in clusters from the leaf axils. Behind the petals, the calyx of sepals is backed by three narrow segments – the epicalyx. The fruit is a ring of tiny wedge-shaped nutlets, which are edible.

GROWS *on wasteland and along field margins, hedgerows, road verges, or grassy coastal sites.*

BIENNIAL/ PERENNIAL

shallow toothed lobes

thin dark veins on petals

ring of nutlets

2-lobed petals

NOTE

The leaves have a moist, sticky quality and may be added to soups as a thickener. This property also makes them excellent to use as a poultice for bruises, insect bites, and other inflammations.

PLANT HEIGHT *50–100cm.*
FLOWER SIZE *2–5cm wide.*
FLOWERING TIME *June–September.*
LEAVES *Alternate, shallowly palmately lobed, and toothed, covered in felty hair.*
FRUIT *Ring of nutlets within persistent calyx.*
DISTRIBUTION *Throughout the region, including N. Africa.*
SIMILAR SPECIES *Small Tree Mallow (p.79).*

Tree Mallow

Lavatera arborea (Malvaceae)

Impossible to miss in its coastal habitat, this is a robust, tall plant with a woody stem. The large leaves are rounded, with 5–7 lobes that are wrinkled or wavy – an adaptation that helps the plant to conserve moisture in a dry environment. The cup-shaped flowers are a deep magenta-pink, with dark lines radiating out from a blackish centre and pale pink anthers.

FOUND *on coasts, on shingle beaches, cliffs, wasteland, rocks, and sand dunes.*

stout stem

dark-veined petals

dark flower centre

wavy lobes

BIENNIAL

PLANT HEIGHT *1–2.5m.*
FLOWER SIZE *3–4cm wide.*
FLOWERING TIME *June–September.*
LEAVES *Alternate, palmate, lobed.*
FRUIT *Cluster of nutlets in a ring.*
DISTRIBUTION *W. and C. Mediterranean*
SIMILAR SPECIES *Sea Mallow (L. maritima), which has pale pink petals.*

Small Tree Mallow

Lavatera cretica (Malvaceae)

This softly hairy mallow is a more understated plant than Tree Mallow, with a weedier appearance. The delicate pink flowers have a shiny surface, with dark pink or purple veins, and a pronounced notch. Usually, only one flower in a cluster is open at any one time. The name *cretica* suggests that the plant comes from the island of Crete.

OCCURS *on waste or disturbed ground, road verges, and field margins, in dry and open areas.*

5–7 lobes

notched petals

flowers pale at centre

ANNUAL/BIENNIAL

veined petals

PLANT HEIGHT *20–120cm.*
FLOWER SIZE *2cm wide.*
FLOWERING TIME *March–June.*
LEAVES *Alternate, almost rounded, hairy, with lobed and toothed margins.*
FRUIT *Ring of up to 12 ribbed nutlets.*
DISTRIBUTION *Throughout the region.*
SIMILAR SPECIES *Common Mallow (p.78).*

Hibiscus

Hibiscus rosa-sinensis (Malvaceae)

PLANTED *in parks and gardens, or as a street tree. This species never becomes naturalized.*

This exotic-looking shrub from China thrives in the warm climate of the Mediterranean and is widely planted. There are pink and white forms but brilliant scarlet is the common colour. The stamens and stigmas are held at the tip of an exceptionally long column protruding from the mouth of the flower.

red, pink, or white flowers

prominent column

5 reflexed petals

PERENNIAL

toothed leaf margin

PLANT HEIGHT *1–5m.*
FLOWER SIZE *15cm wide.*
FLOWERING TIME *May–September.*
LEAVES *Oval, glossy, and dark green.*
FRUIT *Capsule, but rarely sets fruit.*
DISTRIBUTION *Throughout the region.*
SIMILAR SPECIES *Common Hibiscus (H. syriacus), which has a shorter column.*

Tamarix africana

Tamarix africana (Tamaricaceae)

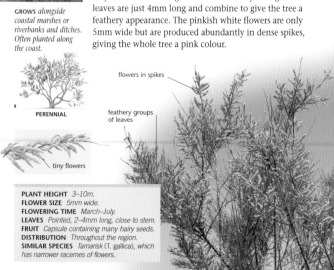

GROWS *alongside coastal marshes or riverbanks and ditches. Often planted along the coast.*

There are several *Tamarix* species in the region, but it is very difficult to distinguish them. The tiny blue-green leaves are just 4mm long and combine to give the tree a feathery appearance. The pinkish white flowers are only 5mm wide but are produced abundantly in dense spikes, giving the whole tree a pink colour.

flowers in spikes

PERENNIAL

feathery groups of leaves

tiny flowers

PLANT HEIGHT *3–10m.*
FLOWER SIZE *5mm wide.*
FLOWERING TIME *March–July.*
LEAVES *Pointed, 2–4mm long, close to stem.*
FRUIT *Capsule containing many hairy seeds.*
DISTRIBUTION *Throughout the region.*
SIMILAR SPECIES *Tamarisk (T. gallica), which has narrower racemes of flowers.*

Grey-leaved Cistus

Cistus albidus (Cistaceae)

The *Cistus* species are evergreen and often aromatic shrubs, characterized by their rose-like flowers with crumpled petals. These often fall from the plant in the heat of the early afternoon sun, so the ground is covered with their remains like confetti. The Grey-leaved Cistus is a common and widespread species with pink flowers. The name *albidus* (from the Latin word meaning whitish) refers to the dense white hair that cover the leaves, giving them a felted appearance.

OCCURS *typically on garigue or low maquis, in open woodland and other dry, rocky places; usually on limestone soil.*

PERENNIAL

5 pink petals

flat-margined leaf

numerous yellow anthers

wrinkled leaf surface

papery petals

PLANT HEIGHT *0.5–1m.*
FLOWER SIZE *Up to 6cm wide.*
FLOWERING TIME *April–June.*
LEAVES *Opposite, oblong to elliptical, covered with white hair.*
FRUIT *Dry capsule containing numerous seeds.*
DISTRIBUTION *Throughout the region.*
SIMILAR SPECIES *C. crispus, which has wavy, undulating leaves and smaller, more deeply coloured flowers.*

NOTE

A typical species of the garigue habitat, this plant has strong-tasting leaves that are not palatable to browsing animals, which protects them from being eaten. The leaves may be used as a tea.

Pomegranate

Punica granatum (Punicaceae)

Originally from S.W. Asia and cultivated in the Mediterranean region since ancient times, this occasionally spiny shrub or tree is famous for its fruit, which contain several seeds in a juicy pulp. The flowers have five to seven crumpled, scarlet petals and a waxy red calyx.

GROWN *for its fruit or as ornament in gardens and hedges; naturalized in scrub and maquis.*

glossy leaves

PERENNIAL

bright red crumpled petals

numerous stamens

fruit has leathery skin

PLANT HEIGHT *2–5m.*
FLOWER SIZE *3–4cm wide.*
FLOWERING TIME *May–September.*
LEAVES *Opposite, oblong, untoothed, glossy.*
FRUIT *Rounded, reddish brown berry with many seeds surrounded by pinkish juicy pulp.*
DISTRIBUTION *Throughout the region.*
SIMILAR SPECIES *None.*

Ivy-leaved Sowbread

Cyclamen hederifolium (Primulaceae)

This cyclamen flowers in autumn and has pink, recurved flowers with a darker V-shaped patch at the fold of each petal. The heart-shaped leaves have toothed margins and are mottled with grey on the upper surface, purplish below. The stems coil up on fruiting.

FORMS *patches in deciduous woods, scrub, maquis, and olive groves, in semi-shaded areas.*

PERENNIAL

marbled leaf surface

pink, upright petals

reflexed petals

V-shaped magenta blotch

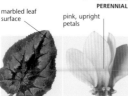

PLANT HEIGHT *5–10cm.*
FLOWER SIZE *1.4–2.2cm long.*
FLOWERING TIME *September–October.*
LEAVES *Heart-shaped, mottled, toothed.*
FRUIT *Capsule on coiled stem.*
DISTRIBUTION *France and Italy.*
SIMILAR SPECIES *C. repandum, which has deep magenta flowers appearing in spring.*

Oleander

Nerium oleander (Apocynaceae)

This evergreen shrub produces its showy flowers in the
height of summer. The vivid pink flowers are hard to miss,
though they may also be red or occasionally white. They
have five rather rounded petals, with a fringed "beard"
in the centre, and grow in dense clusters at the stem tips.
The leathery, dull green leaves grow in opposite pairs,
or in whorls of three or four. The fruit is an upright,
woody follicle, whose sides peel back to release
many feathery seeds. The plant is a favourite
for municipal planting schemes.

GROWS *naturally on
stream and river banks,
and rocky watercourses,
but widely planted in
gardens or alongside
roads and car parks.*

fringed
"beard"
in centre

salver-shaped
flowers

PERENNIAL

prominent
midrib

rounded
petals

ripe follicle
shedding
seeds

NOTE

*The whole plant is extremely poisonous,
causing heart failure, and death has been
known in children from eating only one leaf.
Contact with the milky sap of Oleander can
also cause severe skin irritation.*

PLANT HEIGHT *Up to 4m.*
FLOWER SIZE *3–4cm wide.*
FLOWERING TIME *June–September.*
LEAVES *Narrow lance-shaped, opposite or in whorls, dull green with
leathery texture and a prominent midrib.*
FRUIT *Large follicle 0.8–1.5cm long, splitting to release seeds.*
DISTRIBUTION *Throughout the region.*
SIMILAR SPECIES *None.*

Sea Bindweed

Calystegia soldanella (Convolvulaceae)

CRAWLS over ground on coastal dunes and other sandy or shingly places, but always on the coast.

NOTE

The long, flexible stems are quite strong and may be used as makeshift string, particularly for binding two pieces of wood together, but it is not long-lasting.

This common and attractive plant of sandy coasts has long, flexible, hairless stems that creep over the ground. Some stems run just under the soil surface and emerge to form a new plant. The leaves are characteristic, being distinctly kidney-shaped and with a succulent, fleshy texture to store moisture. They are glossy and can be up to twice as wide as they are long. The trumpet-shaped flowers are produced singly and are bright pink, with a white stripe down the centre of each of the five petals. Surrounding the sepals are two papery scales or bracts, a feature which distinguishes the *Calystegia* species from bindweeds of the related genus *Convolvulus*.

PERENNIAL

white stripe

kidney-shaped leaf

trailing stems

solitary flower

PLANT HEIGHT Stems up to 1m long.
FLOWER SIZE 40cm wide.
FLOWERING TIME May–August.
LEAVES Alternate, fleshy texture, and glossy green.
FRUIT Many-seeded capsule.
DISTRIBUTION Atlantic and Mediterranean coasts throughout the region.
SIMILAR SPECIES Ipomoea sagittata of salt marshes in S. Spain, S. Italy, and the islands, which has arrow-shaped leaves and pink flowers.

Mallow-leaved Bindweed

Convolvulus althaeoides (Convolvulaceae)

The flowers of this plant, like most bindweeds, only open in bright light; in dull weather they remain rolled up like a furled umbrella. When open, the flowers are quite striking, with their magenta-pink coloration and, unusually for bindweeds, a darker centre. The leaves are variable – the leaves at the top are roughly triangular and strongly lobed, while those towards the base are heart-shaped in outline.

OCCURS *on roadsides, dry fields, banks, hillslopes, and on sandy ground.*

PERENNIAL

unstriped flower

dark centre

lower stem leaf

dark-throated flower

PLANT HEIGHT *Up to 1m.*
FLOWER SIZE *5cm wide.*
FLOWERING TIME *April–July.*
LEAVES *Lower leaves with wavy margins.*
FRUIT *Dry capsule.*
DISTRIBUTION *Throughout the region.*
SIMILAR SPECIES *Pink Convolvulus (C. cantabrica), which has elliptical leaves.*

Convolvulus lanuginosus

Convolvulus lanuginosus (Convolvulaceae)

This non-creeping bindweed forms tufts on dry ground. It is well adapted to arid conditions, with leaves reduced to a minimum and all the surfaces, apart from the petals, covered with silvery grey silky hair to minimize moisture loss. This gives the whole plant a fine downy appearance, (*lanuginosus* means woolly). The flowers are borne in tight clusters. They may be pale pink or white, but always have conspicuous stripes on the undersides of the petals.

FORMS *loose tufts in dry rocky places, open areas of maquis; usually on limestone and often in the mountains.*

pale pink flower

narrow leaf

PERENNIAL

striped below

narrow, silvery stems

PLANT HEIGHT *20–30cm.*
FLOWER SIZE *2–2.5cm wide.*
FLOWERING TIME *April–June.*
LEAVES *Lance-shaped or elliptical.*
FRUIT *Hairless capsule.*
DISTRIBUTION *S. and E. Spain, S. France.*
SIMILAR SPECIES *Pink Convolvulus (C. cantabrica) has pinker, unstriped flowers.*

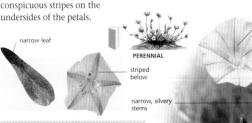

Pale Bugloss

Echium italicum (Boraginaceae)

OCCURS *on roadsides, waste ground, fields, vineyards, and rocky or grassy habitats.*

This robust species is easily identified by its tall, pyramidal shape caused by having shorter branches towards the top. The very pale blue or pink flowers are produced in long, curving cymes. Each is a short tube with five-pointed teeth, long protruding stamens, and a bristly calyx. The narrow, bristly leaves are found mostly towards the base.

BIENNIAL

shorter branches at top

narrow stem-leaf

protruding stamens

blue or pink flowers

PLANT HEIGHT *Up to 1m.*
FLOWER SIZE *1–1.2cm long.*
FLOWERING TIME *April–July.*
LEAVES *Narrow, lance-shaped, bristly.*
FRUIT *Three-sided nutlet.*
DISTRIBUTION *Throughout the region.*
SIMILAR SPECIES *E. asperrimum, which has fleshy pink flowers.*

Vervain

Verbena officinalis (Verbenaceae)

GROWS *in bare, rocky places, wasteland, roadsides, and old tracks; avoids acid soil.*

This wiry, hairy, and rather rough plant has long, square, branching stems bearing spikes of surprisingly small flowers. These are pink in colour with white centres, and each has five asymmetric lobes, making them appear almost two-lipped. The opposite leaves are strongly pinnately-lobed, and coarsely toothed.

PERENNIAL

deeply lobed leaf

narrow flower spikes

tough, wiry stems

PLANT HEIGHT *50–75cm.*
FLOWER SIZE *4–5mm wide.*
FLOWERING TIME *May–September.*
LEAVES *Opposite and toothed.*
FRUIT *Four-ribbed nutlets.*
DISTRIBUTION *Throughout the region.*
SIMILAR SPECIES *V. supina, which is a prostrate annual of damp, sandy meadows.*

Phlomis herba-venti

Philomis herba-venti (Lamiaceae)

Phlomis species are characterized by their hooded flowers in dense whorls. This attractive herbaceous plant has deep pink flowers with a folded upper lip that forms the narrow hood. All the flowers open at about the same time. Its stems are stiff and erect and the hairy leaves are spear-shaped with a wrinkled surface.

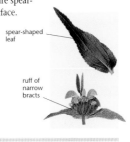

FOUND *in dry, stony, or rocky ground, cultivated fields, roadsides, and garigue; usually in the open.*

dense whorl of flower buds

PERENNIAL

spear-shaped leaf

ruff of narrow bracts

narrow flowerhead

PLANT HEIGHT *Up to 70cm.*
FLOWER SIZE *1.5–2cm long.*
FLOWERING TIME *May–July.*
LEAVES *Greyish, hairy, small-toothed.*
FRUIT *Four nutlets within the calyx.*
DISTRIBUTION *Throughout the region.*
SIMILAR SPECIES *P. purpurea of Portugal and Spain, which is a 2m high shrub.*

Spotted Deadnettle

Lamium maculatum (Lamiaceae)

This common wayside plant is popular in gardens, where its natural tendency to produce variegated leaves has led to many forms with silvery-blotched leaves, which often find their way back into the wild. The pinkish red, two-lipped flowers have dark spots on the lower lip and are found in whorls in the upper leaf axils.

INHABITS *shady places on roadsides, woodland margins, hedgerows, and olive groves.*

PERENNIAL

variegated leaf form

two-lipped flower

strongly-toothed leaves

whorls of pink flowers

PLANT HEIGHT *20–60cm.*
FLOWER SIZE *2–3.5cm long.*
FLOWERING TIME *February–October.*
LEAVES *Triangular-oval, sometimes blotched.*
FRUIT *Four nutlets.*
DISTRIBUTION *Throughout the region.*
SIMILAR SPECIES *L. garganicum, which has a long petal tube, much longer than its calyx.*

Common Thyme

Thymus vulgaris (Lamiaceae)

OCCURS *in the open on rocky ground, garigue, and clearings in woodland or maquis; on limestone soil.*

This aromatic shrub, often somewhat woody at the base, is the source of the widely used culinary thyme, and is easily identified by rubbing a few of the leaves between the fingers and testing their fragrance. The younger shoots and the leaves have a covering of fine white hair and the tiny leaves are in opposite pairs or clusters. The flowers are borne in small clusters at the stem tips and range in colour from almost white to pink or very pale purple. Each two-lipped flower has projecting stamens.

elliptical leaves

PERENNIAL

prominent stamens

tight cluster of flowers

3-lobed lower petal

PLANT HEIGHT *10–30cm.*
FLOWER SIZE *5–6mm long.*
FLOWERING TIME *April–July.*
LEAVES *Opposite, aromatic, with downturned margins.*
FRUIT *Four tiny nutlets enclosed in the calyx.*
DISTRIBUTION *Spain, S. France, and Italy.*
SIMILAR SPECIES *T. longicaulis of France and Italy, which has long, creeping branches, much longer leaves, and purple flowers.*

NOTE

Apart from its culinary uses, Thyme is also valued medicinally. It has antiseptic properties and treats respiratory diseases. However, it must be avoided by pregnant women.

Coridothymus capitatus

Coridothymus capitatus (Lamiaceae)

Although there are many very similar-looking thymes in the region, *Coridothymus capitatus* is quite distinctive. The stems have neat, regular clusters of long and short leaves along their length. All the brightly coloured flowers are clustered into a club-shape at the stem tips. The bracts below each flower overlap to give a cone-like effect.

FOUND *in dry places, hillsides, roadsides, and waste ground; always out in the open, usually on limestone.*

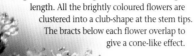

purple-pink flowers

bracts overlap at stem tip

leaves in clusters

flowers formed into a "club"

PERENNIAL

PLANT HEIGHT *20–50cm.*
FLOWER SIZE *Up to 1cm long.*
FLOWERING TIME *May–September.*
LEAVES *Larger leaves 1cm long, linear; shorter leaves borne in their axils.*
FRUIT *Four nutlets within the calyx.*
DISTRIBUTION *Throughout except for France.*
SIMILAR SPECIES *None.*

Nettle-leaved Figwort

Scrophularia peregrina (Scrophulariaceae)

Although robust and tall plants, figworts are often rather inconspicuous. This species is distinguished by its nettle-like, triangular leaves with toothed margins. The pouch-like reddish brown flowers are two-lipped, and are produced in lax clusters on branching side-shoots. Each flower has a leaf-like bract at the base.

GROWS *in cultivated and waste ground, vineyards, roadsides, and rocky places; also alongside old walls.*

loose flower clusters

nettle-like leaf

small, pouched flowers

rounded fruit capsule

PLANT HEIGHT *30–90cm.*
FLOWER SIZE *8mm long.*
FLOWERING TIME *April–June.*
LEAVES *Opposite, oval or triangular, toothed.*
FRUIT *Rounded capsule with a small beak.*
DISTRIBUTION *Throughout the region.*
SIMILAR SPECIES *S. auriculata, which has large spear-shaped leaves lobed at the base.*

ANNUAL

Snapdragon

Antirrhinum majus (Scrophulariaceae)

This plant is frequently cultivated as an annual for garden use, but in its wild state it often forms a woody base and surprisingly long stems. The flowers have two large pink or purple lips, the lower with a yellow or white "palate" that acts as a landing platform for bumblebees. Only large insects are able to force open the flower to access the nectar inside.

GROWS *on walls or among rocks, on old buildings or cliffs, or cultivated ground. Tolerant of shade.*

flowers on short stalks

untoothed leaf

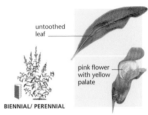

pink flower with yellow palate

long stems

BIENNIAL/ PERENNIAL

PLANT HEIGHT *Up to 1.5m.*
FLOWER SIZE *3–4.5cm long.*
FLOWERING TIME *April–October.*
LEAVES *Linear to oval, often wavy-edged.*
FRUIT *Capsule up to 1.4cm long.*
DISTRIBUTION *From Spain to Italy.*
SIMILAR SPECIES *Large Snapdragon (p.201), which has yellow flowers and is densely hairy.*

Lonicera implexa

Lonicera implexa (Caprifoliaceae)

A rather shrubby, evergreen honeysuckle, this plant has waxy leaves with a pale, milky bloom underneath. The most obvious feature of the leaves, however, is that they are joined together around the stem to form a cup, in which the tight clusters of flowers are formed. They are pink in bud, with a short lower lip.

FOUND *in garigue and maquis, on hillsides, and roadsides; usually on open ground.*

long, pink corolla tube

flowers formed in cup of leaves

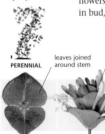

PERENNIAL

leaves joined around stem

short lower lip

PLANT HEIGHT *Up to 2m.*
FLOWER SIZE *4.5cm long.*
FLOWERING TIME *May–July.*
LEAVES *Opposite, oval, and mostly fused together, waxy, especially underneath.*
FRUIT *Orange berry cupped by leaves.*
DISTRIBUTION *Throughout the region.*
SIMILAR SPECIES *None.*

Etruscan Honeysuckle

Lonicera etrusca (Caprifoliaceae)

The commonest honeysuckle of the region, this plant generally relies on other vegetation for support, climbing over other plants or sprawling untidily, although it may occasionally form a shrubby bush of its own. At first, the flowers are a whorl of bright magenta-pink tubes, splitting open to reveal two whitish lobes. Each flower is short-lived, however, and soon fades to a creamy yellow. The oval leaves are joined together only at the very top of the stems just below the flower cluster, but do not cup them closely. Otherwise they are stalked, the stalks becoming progressively shorter up the stem.

CLIMBS *among shrubs or over rocks in open woodland, hedgerows, banks, light maquis, and roadsides. Generally prefers light shade.*

PERENNIAL

long lower lip

magenta buds

4-lobed upper lip

lower leaf

tightly clustered flowers

PLANT HEIGHT *Up to 2.5m.*
FLOWER SIZE *4.5cm long.*
FLOWERING TIME *May–July.*
LEAVES *Opposite, oval to elliptical, grey-green, fused just below the flower.*
FRUIT *Red berry that grows in clusters.*
DISTRIBUTION *Throughout the region.*
SIMILAR SPECIES *Fly Honeysuckle (L. xylosteum), which has smaller white flowers produced in pairs, and leaves that are never joined.*

NOTE

The flowers of honeysuckles are sweetly scented, but more so at night, when they attract long-tongued pollinating moths, which are guided by the white petals.

Red Valerian

Centranthus ruber (Valerianaceae)

GROWS *on coastal rocks and cliff faces, old walls, or sandy, gravelly places along roadsides or near the coast.*

PERENNIAL

Easily recognizable when it is in full flower throughout much of the spring and summer, Red Valerian is particularly conspicuous when it is clinging to the walls of an ancient castle or monument. It has erect, hairless stems, often branched at the top, bearing opposite pairs of grey-green, waxy leaves. The numerous flowers in broad clusters are notable not only for their curious unequally lobed petals, but also for the very long corolla tube with a spur at the base. The pink form is the most common, although deep red and white forms are often found.

flowers in clusters

thick stems

oval leaf

long, slender flower tube

spur at flower base

NOTE

The leaves of this plant are used as a salad vegetable in some parts of Europe, though they are an acquired taste, being rather bitter. The roots are collected and sold for use in soups.

PLANT HEIGHT *50–80cm.*
FLOWER SIZE *0.8–1.2cm long.*
FLOWERING TIME *April–July.*
LEAVES *Opposite, oval, fleshy, and untoothed.*
FRUIT *One-seeded nut with a feathery pappus.*
DISTRIBUTION *Throughout the region, introduced to much of Europe.*
SIMILAR SPECIES *C. angustifolius of France and Italy, which has smaller flowerheads and narrow, linear leaves.*

Valeriana tuberosa

Valeriana tuberosa (Valerianaceae)

Although the flowers of this species have five unequal lobes and are superficially like those of Red Valerian (p.92), they have no spur and the flower tube is shorter. They are also borne in smaller, more compact heads. The stem is solitary, and bears delicate upper leaves that are pinnately divided into narrow lobes. The leaves at the base of the stem are simple and elliptical.

OCCURS *in grassy, rocky places, cliffs, hillsides, open woodland, and in sheltered areas on limestone soil.*

protruding stamens

pink flowers

small, compact heads

PERENNIAL

lobed upper leaf

spoon-shaped lower leaf

PLANT HEIGHT *Up to 50cm.*
FLOWER SIZE *About 5mm long.*
FLOWERING TIME *April–June.*
FRUIT *Single-seeded nut with pronounced feathery tuft.*
DISTRIBUTION *Found throughout, except on most islands.*
SIMILAR SPECIES *V. tripteris, which is shorter.*

Grass-leaved Scabious

Scabiosa graminifolia (Dipsacaceae)

There are many *Scabiosa* and related species in the region, and they provide welcome colour in parched grasslands during the summer. This species is readily identifiable by virtue of its narrow, silky, grass-like leaves, which have a dense covering of fine hair. The flowers are in compact heads, the outer florets with much larger petal-lobes than the inner ones.

FOUND *in grassy or bare, rocky places, often in exposed regions, and particularly in mountainous areas.*

large-lobed outer florets

narrow leaf

single flowerhead

PERENNIAL

papery cells of fruit

PLANT HEIGHT *Up to 40cm.*
FLOWER SIZE *Flowerhead 4cm wide.*
FLOWERING TIME *May–July.*
LEAVES *Opposite, linear, with silky hair.*
FRUIT *Spherical head with papery chambers.*
DISTRIBUTION *Spain, France, and Italy.*
SIMILAR SPECIES *Many similar species in the region; best way to identify is leaf-shape.*

Carduus pycnocephalus

Carduus pycnocephalus (Asteraceae)

One of the most widespread of many thistle species in the region, *Carduus pycnocephalus* is a slender plant with silky-haired stems that have spiny wings along their length. The lobed leaves are armed with spines up to 1.2cm long. Its flowerheads occur in clusters of one to three, producing a small tuft of pink or purple tubular florets that never fan out widely. The bracts underneath curve outwards slightly, and widen at the base. The name *pycnocephalus* comes from the Greek *pycnos* (dense), and *cephalus* (head), and refers to the tightly-packed flowerheads.

OCCURS *in small clumps or colonies on roadsides, waste ground, field margins, and abandoned olive groves.*

narrow tuft of florets

thickened, spiny bracts

spiny-winged stems

ANNUAL/BIENNIAL

pink-purple florets

leaves may have white veins

NOTE

Carduus *species always have spiny-winged stems and achenes with simple hair. The similar* Cirsium *species have a pappus of feathery hair and may or may not have winged stems.*

PLANT HEIGHT *0.5–1m.*
FLOWER SIZE *Up to 2cm wide.*
FLOWERING TIME *March–June.*
LEAVES *Lobed and spiny, sometimes marbled.*
FRUIT *Achene with a tuft of simple hair.*
DISTRIBUTION *Throughout the region.*
SIMILAR SPECIES *Syrian Thistle (Notobasis syriaca), which has wingless stems and a ruff of lobed spines below the flowerhead.*

Galactites

Galactites tomentosa (Asteraceae)

This is one of the earliest thistle-type species to flower in the region. The branched outer florets of the flowerheads are longer than those in the centre, and radiate outwards to form a ring, giving the head a flattened appearance. The branched florets and spiny bracts make this plant unique.

FOUND on dry roadsides, fallow ground, stony or sandy pastures, and waste places.

short inner florets

longer outer florets

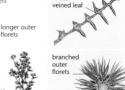

white-veined leaf

branched outer florets

ANNUAL/BIENNIAL

PLANT HEIGHT 20–100cm.
FLOWER SIZE 2–3cm wide.
FLOWERING TIME April–July.
LEAVES Oblong, pinnately lobed, narrow spiny teeth.
FRUIT Achene with long, feathery hair.
DISTRIBUTION Throughout the region.
SIMILAR SPECIES None.

Tyrimnus

Tyrimnus leucographus (Asteraceae)

This thistle is easily recognized by its very long stems topped with a single flowerhead. The tuft of florets fan out slightly, and vary in colour from whitish, flushed with pink or purple, to all pink. The pointed flower bracts are strongly overlapping, and often covered with cobwebby hair. The leaves are mostly basal, but the lower stems are leafy with spiny wings.

FORMS colonies in dry waste habitats, sandy and stony places, abandoned vineyards, and olive groves.

ANNUAL/BIENNIAL

pink-flushed florets

"shaving brush" of florets

narrow, spiny stem leaf

overlapping, cottony bracts

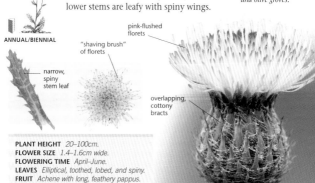

PLANT HEIGHT 20–100cm.
FLOWER SIZE 1.4–1.6cm wide.
FLOWERING TIME April–June.
LEAVES Elliptical, toothed, lobed, and spiny.
FRUIT Achene with long, feathery pappus.
DISTRIBUTION Throughout the region.
SIMILAR SPECIES Mantisalca salmantica has spreading florets and non-spiny, lobed leaves.

Illyrian Scotch Thistle

Onopordom illyricum (Asteraceae)

The *Onopordom* species include some of the bulkiest and most formidable thistles in the region. In this rather variable species, the erect stems are thickly covered with spiny wings and usually with felt-like hair which give the plant a yellowish or silvery appearance. The short, narrow leaves are stalkless and narrow in outline, and have deep spine-tipped lobes along their full length. Most noticeable are the triangular bracts below the purple flowerheads, which are broad at the base with dark spiny tips. The outer bracts strongly recurve downwards.

INHABITS *dry, rocky, or stony places, waste or fallow ground, roadsides, field boundaries, and olive groves, in sunny, open places.*

purple, tubular florets

recurved spiny bracts

BIENNIAL

felted stem with spiny leaves

NOTE

The unripe flowerheads of this thistle may be eaten like the related globe artichoke, but the spiny bracts must be carefully removed after cooking to avoid injury.

narrow, spiny leaves

brush-like flowerheads

PLANT HEIGHT *1–1.50m.*
FLOWER SIZE *4–6cm wide.*
FLOWERING TIME *June–July.*
LEAVES *Stalkless, oblong, pinnately lobed, and covered with white hair.*
FRUIT *Plump achene.*
DISTRIBUTION *Throughout the region.*
SIMILAR SPECIES *Scotch Thistle (O. acanthium), which has linear bracts that are not recurved.*

Milk Thistle

Silybum marianum (Asteraceae)

This common and widespread species is one of the most easily recognized thistles. The spiny leaves, which form large rosettes in the first year, are dark glossy green with a striking pattern of white veins. The smaller stem leaves formed in the second year are also veined, but coil back where they clasp the spineless stems. The solitary flowerheads are most distinctive of all, with bright green bracts that broaden at the base to form a spine-edged cup, narrowing at the end into a long, grooved spine.

OCCURS *on waste and fallow ground, roadsides, and field margins; also in open woodland, and olive groves. Prefers open, sunny places.*

purple, tubular florets

long, grooved spine

BIENNIAL

bracts form spine-edged cup

white-veined leaves

long bracts

NOTE

The plant has a long history of medical use, but recent research shows that it may be very helpful for regenerating damaged liver cells, and to treat liver damage caused by cancer or mushroom poisoning.

PLANT HEIGHT *Up to 1.5m.*
FLOWER SIZE *8cm wide, including bracts.*
FLOWERING TIME *April–June.*
LEAVES *Oblong, pinnately lobed with spines,*
FRUIT *Achene with tuft of white hair.*
DISTRIBUTION *Throughout the region.*
SIMILAR SPECIES *S. eburneum of Spain and N. Africa, which has whitish stems and longer spines on leaves and bracts.*

Red Star-thistle

Centaurea calcitrapa (Asteraceae)

OCCURS *on waste and cultivated ground, bare and sandy places, and roadsides; usually near the coast.*

This is a low, highly branched shrub that always has a rather untidy appearance. The leaves are deeply lobed into long, narrow leaflets that are often spread at odd angles. The flowers often arise where the stems branch, and their most noticeable feature is the long, very sharp, woody spines emerging from the bracts, with shorter spines in between.

BIENNIAL

all ray florets

lobed stem leaves

woody spine

pink-red flowerhead

PLANT HEIGHT *20–60cm.*
FLOWER SIZE *Flowerhead 0.8–1cm wide.*
FLOWERING TIME *June–September.*
LEAVES *Stem leaves lobed with narrow leaflets.*
FRUIT *Simple achene without a pappus.*
DISTRIBUTION *Throughout the region.*
SIMILAR SPECIES *Yellow Star-thistle (p.208), which has similar spines but yellow flowers.*

Crupina

Crupina crupinastrum (Asteraceae)

GROWS *on waste ground, roadsides, hill slopes, pastures, and meadows; sometimes forming large colonies.*

This slender, rather neat-looking, thistle-like plant is leafy only in the lower half. The upper half consists of fine branches, each with a single, small flowerhead. There is a short tuft of pale purple ray-florets, and below them, an attractive collection of narrow, pointed purple bracts.

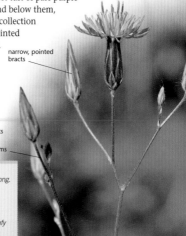

narrow, pointed bracts

narrow, toothed leaflets

ANNUAL

9–15 purple florets

branching stems

PLANT HEIGHT *20–50cm.*
FLOWER SIZE *Flowerheads 1.7–2.2cm long.*
FLOWERING TIME *May–July.*
LEAVES *Pinnately divided.*
FRUIT *Achene with a tuft of golden hair.*
DISTRIBUTION *Throughout the region.*
SIMILAR SPECIES *C. vulgaris, which is leafy all the way up to the stem branches.*

Salsify

Tragopogon porrifolius (Asteraceae)

This is a rather variable plant, but easily identified due to its narrow, grassy-looking leaves, which is unusual within the daisy family. Each leaf tapers to a fine point, but has a wide base which sheaths the stem. The pink or pale purple flowerheads open for only a few hours in the morning, closing by midday. The narrow bracts may be up to twice as long as the ray florets. In the subsp. *australis*, sometimes named *T. sinuatus*, the florets are mauve to deep purple and the bracts droop downwards sharply. The achenes have a long, feathery pappus, which together form a large clock, like an enormous dandelion.

INHABITS *grassy waysides and road verges, cultivated and waste ground; usually as isolated plants.*

narrow, pointed bracts

stamens with dark filaments

BIENNIAL

lilac to purple florets

long bracts

ssp. australis

NOTE

The edible root is highly esteemed, and may be eaten cooked or raw. It has a mild, sweet taste, similar to oysters. There are several cultivars available for producing fast, strong root growth.

PLANT HEIGHT *0.4–1.2m.*
FLOWER SIZE *2.5–5cm wide.*
FLOWERING TIME *April–July.*
LEAVES *Broadly linear, widened at the base.*
FRUIT *Large clock of feathery achenes.*
DISTRIBUTION *Throughout the region; often cultivated.*
SIMILAR SPECIES *Blue Lettuce (p.138); T. hybridum, which is a smaller annual, often with only five florets and much longer bracts.*

Rosy Garlic

Allium roseum (Alliaceae)

OCCURS *in grassy places, roadsides, cultivated ground, and embankments, sometimes forming large colonies where bulbils are produced.*

This delicate and attractive *Allium* species produces hemispherical heads of bell-like or cup-shaped flowers on fairly long stalks. Sometimes, however, some of the flowers are replaced by crimson-coloured bulbils, which eventually fall and produce new plants without the need for pollination or setting seed.

rose-pink flowers

narrow, unkeeled leaves

stalkless bulbils

PERENNIAL

flowerhead without bulbils

PLANT HEIGHT *Up to 60cm.*
FLOWER SIZE *Flowerheads up to 7cm wide.*
FLOWERING TIME *March–June.*
LEAVES *Narrow and tapering, up to 35cm long, flat on both sides with glossy surface.*
FRUIT *Small capsule containing black seeds.*
DISTRIBUTION *Throughout the region.*
SIMILAR SPECIES *A. nigrum (below).*

Allium nigrum

Allium nigrum (Alliaceae)

GROWS *in fields, olive groves, fallow, and cultivated ground; also cultivated in gardens.*

This species produces pink, lilac, or white flowers with a green midvein on each petal, especially below. The flowers are characterized by a large green or black ovary at the centre. It has wide, strap-shaped leaves which surround the base of the stem, and are attached at or below ground level.

flat, strap-shaped leaf

large green ovaries

star-shaped flowers

densely packed flowerhead

PERENNIAL

PLANT HEIGHT *60–90cm.*
FLOWER SIZE *Flowerhead up to 10cm wide.*
FLOWERING TIME *May–June.*
LEAVES *Up to 8cm wide and 50cm long, arching down to the ground.*
FRUIT *Capsule, up to 8mm long.*
DISTRIBUTION *Throughout the region.*
SIMILAR SPECIES *Rosy Garlic (above).*

Field Gladiolus

Gladiolus italicus (Iridaceae)

This beautiful and striking plant is usually seen close to cultivated ground, and is the most common of several species of Gladiolus found in the Mediterranean region. The name "Gladiolus" comes from the Latin meaning "little sword", referring to the shape of the leaves, which sheath each other in the same plane at the base. The remarkable flowers are enclosed by a green bract in bud, and open out to face in alternating directions. The two lower lateral petals have a flame-like white streak, sometimes also seen on the central petal.

FOUND *in cultivated or abandoned fields, olive groves, grassy places, and hillslopes; often in cereal crops, where it may become invasive.*

long bract protects flower bud

PERENNIAL

NOTE

An extract of the flowers may be used as an indicator of pH, turning bright pink in extreme acid conditions, changing to colourless at neutral pH, then green to yellow with increasing alkalinity.

flowers alternate in direction

3 upper and 3 lower petals

sword-shaped leaves

pink petals with "flame" streak

PLANT HEIGHT *50–100cm.*
FLOWER SIZE *5cm long.*
FLOWERING TIME *March–June.*
LEAVES *Upright, tapering, about 60cm long and up to 1.6cm wide.*
FRUIT *Three-lobed capsule containing several seeds.*
DISTRIBUTION *Throughout the region.*
SIMILAR SPECIES *G. communis, which is very similar but is often branched towards the base.*

Red Helleborine

Cephalanthera rubra (Orchidaceae)

The pinkish red flowers of this elegant, rather uncommon orchid, brighten the woods and copses it inhabits. The sepals and petals are alike, finely tapered to a point, the lateral sepals spreading like wings. The central lip has very fine yellow markings. The alternate, pale green leaves are narrow and tapered, and each is folded along its length.

FOUND *singly or in small groups in open woodland glades and rides, along shaded hedgerows; prefers semi-shade.*

loose flower spikes

pointed petals and sepals

leaf folded lengthwise

wing-like sepals

PERENNIAL

PLANT HEIGHT *40–60cm.*
FLOWER SIZE *Lower lip 1.7–2.2cm long.*
FLOWERING TIME *June–July.*
LEAVES *Alternate, long, with central fold.*
FRUIT *Capsule containing many tiny seeds.*
DISTRIBUTION *Throughout the region.*
SIMILAR SPECIES *Dark Red Helleborine (Epipactis atrorubens) has darker flowers.*

Violet Bird's-nest Orchid

Limodorum abortivum (Orchidaceae)

This species appears to feed on decaying matter in the soil, in the way that fungi do, though it may possibly act as a parasite on the roots of living plants. It therefore has no need of green leaves, and they are replaced by a few brown scales on the stem. The flower-spikes are produced singly, or in groups of four.

PREFERS *slightly shaded conditions in grassland, by roadsides, and embankments, usually near pine trees.*

spreading petals and sepals

violet tinge to whole plant

loose flower-spike

yellow-throated flower

PERENNIAL

PLANT HEIGHT *40–80cm.*
FLOWER SIZE *4–4.5cm wide.*
FLOWERING TIME *April–June.*
LEAVES *None, but several purple-brown scales on the stem.*
FRUIT *Many-seeded capsule.*
DISTRIBUTION *Throughout the region.*
SIMILAR SPECIES *Red Helleborine (above).*

Pink Butterfly Orchid

Orchis papilionacea (Orchidaceae)

One of the most conspicuous orchids, this species has relatively few but quite large flowers. It frequently hybridizes with Green-winged Orchid (p.104). Most of its leaves are in a basal rosette, and are linear to lance-shaped, channelled, and unspotted. There may also be several sheathing stem leaves. The bold flowers grow in a head of 3–12 blooms, each with a reddish bract beneath it. The sepals and upper petals form a small pointed hood; the lower lip is broad and rounded or heart-shaped, usually pink with darker pink dots or stripes.

FORMS *extensive colonies in open woodland, rocky hillsides, fields, and, and other grassy or stony habitats.*

densely-clustered flowers

PERENNIAL

unlobed lower lip

unspotted leaves

frilly margin to lower lip

NOTE

Pink Butterfly Orchid is one of the most widespread and variable of the Mediterranean orchids. The lower lip may be dark and heavily streaked, but may be almost white and unspotted.

PLANT HEIGHT *20–40cm.*
FLOWER SIZE *Lower lip 1–1.6cm long.*
FLOWERING TIME *February–May.*
LEAVES *Lance-shaped, unspotted, up to 10cm long.*
FRUIT *Capsule containing numerous tiny seeds.*
DISTRIBUTION *Throughout the region.*
SIMILAR SPECIES *O. tridentata, which forms similar compact heads but has flowers that are smaller with lobed lips.*

Green-winged Orchid

Orchis morio (Orchidaceae)

OCCURS in woodland clearings, grassy roadsides and meadows, scrub, banks, and maquis, sometimes forming colonies.

This species is widespread throughout Europe, but there are two particular subspecies often seen in the Mediterranean region. Subspecies *picta* (main image below) has a dark-spotted lower lip, and the lateral sepals may be purple-veined rather than greenish; subsp. *champagneuxii* has a completely unspotted lip, which is often folded back, and a club-shaped spur. Many hybrids also occur.

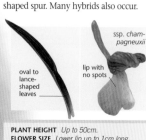

ssp. champagneuxii

lip with no spots

oval to lance-shaped leaves

dark-spotted lip

PERENNIAL

PLANT HEIGHT Up to 50cm.
FLOWER SIZE Lower lip up to 1cm long.
FLOWERING TIME February–May.
LEAVES Mostly in basal rosette, unspotted.
FRUIT Capsule containing several tiny seeds.
DISTRIBUTION Throughout N.W. Europe.
SIMILAR SPECIES Milky Orchid (p.105); Lady Orchid (p.106); Pyramidal Orchid (p.108).

Bug Orchid

Orchis coriophora (Orchidaceae)

PREFERS damp places, hillsides, grassy waysides, and poor meadows; often found on slightly acid soil.

This is a compact orchid whose flower spikes form a tightly packed cylindrical shape. The fragrant flowers are a mixture of red, green, and maroon, with a sharply pointed hood and a spotted lower lip, which has an elongated central lobe. The stem leaves reach up as far as the flowerhead.

flower buds

greenish maroon flowers

sharply pointed hood

narrow, unspotted leaves

long central lobe

PLANT HEIGHT 15–40cm.
FLOWER SIZE Lower lip 0.8–1.1cm long.
FLOWERING TIME March–May.
LEAVES Mostly in basal rosette.
FRUIT Capsule containing several tiny seeds.
DISTRIBUTION Throughout the region, except for the Balearic Islands.
SIMILAR SPECIES None.

PERENNIAL

Milky Orchid

Orchis lactea (Orchidaceae)

The pointed sepals, which form the "hood" of this species, recurve slightly, as though the flower is wearing a little crown. They are often striped with green veins, but unlike Green-winged Orchid they are usually against a white or creamy background, as are the dots and blotches on the lower lip. The flower spike is generally quite small, and the entire plant rarely grows taller than 20cm.

FOUND *in low grass and other vegetation, in garigue, scrub, or other dry, rocky ground.*

pointed sepals

small flowerhead

pointed leaves

PERENNIAL

broad basal leaf

green-veined hood

PLANT HEIGHT *10–20cm.*
FLOWER SIZE *Lower lip up to 1cm long.*
FLOWERING TIME *February–April.*
LEAVES *Three to four oblong basal leaves.*
FRUIT *Capsule containing several tiny seeds.*
DISTRIBUTION *Throughout the region.*
SIMILAR SPECIES *O. tridentata, with pink-violet flowers and a small tooth on the lower lip.*

Wavy-leaved Monkey Orchid

Orchis italica (Orchidaceae)

This common and eye-catching species bears numerous flowers; the petals are drawn out into long lobes, giving the flowerhead a somewhat frilly appearance. Each flower individually resembles the shape of a man, or a monkey with a tail between the "legs". The leaves are also distinctive, with wavy margins, and are sometimes covered with dark blotches.

GROWS *in maquis, garigue, open woodland (especially pine), scrub, and grassy places, often forming colonies.*

blotchy, wavy-edged leaves

"man-like" lower lip

PERENNIAL

oblong flowerhead

pale pink flowers

PLANT HEIGHT *20–40cm.*
FLOWER SIZE *Lower lip 1.2–1.8cm long.*
FLOWERING TIME *March–May.*
LEAVES *Five to eight leaves in basal rosettes.*
FRUIT *Capsule containing many tiny seeds.*
DISTRIBUTION *Throughout the region, except for France, Corsica, and Sardinia.*
SIMILAR SPECIES *Monkey Orchid (O. simia).*

Lady Orchid

Orchis purpurea (Orchidaceae)

A tall, statuesque species, Lady Orchid has flowers with a dark brownish purple hood formed by the upper petals and sepals, which gives the immature flowers a striking look, as though they have been dipped in ink. The pale lower lip is said to resemble a lady, with arms on either side and a wide skirt; it is lobed with a tiny, central tooth, and spotted with purple. The broad, shiny leaves are mostly basal, with one or two small narrow leaves on the long stem. They are roughly elliptic and slightly fleshy to the touch.

OCCURS *among grasses in woodland margins and glades, on road verges, and hill slopes, often in large, widely distributed groups; prefers chalky soil.*

PERENNIAL

broad flower-spike

tall, stout habit

broad leaf

purple spots on lip

NOTE

Orchis *species have two rounded tubers underground, one of which supplies food to the plant, while the other stores it.* Orchis *means testicle in Greek.*

PLANT HEIGHT 30–70cm.
FLOWER SIZE Lower lip 1–1.5cm long.
FLOWERING TIME April–June.
LEAVES Basal, oval to elliptical, shiny green.
FRUIT Capsule containing many tiny seeds.
DISTRIBUTION From N. Spain eastwards.
SIMILAR SPECIES *Burnt Orchid (O. ustulata), which is shorter, with very dark flower buds.*

Giant Orchid

Barlia robertiana (Orchidaceae)

Although not the tallest orchid, this is one of the most imposing orchids of the region, often forming a flower spike that is longer than the supporting stem. It is an early-flowering species, although it may be seen even as late as April. Its very fragrant flowers are quite variable, with green sepals and hood, and a generally pale pinkish lower lip flushed with magenta, red, or green, and is often marked with dark spots or streaks. The stem is usually flushed with red.

FOUND *in grassy places, scrub, open woodland, and often on banks and roadsides. Prefers nutrient-poor grassland on non-acid soil.*

unstalked flowers form a long spike

dark purple-brown hood

glossy leaf without spots

greenish, often spotted lip

lip lobed with '"arms and legs"

PERENNIAL

NOTE

This species has a rather confused taxonomy. It is thought to be related to the Lizard Orchid (p.164), and is also known as Himantoglossom longibracteatum and Loroglossom longibracteatum, both of which mean "strap-shaped tongue with long bracts".

PLANT HEIGHT 30–80cm.
FLOWER SIZE Lower lip 2cm long.
FLOWERING TIME February–April.
LEAVES Oval to elliptical, basal, dark glossy green.
FRUIT Capsule containing many tiny seeds.
DISTRIBUTION Throughout W. Mediterranean region.
SIMILAR SPECIES The size and flowering period precludes confusion with any other species.

Pyramidal Orchid

Anacamptis pyramidalis (Orchidaceae)

Widespread throughout the whole of Europe, this species can also be seen in large numbers in parts of the Mediterranean. The triangular shape of the newly formed flower spike gives this plant its name. The small, neat flowers are pale pink or, more often, deep pink or cerise. They have no veins or spots but each has a long, slender spur at the back, from which butterflies and moths sip nectar. The slender stem has sheath-like leaves along its entire length.

PROLIFERATES *in open grassy places, pastures, scrub, maquis, and roadsides; prefers well-drained, chalky soil.*

PERENNIAL

dense, conical flowerhead

sheath-like upper-leaf

unspotted leaf

deep pink flower

PLANT HEIGHT *20–40cm.*
FLOWER SIZE *Lip 6–8mm long.*
FLOWERING TIME *June–August.*
LEAVES *Alternate, lance-shaped, pale green.*
FRUIT *Capsule containing many tiny seeds.*
DISTRIBUTION *Throughout the region.*
SIMILAR SPECIES *Pale versions of Green-winged Orchid (p.104) and other Orchis species may superficially resemble this species.*

NOTE

The flowers are fragrant with the scent of vanilla during the day, which attracts pollinating moths, but in the evening the scent changes to that of goats, which repels moths.

Heart-flowered Serapias

Serapias cordigera (Orchidaceae)

The tallest and most robust of the tongue orchids, this plant sends up large spikes with tightly packed flowers. Each flower has a hood formed by the pinkish, dark-veined sepals, with a long, similarly-coloured bract behind. The lateral lobes of the flower lip form a cylindrical mouth inside the hood, but the central lobe is greatly extended, drooping down to form a heart-shaped tongue, which is hairy at the base and usually deep maroon or blood red in colour.

GROWS *in damp grassy habitats, scrub, open marshy woodland, streamsides, maquis, heathland, and sandy places.*

pinkish sepals

side lobes curled inside

PERENNIAL

narrow, channelled leaves

heart-shaped lip

NOTE

The Serapias orchids are named after the Egyptian god Serapis, an invention of the pharaoh Ptolemy I, in an attempt to find a common deity for both the Egyptian and the Greek cultures.

PLANT HEIGHT *20–45cm.*
FLOWER SIZE *Lower lip 2–3.5cm long.*
FLOWERING TIME *March–May.*
LEAVES *Narrow, channelled and pointed, continuing up the stem.*
FRUIT *Capsule containing numerous small seeds.*
DISTRIBUTION *Throughout the region.*
SIMILAR SPECIES *S. neglecta, of S.E. France and Corsica, which is shorter with paler, slightly orange-coloured flowers.*

Tongue Orchid

Serapias lingua (Orchidaceae)

OCCURS *in damp meadows and grassy places, scrub, olive groves, sometimes in partial shade and often near the coast.*

This species may be difficult to spot when growing among tall grasses. It has just a few blooms that are well separated, each flower being held horizontally with the "tongue" acting as a landing platform for visiting insects. The lower lip has darker side lobes that are curved round within the hood formed by the sepals. The "tongue" lobe may be yellowish, pink, or red. This slender-stemmed plant has narrow, lance-shaped leaves.

"hood" of striped sepals

long reddish bract

"tongue" held horizontally

PERENNIAL

lance-shaped leaf

dark lateral lip-lobes

narrow leaf clasps stem

NOTE

Tongue orchids offer no rewards such as nectar to visiting insects that pollinate them. Instead, the short tube formed by the flower offers a secure site for small insects to rest overnight.

PLANT HEIGHT *10–30cm.*
FLOWER SIZE *Lower lip 2.4–3.2cm long.*
FLOWERING TIME *March–May.*
LEAVES *Narrow, clasping the stem.*
FRUIT *Capsule containing numerous tiny seeds.*
DISTRIBUTION *Throughout the region.*
SIMILAR SPECIES *S. vomeracea, which has upright flowers with a white-haired, longer lip (3–4cm) that folds downwards.*

Woodcock Orchid

Ophrys scolopax (Orchidaceae)

There are many *Ophrys* species in the Mediterranean region, known collectively as Bee Orchids. They are highly variable, frequently forming subspecies which some authorities recognize as separate species in their own right, and Woodcock Orchid is no exception. Its flowers appear in spikes, with up to 12 flowers in a spike. The lower lips are rounded, sometimes with a forward projecting tooth at the tip, and there are two hairy appendages on the sides. The yellow-edged pattern on the lip varies greatly, even within subspecies.

FOUND *on grassy road verges, hillsides, meadows, open woodland, garigue, and maquis; plants widely spaced apart.*

three, upright pink sepals

O. heldreichii

O. apiformis

rounded lip with tooth

PERENNIAL

NOTE

Ophrys species have no scent or nectar, but the males of certain insects such as *Eucera* bees land on the flowers believing that they are females, and in attempting to mate they pollinate the flower.

PLANT HEIGHT *15–40cm.*
FLOWER SIZE *Lower lip up to 1.2cm long.*
FLOWERING TIME *March–May.*
LEAVES *Lance-shaped, glossy, on lower stem.*
FRUIT *Capsule containing numerous tiny seeds.*
DISTRIBUTION *Throughout the region.*
SIMILAR SPECIES *Bee Orchid (p.112); Late Spider Orchid (O. fuciflora), which has a broad, squarish lower lip.*

Bee Orchid

Ophrys apifera (Orchidaceae)

INHABITS *woodland margins, meadows, maquis, scrub, garigue, road verges, and dune slacks.*

One of the most commonly found *Ophrys* species, this plant has pink sepals, and a rounded lower lip with a short tip which is bent backwards. The two upper petals may be linear or very short, and between them there is a pronounced hood hanging forward.

leaf-like bract

pale green leaf

yellow markings on lip

green hood

dark brown lip

PERENNIAL

PLANT HEIGHT *25–45cm.*
FLOWER SIZE *Lower lip 1–1.3cm long.*
FLOWERING TIME *April–May.*
LEAVES *Shiny, mostly basal, in loose rosettes.*
FRUIT *Capsule containing several tiny seeds.*
DISTRIBUTION *Throughout the region.*
SIMILAR SPECIES *Woodcock Orchid (p.111);
Late Spider Orchid (O. fuciflora).*

Sawfly Orchid

Ophrys tenthredinifera (Orchidaceae)

FOUND *in scrub on stony or grassy ground, maquis, garigue; often close to the coast.*

This attractive species has rather rounded sepals which are usually pink, though sometimes greenish. The upper petals are broadly triangular with blunt tips. The lower lip is squarish or lobed in outline, with a wide margin that is usually yellow, though it may be green or light brown. The speculum has a C- or W-shaped outline.

pink sepals

yellow lip-margin

form with green sepals

robust, leafy stem

PERENNIAL

PLANT HEIGHT *10–45cm.*
FLOWER SIZE *Lower lip up to 1.4cm long.*
FLOWERING TIME *March–May.*
LEAVES *Broadly lance-shaped; some on stem.*
FRUIT *Capsule containing several tiny seeds.*
DISTRIBUTION *Throughout the region.*
SIMILAR SPECIES *Yellow Bee Orchid (p.216),
which has a brighter yellow lip-margin.*

Purple-Blue

Purple and blue flowers may be seen as the same colour by some insects; for example, the red element in purple is invisible to a bee. However, such colours are frequently "highlighted" by a white centre, such as in Coris, below. Many members of the borage family, such as Large Blue Alkanet, produce flowers that are red or purple in bud but become blue when they are mature, so that insects are less inclined to visit the purple flowers, whose pollen may not yet have become fully ripe.

SAGE

SCARLET PIMPERNEL

LUCERNE

LARGE BLUE ALKANET

Love-in-a-Mist

Nigella damascena (Ranunculaceae)

SCATTERED over dry fields, stony land, olive groves, and disturbed or cultivated soil.

This is an attractive but nonetheless inconspicuous plant with a pale blue or white petalled flower, borne singly, above a ruff of feathery bracts. More noticeable are the united follicles of the fruit which inflate as they ripen. The leaves are divided into linear, feathery segments.

hugely inflated fruit

prominent styles

feathery leaves

blue or white petals

ANNUAL

PLANT HEIGHT	10–40cm.
FLOWER SIZE	4–5cm wide.
FLOWERING TIME	May–July.
LEAVES	Alternate, divided.
FRUIT	5–6 united greatly inflated follicles.
DISTRIBUTION	Throughout the region.
SIMILAR SPECIES	N. arvensis, which has smaller flowers and non-inflated fruit.

Eastern Larkspur

Consolida orientalis (Ranunculaceae)

GROWS on disturbed soil of arable fields, waysides, olive groves, and other cultivated places; also in gardens.

Eastern Larkspur is a small, upright plant with highly divided leaves that almost give the appearance of whorls. The complex light to dark blue petals form a "horned pouch" at the front and a curved spur at the back, with four or five broad petals in between.

ANNUAL

complex petal arrangement

curved spur

flowers in a raceme

fruit is a single follicle

PLANT HEIGHT	Up to 50cm.
FLOWER SIZE	2–2.8cm wide.
FLOWERING TIME	April–July.
LEAVES	Divided into numerous linear lobes.
FRUIT	Single follicle, turning black.
DISTRIBUTION	Throughout the region.
SIMILAR SPECIES	Forking Larkspur (C. regalis), which has branching flower stems.

Hepatica

Hepatica nobilis (Ranunculaceae)

An evergreen plant, Hepatica has distinctive leaves, recognizable long after the flowers had died. They have three oval lobes, mottled purplish below, with strongly marked veins. The flowers have six or seven oval, deep blue petals with contrasting white anthers, and are borne on hairy, unbranched stems.

GROWS *in clumps or carpets among leaf-litter in woods or rocky places.*

oval petals

white anthers

PERENNIAL

blue or pinkish petals

3-lobed, mottled leaves

PLANT HEIGHT *10–20cm.*
FLOWER SIZE *1.5–2.5cm wide.*
FLOWERING TIME *March–May.*
LEAVES *Basal, three-lobed with heart-shaped base, fleshy, glossy green, veined or mottled.*
FRUIT *Cluster of achenes.*
DISTRIBUTION *Throughout in montane areas.*
SIMILAR SPECIES *None.*

Narrow-leaved Lupin

Lupinus angustifolius (Fabaceae)

This slender lupin has short-haired, alternately branching stems. The long-stalked leaves have a fan of five to nine very narrow leaflets not more than 5mm wide. The flowers range from light to dark blue, usually with darker veins on the standard and wing petals, and are borne alternately on the stem.

FORMS *colonies in maquis, garigue, open fields, and vineyards; on acid, sandy soil.*

up to 9 leaflets

long raceme of flowers

linear leaflets

pod with 4–6 seeds

ANNUAL

veined, blue petals

PLANT HEIGHT *30–80cm.*
FLOWER SIZE *Up to 1.2cm long.*
FLOWERING TIME *March–May.*
LEAVES *Digitate, with 5–9 narrow leaflets.*
FRUIT *Brown or black pod, with 4–6 seeds.*
DISTRIBUTION *Throughout the region.*
SIMILAR SPECIES *L. varius, which is very hairy, has broader leaves and white-blotched flowers.*

Lucerne

Medicago sativa (Fabaceae)

Also known as Alfalfa, this plant has been introduced throughout Europe as a fodder crop for cattle, and to improve the fertility of the soil due to nitrogen-fixing bacteria in its roots. As a consequence, it is no longer known as a truly wild plant, although it frequently escapes from cultivation. The trifoliate leaves are divided into long, slender leaflets, and the loose clusters of flowers vary greatly in colour from pale pink to deep violet. The fruit is a small, straight, curved, or spiral pod.

FORMS colonies on cultivated and waste ground, roadsides, and disturbed, rough, and grassy areas.

NOTE

The sprouted seeds are highly nutritious and make an excellent addition to salads. However, recent research suggests that large quantities may cause liver damage in susceptible people.

PERENNIAL

pink to violet flowers

flowers in clusters

long, narrow leaflets

toothed leaflet tip

coiled seed pod

PLANT HEIGHT 40–90cm.
FLOWER SIZE 7–11mm long.
FLOWERING TIME June–July.
LEAVES Alternate, trifoliate, elliptical leaflets.
FRUIT Spiralled pod, 5–6mm wide, with a hole in the centre.
DISTRIBUTION Throughout the region.
SIMILAR SPECIES Pitch Trefoil (p.117), which has larger leaflets and larger flower clusters.

Pitch Trefoil

Bituminaria bituminosa (Fabaceae)

Until recently this plant's Latin name was *Psoralea bitiminosa*. It is a common wayside plant of the region, occurring in a wide variety of habitats and with a long flowering season. Superficially similar to Lucerne (p.116), it has a more open, spreading habit. It can readily be identified by the leaves alone, which have a dark, glossy surface outlined by a narrow margin of white, downy hair. When crushed, the leaves give off an overpowering, tar-like smell – a familiar scent of the Mediterranean area – which is noticeable even when brushing past the thin, wiry stems.

OCCURS *in dry places such as waste or cultivated ground, roadsides, rocky places, and garigue. It may be found close to the sea or even in light woodland.*

hairy, wiry stems

bi-coloured violet flowers

PERENNIAL

leaves with silvery margin

NOTE

The plant contains Psoralen, a light-sensitive compound which is sometimes used in the treatment of the skin disease psoriasis. Patients take the drug internally or externally and are then exposed to controlled amounts of ultraviolet light.

calyx with immature pod

PLANT HEIGHT *30–100cm.*
FLOWER SIZE *1.5–2cm long.*
FLOWERING TIME *March–August.*
LEAVES *Trifoliate with slender, elliptical leaflets, dark, glossy green.*
FRUIT *Flattened pod, 1.5cm long with a curved spur.*
DISTRIBUTION *Throughout the region.*
SIMILAR SPECIES *Lucerne (p.116); P. americana which has more rounded and toothed leaflets.*

Erodium ciconium

Erodium ciconium (Geraniaceae)

This storksbill may form considerable colonies at the edges of arable fields in spring. It is best viewed in the morning, as the petals start to fall soon after opening. The lilac-blue coloration of the flowers is quite distinctive, separating it from the more usual pink of other storksbills. The "beaks" of the fruit are exceptionally long, and are held vertically erect so that en masse they take on the appearance of a townscape of church spires. The leaves are pinnately divided into more or less rounded, toothed leaflets.

OCCURS *in colonies on roadsides, cultivated and waste places, and olive groves, or close to walls; on dry, sandy soil.*

ANNUAL/BIENNIAL

veined, blue-violet petals

fruits held erect

deeply lobed leaves

beak to 10cm long

NOTE

The name Erodium is from the Greek erodios, *meaning heron.* Ciconium *means stork, so the plant is named twice in reference to its long, beak-like fruit. The name of the similar* E. gruinum *means heron-crane.*

PLANT HEIGHT *20–50cm.*
FLOWER SIZE *1.4–1.6cm wide.*
FLOWERING TIME *February–April.*
LEAVES *Up to 9cm long; pinnate, with small toothed leaflets between the larger ones.*
FRUIT *Five mericarps joined into a beak, 6–10cm long.*
DISTRIBUTION *Throughout the region except for Portugal.*
SIMILAR SPECIES *E. botrys, which has more deeply divided leaves.*

Beautiful Flax

Linum narbonense (Linaceae)

It is difficult to miss this plant in sunny weather, when its bright azure-blue flowers open. Unlike other flaxes, Beautiful Flax retains its petals after midday, but they are nevertheless very delicate and short-lived. At a distance, the flowers may be mistaken for those of *Aphyllanthes* (p.139), which grows in similar habitats, but that plants' rush-like leaves distinguish it immediately from Beautiful Flax.

INHABITS *open, rocky, or grassy areas on well-drained, sandy soil; also abandoned fields and vineyards.*

white centre to flower

stems branched at top

linear leaves

PERENNIAL

5 bright blue petals

PLANT HEIGHT *Up to 50cm.*
FLOWER SIZE *3–4cm wide.*
FLOWERING TIME *April–June.*
LEAVES *Greyish, with one or three veins.*
FRUIT *Rounded capsule.*
DISTRIBUTION *Throughout the region, eastwards to the Adriatic.*
SIMILAR SPECIES *Pale Flax* (L. bienne).

Nicean Milkwort

Polygala nicaensis (Polygalaceae)

Milkworts have a curious petal arrangement. The three true petals are joined together; the central one is usually white and with a conspicuously fringed lip. Two sepals form the "wings" of the flower, and usually give the blooms a deep colour, as they may be dark or paler blue, pink, or occasionally white.

OCCURS *in dry, grassy, or stony places such as roadsides, garigue, or maquis; often among long grass.*

narrow, lance-shaped leaves

PERENNIAL

flowers in loose spikes

fringed, central petal

PLANT HEIGHT *15–30cm.*
FLOWER SIZE *8–11mm long.*
FLOWERING TIME *April–July.*
LEAVES *Narrow, lance-shaped, stalkless.*
FRUIT *Small, rounded capsule.*
DISTRIBUTION *S. France and N.W. Italy.*
SIMILAR SPECIES *Common Milkwort* (P. vulgaris), which is shorter with smaller flowers.

Sea Holly

Eryngium maritimum (Apiaceae)

GROWS *in small patches or extensive colonies along the coast, chiefly on sand dunes and sometimes on shingle.*

This member of the carrot family is unmistakable for many reasons. Most distinctive are its bluish or greenish grey leaves. They are stiff and waxy, undulating like dried leather, and are coarsely toothed, with each tooth ending in a sharp spine. The upper leaves are unstalked while the lower leaves are long-stalked. A tight ruff of bracts below the flowerhead is similarly spined, but may have a blue-violet tint, reflecting the colour of the blue flowers. The final clue to identity is the habitat, for the plant is restricted to sandy coasts.

waxy, grey-green leaves

whitish leaf veins

rounded flowerhead

tiny blue flowers

spiny bracts below flowerhead

NOTE

The root of this plant was popular in the 17th century as a candied sweetmeat; the candied root was also used as an expectorant.

PLANT HEIGHT *30–60cm.*
FLOWER SIZE *Flowerhead 1.5–3cm wide.*
FLOWERING TIME *June–September.*
LEAVES *Basal and alternate, lobed, and toothed into spines.*
FRUIT *Mericarp with overlapping scales.*
DISTRIBUTION *Throughout the region.*
SIMILAR SPECIES *Field Eryngo (p.157); E. aquifolium of S. Spain; E. amethystinum of Italy, which has pinnate leaves and small flowerheads.*

PERENNIAL

Scarlet Pimpernel

Anagallis arvensis (Primulacea)

The flowers of this diminutive plant may be bright scarlet or deep blue, often with the two colour forms growing together. However, the flowers only open in bright sunshine. The margins of the petals are hairy or finely toothed, which separates this species from the very similar *Anagallis foemina*, which has untoothed petals.

OCCURS *on wasteland, fields and field margins, garigue, and dry, sandy ground close to the sea.*

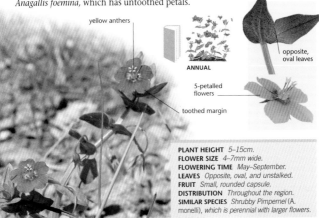

yellow anthers

ANNUAL

opposite, oval leaves

5-petalled flowers

toothed margin

PLANT HEIGHT *5–15cm.*
FLOWER SIZE *4–7mm wide.*
FLOWERING TIME *May–September.*
LEAVES *Opposite, oval, and unstalked.*
FRUIT *Small, rounded capsule.*
DISTRIBUTION *Throughout the region.*
SIMILAR SPECIES *Shrubby Pimpernel (A. monelli), which is perennial with larger flowers.*

Coris

Coris monspeliensis (Primulaceae)

Superficially resembling a kind of Thyme (p.88), each flower of this unusual member of the Primrose family has five distinct petals in a "star" arrangement. Each of the densely packed flowers has three long and two shorter petals. The petals may be pink or purple as well as the more usual blue.

FOUND *in open, rocky, or sandy areas, and garigue, usually near the coast, or sometimes in the mountains.*

dense, linear leaves

BIENNIAL/PERENNIAL

lobed, unequal petals

bell-shaped calyx

flower clusters at stem tips

PLANT HEIGHT *Up to 30cm.*
FLOWER SIZE *1.2cm wide.*
FLOWERING TIME *April–July.*
LEAVES *Alternate, with small teeth.*
FRUIT *Rounded capsule, 2mm wide.*
DISTRIBUTION *Throughout the region.*
SIMILAR SPECIES *Coris hispanica of S. Spain, which has white or pale pink flowers.*

Common Sea Lavender

Limonium vulgare (Plumbaginaceae)

The erect, wiry stems of this salt marsh plant branch at the top and bear tight heads of tiny, pink to lilac, five-petalled flowers, each flower surrounded by papery bracts. The narrow, basal leaves have a leathery texture. Each leaf has a single prominent vein, and tapers to a stalk about half the length of the leaf blade.

FORMS *extensive carpets on the mud of salt marshes, colouring large areas with its flowers.*

tough, leafless stems

tight flower clusters

PERENNIAL

single-veined leaf

papery bracts

PLANT HEIGHT 20–40cm.
FLOWER SIZE 6–8mm long.
FLOWERING TIME July–October.
LEAVES Basal, oblong to elliptical.
FRUIT Small capsule with papery calyx.
DISTRIBUTION Throughout the region.
SIMILAR SPECIES Matted Sea Lavender (L. bellidifolium), which has three-veined leaves.

Winged Sea Lavender

Limonium sinuatum (Plumbaginaceae)

This attractive sea lavender is frequently seen inland as well as close to the coast. The flowers are borne in compact clusters on branching stems. The petals of each flower are creamy white or yellowish, and stand out against the mauve sepals forming a cup beneath them. The stems have three or four narrow wings running along their length, with the leaves forming a rosette at the base.

OCCURS *in rocky and sandy places, short grassland, and dry coastal sites, sometimes inland.*

toothed leaf

flowers in a flattish cluster

PERENNIAL

mauve sepals

white petals

PLANT HEIGHT 20–40cm.
FLOWER SIZE 1.5cm long.
FLOWERING TIME April–September.
LEAVES Rosette of pinnately divided leaves.
FRUIT Single-seeded capsule.
DISTRIBUTION Throughout the region.
SIMILAR SPECIES The white or yellowish petals make this species distinctive.

Greater Periwinkle

Vinca major (Apocynaceae)

Unmistakable when in flower, this attractive plant has long, trailing stems that twine over other vegetation for a considerable distance. The large blooms have five blue-violet petals, which are often slightly twisted like a propeller or the screw of a ship. These join to form a short, angled tube at the base, which is paler inside. The broad leaves are in pairs and rounded at the base. They have a deep, glossy green surface and a margin of very fine hair. Greater Periwinkle is often cultivated in gardens, sometimes with variegated leaves.

CREEPS *over grasses and other vegetation in woodland margins, scrub, riverbanks, and hedgerows, to form large patches.*

PERENNIAL

NOTE

Although poisonous, Greater Periwinkle contains an alkaloid "vincamine", which is used medicinally to treat excessive bleeding, and "reserpine", which can reduce blood pressure.

pale centre to flower

blue-violet petals

glossy leaf surface

slightly twisted petals

PLANT HEIGHT *Up to 30cm.*
FLOWER SIZE *3–5cm wide.*
FLOWERING TIME *February–May.*
LEAVES *Opposite, oval, shiny dark green.*
FRUIT *Forked capsule, 4–5cm long.*
DISTRIBUTION *Throughout the region.*
SIMILAR SPECIES *Intermediate Periwinkle* (V. difformis), *which has pale blue, almost white flowers on longer stems.*

Purple Gromwell

Buglossoides purpurocaerule (Lithospermum)

INHABITS *semi-shaded areas such as chalky woodland margins, hedgerows, and banks.*

Leafy, non-flowering as well as flower-bearing shoots are produced on this plant, but the brightly coloured flowers are still easily spotted even in shady situations. The flowers are clustered together with many narrow bracts, and are pinkish violet at first but soon change to a deep violet. The fruit are tiny white nutlets, like porcelain beads, that remain attached to the hairy stems into the late summer.

narrow, untoothed leaf

dark green leaves

flowers in small clusters

5 deep violet petals

woody stem

PERENNIAL

PLANT HEIGHT *40–60cm.*
FLOWER SIZE *1.4–1.9cm long.*
FLOWERING TIME *March–June.*
LEAVES *Alternate, lance-shaped, hairy.*
FRUIT *Up to four hard, shiny white nutlets.*
DISTRIBUTION *Throughout the region.*
SIMILAR SPECIES *Shrubby Gromwell (L. fruticosum), which is a taller, shrubbier plant.*

Purple Viper's Bugloss

Echium plantagineum (Boraginaceae)

GROWS *in sandy field margins, waste ground, roadsides, and embankments.*

This common and conspicuous plant of the region may be confused with the equally common and more widespread Viper's Bugloss (*E. vulgare*). This plant, however, feels softer and less bristly to the touch than most buglosses. The larger flowers, initially red, become purple as they mature rather than deep blue, and it has a more branching habit. Purple Viper's Bugloss is often found close to the sea or on the seashore.

ANNUAL/BIENNIAL

2 protruding stamens

flowers mature from red to purple

prominent veins

PLANT HEIGHT *30–60cm.*
FLOWER SIZE *2–3cm long.*
FLOWERING TIME *April–July.*
LEAVES *Upper leaves are softly bristly.*
FRUIT *Three-sided nutlet.*
DISTRIBUTION *Throughout the region.*
SIMILAR SPECIES *E. parviflorum, which is shorter with flowers only 1.2cm long.*

Large Blue Alkanet

Anchusa azurea (Boraginaceae)

The Large Blue Alkanet is easily recognizable along roadsides and field margins on account of the brilliant colour of its flowers. The buds are purple at first, soon changing to a deep ultramarine on opening fully. In common with other members of its family, the flowerheads are formed in a coil, opening at the base first with the coil unrolling as more flowers mature. The very hairy stems and sepals are often tinged red or purple. Its open, branched habit is a further clue to identification.

OCCURS as scattered plants in fields, olive groves, waysides, and cultivated ground, in full sun on dry soil.

long basal leaf

flowers open in coils

PERENNIAL

5 blue petals

robust, bristly stems

branched stems

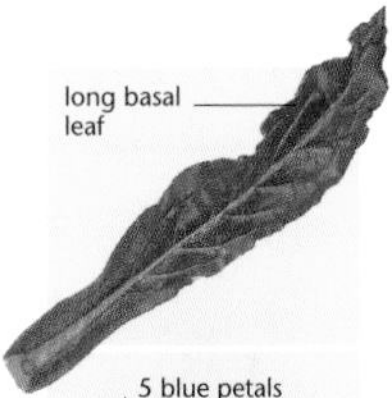

PLANT HEIGHT *40–120cm.*
FLOWER SIZE *2cm wide.*
FLOWERING TIME *March–June.*
LEAVES *Up to 30cm long at the base, upper leaves clasping the stem.*
FRUIT *Oblong nutlet up to 1cm long.*
DISTRIBUTION *Throughout the region.*
SIMILAR SPECIES *Alkanet (A. officinalis), which has smaller, violet flowers; Bugloss (A. arvensis), which is smaller with very rough leaves.*

NOTE

Especially suited for a dry garden, the Large Blue Alkanet has been cultivated outside its native range for its attractive flowers. The flowers may be used as a decorative addition to salads.

Borage

Borago officinalis (Boraginaceae)

OCCURS *in arable fields, wasteland, and disturbed soil; favours dry, sunny places.*

Borne in loose, branched clusters, the nodding, ultramarine blue flowers of this plant have a curious appearance as the black stamens form a cone inside the white centre of the flower. This roughly hairy plant has transparent, glass-like bristles, which give it a frosted appearance as well as some protection from grazing animals. Borage is a widespread plant that has long been cultivated throughout the region. The leaves may be cooked and eaten like cabbage or spinach, and the flowers make an attractive, cucumber-flavoured addition to drinks.

ANNUAL

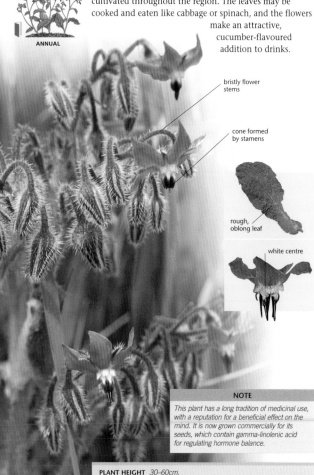

bristly flower stems

cone formed by stamens

rough, oblong leaf

white centre

NOTE

This plant has a long tradition of medicinal use, with a reputation for a beneficial effect on the mind. It is now grown commercially for its seeds, which contain gamma-linolenic acid for regulating hormone balance.

PLANT HEIGHT *30–60cm.*
FLOWER SIZE *2–2.5cm wide.*
FLOWERING TIME *May–September.*
LEAVES *Alternate, basal, oval to oblong, untoothed, stalked.*
FRUIT *Four nutlets at the base of the calyx.*
DISTRIBUTION *Throughout the region.*
SIMILAR SPECIES *B. pygmaea of Corsica and Sardinia, which is much smaller with bell-shaped flowers, rather like a Campanula species.*

Blue Hound's-tongue

Cynoglossum creticum (Boraginaceae)

This is an upright plant with soft leaves that clasp the hairy stems. The flowers are produced in small, nodding cymes at the stem tips and are notable for their deep, lilac-blue colour, netted and veined in a deep inky blue. The fruit are clusters of four large, hooked nutlets.

GROWS *in open grassy ground, roadsides, olive groves, vineyards, or by streams and ditches.*

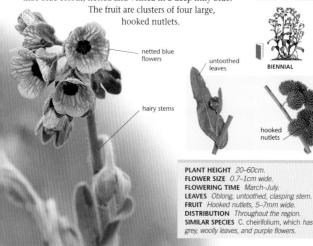

netted blue flowers

untoothed leaves

hairy stems

BIENNIAL

hooked nutlets

PLANT HEIGHT *20–60cm.*
FLOWER SIZE *0.7–1cm wide.*
FLOWERING TIME *March–July.*
LEAVES *Oblong, untoothed, clasping stem.*
FRUIT *Hooked nutlets, 5–7mm wide.*
DISTRIBUTION *Throughout the region.*
SIMILAR SPECIES *C. cheirifolium, which has grey, woolly leaves, and purple flowers.*

Tree Germander

Teucrium fruticans (Lamiaceae)

This plant forms a shrub with a woody base. The leaves are untoothed, with a dark, glossy upper surface, but densely felted below. As in other *Teucrium* species, the upper lip of the flowers is absent, but the pale blue lower lip has a long central lobe. Tree Germander is grown as an ornamental shrub.

FORMS *thickets in garigue, maquis, and other wooded ground near the coast.*

glossy above

prominent stamens

long lower lip

clustered flowers

PERENNIAL

PLANT HEIGHT *Up to 1.5m.*
FLOWER SIZE *1.5–2.5cm.*
FLOWERING TIME *February–June.*
LEAVES *Opposite, oval, white-felted beneath.*
FRUIT *Four nutlets within the calyx.*
DISTRIBUTION *Throughout the region.*
SIMILAR SPECIES *T. marum, which has smaller, purplish flowers in denser clusters.*

Rosemary

Rosmarinus officianalis (Lamiaceae)

FOUND *growing among rocks on the steep banks of roadsides or hillsides, or in maquis, garigue, and open woodland, in the sun or shade.*

PERENNIAL

Rosemary is a familiar plant of the herb garden, but the wild form often grows as a straggly bush of considerable size. The flowers are generally much paler blue than many garden varieties, and may be almost white. They are usually clustered towards the tops of the upright stems, though sometimes only a few are open at any one time, as the plant has a long flowering season. The highly aromatic leaves, present throughout the year, are densely clustered around the stems at an upswept angle, and are silvery white below.

clustered leaves

pale blue flower

prominent stamens

NOTE

The leaves are well known for their culinary uses; the flowers have a milder taste and may be added to peas or spinach. The volatile oil is used in aromatherapy as a stimulant tonic.

small, linear leaves

2-lipped flower

PLANT HEIGHT *Up to 1.5m.*
FLOWER SIZE *1–1.5cm long.*
FLOWERING TIME *January–May, occasionally at other times.*
LEAVES *Linear, leathery, deep glossy green with inrolled margins, white below.*
FRUIT *Four brown nutlets at base of calyx.*
DISTRIBUTION *Throughout the region.*
SIMILAR SPECIES *R. eriocalyx of S. Spain is greyish with shorter leaves.*

Common Lavender

Lavandula angustifolia (Lamiaceae)

Common Lavender is a medium-sized woody perennial which bears flowers at the tips of thin, tall stems each year. The flowers are bluish purple and tightly clustered in whorls, with only a few fully open at any time, but the purple sepals give a dark appearance to the entire flowerhead. Any doubts over its identity can instantly be dispelled by the strong fragrance of the flowers, also present to a lesser extent in the leaves. The leaves are evergreen and extremely narrow – the name *angustifolia* means narrow-leaved.

OCCURS *in scattered clumps over stony or rocky ground and in open woodlands, usually over limestone. Also widely planted in fields.*

PERENNIAL

tightly clustered flowers

small, 2-lipped flowers

grey-green leaves

stiff, upright stems

NOTE

Lavender oil is extracted from the flowers. It has a soothing effect on the nervous system, as well as antiseptic and insect repellent properties, in addition to its use as a perfume.

PLANT HEIGHT *Up to 1m.*
FLOWER SIZE *1.2cm long.*
FLOWERING TIME *June–August.*
LEAVES *Narrow, almost linear, in opposite pairs, woolly when young.*
FRUIT *Four brown nutlets.*
DISTRIBUTION *Throughout the region.*
SIMILAR SPECIES *Toothed Lavender (L. dentata), which has clearly toothed leaves and small purple bracts at the tip of the flowerhead.*

French Lavender

Lavandula stoechas (Lamiaceae)

A much earlier-flowering species than Common Lavender, French Lavender is more likely to be found on acid soil. It is also considerably showier, with plumes of tall purple or blue papery bracts on top of the flowerheads. These serve to attract insects to the true flowers, which are small, very dark purple trumpets arranged in neat columns, each emerging from a cluster of woolly sepals. The narrow, grey-woolly leaves are wider than those of Common Lavender and have inrolled margins.

GROWS *in widespread clumps in stony places, garigue, maquis, or in clearings in pine woods, preferring slightly acid, sandy soil.*

papery bracts on top

neat columns of flowers

narrow leaves

PERENNIAL

small purple flowers

NOTE

French Lavender produces more essential oil than Common Lavender, but it is of inferior quality, though it is still used in the perfume industry. It is often grown in gardens.

PLANT HEIGHT *Up to 1m.*
FLOWER SIZE *Bracts up to 5cm long.*
FLOWERING TIME *March–June.*
LEAVES *Lance-shaped, grey-green, untoothed with inrolled margins.*
FRUIT *Four brown nutlets.*
DISTRIBUTION *Throughout the Mediterranean region.*
SIMILAR SPECIES *L. viridis, of S.W. Spain and Portugal, which has green bracts and white flowers.*

Sage

Salvia officinalis (Lamiaceae)

This plant is the source of culinary sage, and the leaves are instantly recognizable as the familiar plant of the kitchen garden, both by their shape and scent. They have a finely wrinkled surface, a soft, velvety texture, and often have two smaller leaflets or lobes at the base. The undersides and stems are covered with a fine, woolly down which gives them a greyish appearance. Its fairly large pale blue or lilac flowers are cupped by strongly-ribbed, reddish purple sepals, and are held in loose whorls on tall stems. The upper petals form a narrow hood and the three-lobed lower lip is longer.

FOUND *in conspicuous clumps on roadsides, stony, or grassy ground, in dry, open places such as garigue.*

PERENNIAL

greyish stems

shorter upper lip

2-lipped calyx

wrinkled surface to leaf

coarse, reddish sepals

NOTE

Now largely used as a condiment to flavour and aid the digestion of fatty meats, Sage has a history of medicinal use, and is said to be good for throat or mouth infections.

PLANT HEIGHT *30–60cm.*
FLOWER SIZE *Up to 3.5cm long.*
FLOWERING TIME *May–July.*
LEAVES *Oblong, often white-felted below, with very finely toothed margins.*
FRUIT *Four brown, oval nutlets.*
DISTRIBUTION *Spain and S. France, though widely planted elsewhere.*
SIMILAR SPECIES *Wild Clary (p.132); S. triloba of the E. Mediterranean, which has woollier leaves and obviously three-lobed leaves.*

Wild Clary

Salvia verbenaca (Lamiaceae)

OCCURS *along roadsides, waste places, and cultivated fields such as olive groves and vineyards.*

This rather variable type of sage may either be short or tall and is less robust and leafy than Sage (p.131). Most of its leaves are clustered towards the base of the plant, and are pinnately-lobed with large, blunt teeth and wrinkled on the upper surface. The small, pale blue or violet flowers are produced in loose whorls on several erect stems. Each flower has a hooded upper lip and protruding, forked style.

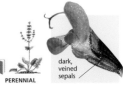

small bracts below each cluster

flowers in whorls

dark, veined sepals

PERENNIAL

PLANT HEIGHT *20–80cm.*
FLOWER SIZE *0.6–1cm long.*
FLOWERING TIME *January–May.*
LEAVES *Opposite, oblong with rounded teeth.*
FRUIT *Four nutlets within the calyx.*
DISTRIBUTION *Throughout the region.*
SIMILAR SPECIES *Whorled Clary (S. verticillata), which has lyre-shaped leaves.*

Clary

Salvia sclarea (Lamiaceae)

FOUND *in rocky or grassy habitats, fallow ground, roadsides, and sometimes cultivated for its essential oil.*

This large and robust sage has aromatic leaves with a strong fragrance that is used in aromatherapy. It is easily recognized by its bicoloured flowers which have a pale blue, lilac, or pink upper lip and a whitish lower lip, with colourful bracts beneath them. The leaves are soft, broad, and wrinkled with woolly hair below.

heart-shaped leaves

large, branching flower clusters

colourful flowers and bracts

long, arching upper lip

BIENNIAL/PERENNIAL

PLANT HEIGHT *Up to 1m.*
FLOWER SIZE *2–3cm long.*
FLOWERING TIME *May–August.*
LEAVES *Oval, toothed, woolly below.*
FRUIT *Four nutlets within the calyx.*
PLANT HEIGHT *Throughout the region.*
SIMILAR SPECIES *S. aethiops, which has white flowers and downy white stems.*

Jersey Toadflax

Linaria pelisseriana (Scrophulariaceae)

This is a delicate-looking plant with erect, narrow leaves on tall, wiry stems that barely look as if they can support their own weight. The purplish violet flowers are clustered towards the tops of the stems, and have an upper lip which is lobed into two; the lobed lower lip has two pale bosses called the palate, and a long downward-pointing spur.

INHABITS *dry fields, open places, waste ground, cultivated land, and open garigue, on sandy soil.*

ANNUAL

spur up to 9mm long

flowers with paler palate

globular fruit capsule

PLANT HEIGHT	*20–50cm.*
FLOWER SIZE	*1.5–2cm long.*
FLOWERING TIME	*March–May.*
LEAVES	*Whorled below, alternate above.*
FRUIT	*Rounded capsule with winged seeds.*
DISTRIBUTION	*Throughout the region.*
SIMILAR SPECIES	*Purple Toadflax (L. purpurea), has denser purple flowerheads.*

Ivy-leaved Toadflax

Cymbalaria muralis (Scrophulariaceae)

This plant, originally from Italy and the E. Mediterranean, is now found on rocks and old walls throughout much of Europe. The long, trailing stems are reddish, with fleshy, lobed leaves similar in shape to those of Ivy *(Hedera helix)*. The long-stemmed flowers have two lilac or violet lips, with two central yellow patches and a short spur.

GROWS *on old walls, pavements, and rocky places, generally on vertical surfaces, in full or partial shade.*

PERENNIAL

5–9 broad lobes

short spur

lilac or violet petals

slender, reddish stems

PLANT HEIGHT	*10–25cm.*
FLOWER SIZE	*0.9–1.5cm long.*
FLOWERING TIME	*May–September.*
LEAVES	*Alternate, palmately lobed, fleshy.*
FRUIT	*Small capsule, opens by irregular slits.*
DISTRIBUTION	*Throughout the region.*
SIMILAR SPECIES	*Kickxia species of cultivated fields, have yellow and dark purple flowers.*

Shrubby Globularia

Globularia alypum (Globulariaceae)

This many-branched evergreen shrub has small, leathery, spoon-shaped leaves. Forming dense, rounded heads, the bright blue flowers have strap-shaped, toothed petals and slightly protruding stamens. Each head is cupped by overlapping, pointed bracts.

FORMS *mounds in dry, rocky places, maquis, garige, and exposed stony ground.*

PERENNIAL

protruding anthers

toothed petal tips

small, leathery leaves

bright blue flowerhead

PLANT HEIGHT	Up to 1m.
FLOWER SIZE	Flowerhead 1.5–2.5cm wide.
FLOWERING TIME	January–May.
LEAVES	Evergreen, up to 2cm long.
FRUIT	Dry fruit enclosed by the calyx.
DISTRIBUTION	Throughout the region.
SIMILAR SPECIES	G. cambessedesii of Majorca, which is shorter with larger flowers.

Common Globularia

Globularia vulgaris (Globulariaceae)

This rather short but attractive herbaceous perennial has a basal rosette of stalked oval or spoon-shaped leaves, and smaller oblong leaves that clasp the stem. The solitary flowerheads consist of numerous flowers with linear petals, often darker in the centre where they are still in bud.

GROWS *in dry, grassy, and stony habitats, roadsides, scrub, sunny and rocky hillsides.*

stalked basal leaf

dark centre to flowerhead

ruff of linear petals

unbranched stems

PERENNIAL

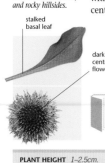

PLANT HEIGHT	1–2.5cm.
FLOWER SIZE	2.5cm wide.
FLOWERING TIME	April–June.
LEAVES	Oval basal leaves; stem leaves oblong.
FRUIT	Dry fruit remaining in calyx.
DISTRIBUTION	Portugal, Spain, and S. France.
SIMILAR SPECIES	G. punctatum, which is larger with slightly smaller flowerheads.

Hemp Broomrape

Orobanche ramosa (Orobanchaceae)

This plant's most distinguishing feature is reflected in the name *ramosa*, meaning branched – an uncommon feature in broomrapes. It has slender, very hairy stems, and loose spikes of blue and white two-lipped flowers, with a distinct curve to the tube. Small scales replace the leaves on this plant.

PARASITIZES *a range of plants, mostly members of the potato family, including tobacco and* Solanum *species.*

tubular flowers

leafless stems

3-lobed lip

PERENNIAL

papery bracts

PLANT HEIGHT *10–30cm.*
FLOWER SIZE *1–2.2cm long.*
FLOWERING TIME *March–June.*
LEAVES *Oval, pointed scales.*
FRUIT *Many-seeded capsule.*
DISTRIBUTION *Throughout the region.*
SIMILAR SPECIES O. lavandulacea, *which grows on Pitch Trefoil (p.117).*

Large Venus's Looking Glass

Legousia speculum-veneris (Campanulaceae)

Although a short plant, the brilliant violet-purple colour of it's flowers immediately catches the eye. The flowers open widely in the sunshine to form a five-pointed star with a white "eye" in the centre, and have narrow sepals just shorter than the petals. The stem is branched, with alternate, oblong, usually unstalked, leaves towards the base.

INHABITS *cultivated fields and wasteland on disturbed soil. Declining due to changing farming practices.*

5 petals

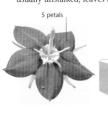

narrow sepals

central white "eye"

ANNUAL

PLANT HEIGHT *10–40cm.*
FLOWER SIZE *1.5–2.3cm wide.*
FLOWERING TIME *March–June.*
LEAVES *Oblong, with slightly wavy margins.*
FRUIT *Capsule 1–1.5cm long.*
DISTRIBUTION *Throughout the region.*
SIMILAR SPECIES L. hybrida, *which is shorter with a very long calyx tube and tiny petals.*

Globe Thistle

Echinops ritro (Asteraceae)

INHABITS *dry, grassy places, stony pastures, garigue, rocky hillsides; often grown in gardens.*

Globe Thistle is a variable plant, particularly in terms of its height, but remains instantly recognizable. Its blue flowerheads are arranged in a spiky ball, almost like a Christmas decoration, each surrounded by stiff, blue-green bracts. It has spiny leaves that are densely woolly below.

lower leaves up to 15cm long

PERENNIAL

florets radiate outwards

spiny-margined leaves

stiff, blue-green bracts

PLANT HEIGHT *20–80cm.*
FLOWER SIZE *Flower cluster 3.5–5cm wide.*
FLOWERING TIME *July–September.*
LEAVES *Lance-shaped, spiny, felted below.*
FRUIT *Achene with tuft of bristly hair.*
DISTRIBUTION *Throughout the region.*
SIMILAR SPECIES *Echinops sphaerocephalus, which has larger, greyish white flowerheads.*

Carduncellus monspeliensium

Carduncellus monspeliensium (Asteraceae)

OCCURS *in rocky and stony places, garigue, open scrub, and other dry habitats.*

Usually found in hills and mountains, this plant is notable for its vivid lilac-blue flowers. It has a very short stem, with pinnately divided leaves that have spine-tipped lobes or teeth. Borne in rounded clusters, the flowers have broad bracts, branched florets, and dark blue stamens.

PERENNIAL

branched florets

broad, spiny bracts

rounded flowerhead

narrowly-lobed leaves

PLANT HEIGHT *5–20cm.*
FLOWER SIZE *2–3cm wide.*
FLOWERING TIME *May–July.*
LEAVES *Pinnately lobed, spine-tipped.*
FRUIT *Achene with several rows of hair.*
DISTRIBUTION *Spain, Balearic Islands, S. France, and Italy.*
SIMILAR SPECIES *C. caeruleus, which is taller.*

Chicory

Cichorium intybus (Asteraceae)

The tall, flowering spikes of Chicory are an unmistakable sight among the grass on road verges and wasteland, but they are only visible in the morning. In common with many blue-flowered members of the daisy family the Chicory flowers close by midday and the thin, wiry stems disappear into the surrounding vegetation. Each flower is made up of broad, bright sky blue, strap-like ray florets. The upper leaves are barely toothed, while the lower ones have backward-pointing lobes like those of Dandelion (*Taraxacum* sp.).

FOUND *in grassy places and fields, and on road verges, wasteland, and embankments; on chalky soil.*

slightly toothed upper leaf

green flower bracts

PERENNIAL

spreading ray florets

sky blue flowerheads

stiff, upright stem

NOTE

Chicory has long been cultivated as a salad vegetable, where the shoots are forced or blanched. The roots and young shoots may also be dried, roasted, ground, and then blended with coffee.

PLANT HEIGHT *60–100cm.*
FLOWER SIZE *2.5–4cm wide.*
FLOWERING TIME *July–October.*
LEAVES *Alternate, upper leaves are spear-shaped.*
FRUIT *Achene without a pappus.*
DISTRIBUTION *Throughout the region.*
SIMILAR SPECIES *Blue Lettuce (p.138); Cupidone (p.138); and Spiny Chicory (C. spinosum), which is a small densely-branched shrub.*

Cupidone

Catananche caerulea (Asteraceae)

Cupidone is an eye-catching plant of late summer, when its bright blue flowers shine out among the surrounding dry grass. It is a much neater plant than the similar Chicory (p.137), but may always be identified by the delicate, glass-like translucent bracts below the flowerhead, each with a dark central vein.

INHABITS *dry grassland, roadsides, garigue, pastures, and open woodland, particularly on limestone soil.*

papery, translucent bracts

leaf with narrow lobes

PERENNIAL

blue ray florets

dark centre to flowerhead

PLANT HEIGHT *40–80cm.*
FLOWER SIZE *Up to 6cm wide.*
FLOWERING TIME *June–September.*
LEAVES *Almost linear, with small teeth.*
FRUIT *Achene with narrow scales.*
DISTRIBUTION *W. Mediterranean, up to Italy.*
SIMILAR SPECIES *Chicory (p.137); Blue Lettuce (below); C. lutea has yellow flowers.*

Blue Lettuce

Lactuca perennis (Asteraceae)

The blue or lilac flowers of this plant may easily go unseen, for they are open only during the early morning and are often closed up to two or three hours before midday in sunny weather. It is a rather weak, straggly plant, with mostly basal leaves that are finely divided into narrow, toothed lobes, and which exude a milky latex when cut.

FOUND *on rocky or stony ground, alongside old walls, and other dry habitats, on limestone.*

strap-shaped ray florets

flowerheads in branched clusters

PERENNIAL

narrow, toothed leaflets

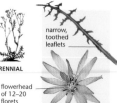

long, narrow buds

flowerhead of 12–20 florets

PLANT HEIGHT *30–80cm.*
FLOWER SIZE *Up to 3cm wide.*
FLOWERING TIME *April–July.*
LEAVES *Pinnate, grey-green with a pale midrib.*
FRUIT *Achene with a pappus of rough hair.*
DISTRIBUTION *Throughout W. Mediterranean.*
SIMILAR SPECIES *Cupidone (above); Salsify (p.99) with pinker flowers; and Chicory (p.137).*

Aphyllanthes

Aphyllanthes monspeliensis (Aphyllanthaceae)

Where it occurs, this attractive species may seem to be almost ubiquitous, peppering the countryside with its bright flowers in late spring and early summer. When not in flower, however, Aphyllanthes recedes into obscurity, as its leaves, which are little more than narrow sheaths that clasp the bases of the hairless and ridged stems, look deceptively like a clump of rushes or grass. The flowers are generally pale blue in colour, though sometimes darker, and very occasionally white; each tepal has a dark central vein. Aphyllanthes is quite unmistakeable, though Beautiful Flax (p.119) may seem similar at a distance.

GROWS *in tufts, often over a wide area; in grassy or rocky places, meadows, roadsides, woodland clearings, and embankments.*

pale blue flowers

papery bracts

NOTE

This plant was a member of the Liliaceae family, which is sometimes split into smaller families, but botanists now recognize it as the Aphyllanthaceae family's sole species.

PERENNIAL

rush-like grey-green stems

6 rounded tepals

dark, central vein

PLANT HEIGHT *30–50cm.*
FLOWER SIZE *Up to 2.5cm wide.*
FLOWERING TIME *April–June.*
LEAVES *Linear, brownish membranous sheaths.*
FRUIT *Capsule containing three seeds.*
DISTRIBUTION *Western Mediterranean, as far east as N.W. Italy.*
SIMILAR SPECIES *Beautiful Flax (p.119), which has darker flowers and numerous small leaves.*

Tassel Hyacinth

Muscari comosum (Liliaceae)

OCCURS *in well-drained or disturbed soil of roadsides, cultivated ground, and in rough, grassy places.*

There are two kinds of flowers on the fleshy, erect stems of this plant. The tassel of long-stemmed purple flowers, forming a top-knot at the top of the flowerhead, are sterile and serve to attract insects. The dark purple-brown flowers below droop downwards and become paler with a whitish rim. These are the fertile flowers which develop into three-lobed fruit capsules.

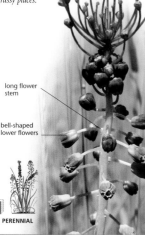

long flower stem

bell-shaped lower flowers

strap-like leaves

pale brown fertile flowers

PERENNIAL

PLANT HEIGHT *25–50cm.*
FLOWER SIZE *Fertile flower 5–9mm long.*
FLOWERING TIME *March–June.*
LEAVES *Basal, glossy, and channelled.*
FRUIT *Three-parted capsule.*
DISTRIBUTION *Throughout the region.*
SIMILAR SPECIES *M. gussonei of Italy and Sardinia, which has much shorter tassels.*

Common Grape Hyacinth

Muscari neglectum (Liliaceae)

FORMS *large colonies in grassy and rocky habitats, olive groves, meadows, scrub, and cultivated ground.*

linear, channelled leaves

white teeth

fertile flowers

Like Tassel Hyacinth, the uppermost flowers of the spike in this species are sterile, but are restricted to just a few small, violet-blue blobs that look like unopened flower buds. The true flowers are very dark blue-black, with a ring of white teeth around the mouth of the flower. These go on to form the rather distinctive three-lobed fruit which are heart-shaped in profile.

violet sterile flowers

stem with waxy bloom

PLANT HEIGHT *Up to 30cm.*
FLOWER SIZE *4–7mm long.*
FLOWERING TIME *February–May.*
LEAVES *Linear, channelled, bright green.*
FRUIT *Green capsule, ripening brown.*
DISTRIBUTION *Throughout the region.*
SIMILAR SPECIES *M. commutatum, of Italy and Sicily, which has dark indigo-violet flowers.*

PERENNIAL

Scilla peruviana

Scilla peruviana (Liliaceae)

This spectacular and exotic-looking species is difficult to miss when its large conical racemes burst into bloom in spring. It is variable in appearance – the raceme may contain up to 100 individual blooms, but sometimes there may be only 20. The lowest blooms have long stalks and are held almost horizontally from the stem, while the uppermost are almost stalkless. Very rarely, white flowers are produced, in which case the stamens are often green instead of the more usual blue. It makes an excellent garden plant for dry sites, although it is not commonly grown. The plant grows from a large bulb just below the ground surface.

GROWS *in damp and sandy habitats, open woodland, scrub, and roadsides; also found frequently near the coast.*

PERENNIAL

deep violet flower buds

6-petalled flowers

conical flowerheads

glossy leaf surface

strap-like leaf

long flower stalks below

each head from a single bulb

PLANT HEIGHT *Up to 50cm.*
FLOWER SIZE *1–2cm wide.*
FLOWERING TIME *March–May.*
LEAVES *1.5–4cm wide and up to 60cm long, flopping on the ground.*
FRUIT *Capsule, with a long, pointed beak.*
DISTRIBUTION *Throughout except for the Balearic Islands and Corsica.*
SIMILAR SPECIES *S. hyacinthoides, which has a stem up to 80cm tall, and a longer, looser flowerhead.*

NOTE

This truly native species of the Mediterranean reached Linnaeus, the 18th century botanist, from Spain on a ship called The Peru, and some confusion led to the name "peruviana".

Iris lutescens

Iris lutescens (Iridaceae)

This species is also known as *Iris chamaeiris* ("chamae" means "dwarf"), refering to the diminutive size of the plant in comparison to many other irises. It is perhaps a better description than "lutescens", which means "yellow-coloured", as the plant occurs in two distinct colour forms, both equally common and usually growing together. The purple form has intensely coloured standard petals, and darker fall petals with a white or yellow beard of stamens. Yellow forms often have fall petals heavily streaked with brown or violet, although completely yellow flowers also occur.

violet standard petal

PERENNIAL

NOTE

The word "iris" comes from the name of the goddess of the rainbow in classical Greek mythology, and refers to the varied colours of the flowers, within the different Iris species.

beard of stamens

darker fall petal

all yellow colour form

purple flower form

PLANT HEIGHT *Usually about 30cm.*
FLOWER SIZE *6–7cm long.*
FLOWERING TIME *March–April.*
LEAVES *Sword-shaped, slightly curved, up to 30cm long.*
FRUIT *Capsule containing pear-shaped seeds.*
DISTRIBUTION *Portugal, Spain, S. France, and Italy.*
SIMILAR SPECIES *Iris subbiflora, which has violet flowers with a violet or white beard; Iris pseudopumila, which has a longer corolla tube.*

German Iris

Iris germanica (Iridaceae)

A tall, robust species, German Iris is so commonly cultivated and grown in gardens that its true origins remain uncertain. It is rather variable, with distinct forms recognized in different parts of the Mediterranean. It always has fragrant, rich purple-blue flowers, three or four on a stem, with a yellow beard and dark veining on the fall petals, and purple-tinged spathes.

FORMS *large clumps along field margins, besides ditches, in cultivated ground, olive groves, and also in abandoned vineyards.*

yellow beard

flat, grey-green leaves

plain purple standard petal

PERENNIAL

purple-tinged spathe

several flowers on a stem

PLANT HEIGHT *Up to 1m.*
FLOWER SIZE *9–11cm long.*
FLOWERING TIME *April–June.*
LEAVES *Sword-shaped, 2–4cm wide.*
FRUIT *Three-parted capsule.*
DISTRIBUTION *Throughout the region.*
SIMILAR SPECIES *Iris pallida of N. Italy, which has paler blue flowers with silvery spathes.*

Barbary Nut

Gynandriris sisyrinchium (Iridaceae)

This commonly found iris-like plant grows from a corm, not a rhizome as in true irises. It usually has just two thin, arching, thread-like deep green leaves, and produces narrow, torpedo-shaped buds, one above the other. Up to six short-lived iris-like flowers emerge from these buds, opening at about midday and withering by evening, with a white patch on the fall petals.

GROWS *in cultivated, waste, fallow, stony, or sandy ground, olive groves, roadsides, and field margins.*

beardless fall petal

violet flowers

thin, grooved leaves

white patch on fall petal

up to 6 flowers on stem

PLANT HEIGHT *10–50cm.*
FLOWER SIZE *3–4cm wide.*
FLOWERING TIME *February–May.*
LEAVES *Channelled, 5–7mm wide.*
FRUIT *Three-parted capsule.*
DISTRIBUTION *Throughout the region.*
SIMILAR SPECIES *G. monophylla, which is smaller, with only one leaf.*

PERENNIAL

Green-Brown

This chapter includes those plants whose flowers are pollinated by the wind, such as Hare's Tail grass, below, and therefore are not dependent on colour. Some others make use of scent as the main attracting force to entice pollinating insects. These include the highly adapted *Ophrys* orchids, which have pheromone-scented flowers that mimic the female body-form of particular species of bees and wasps. The male bee or wasp attempts to mate with the flower, and in doing so, transfers pollen to it.

EARLY SPIDER
ORCHID

FIELD ERYNGO

ARISTOLOCHIA
PISTOLOCHIA

THYMELAEA
SANAMUNDA

Osyris

Osyris alba (Santalaceae)

This rather broom-like shrub is a member of the sandalwood family and has slender, stiff, upright stems.

stems unbranched at top

The small and somewhat leathery leaves are almost linear and have a pointed tip. The sweetly-scented male and female flowers are borne on separate plants, the male flowers more clustered than the females. Both are greenish yellow and are formed from three cup-shaped petals.

FORMS *small thickets in dry, grassy, or scrubby places, maquis, abandoned fields, and shrubby wasteland.*

simple, pointed leaves

slender stems

PERENNIAL

3-parted flowers

clustered male flowers

PLANT HEIGHT 0.5–1.2m.
FLOWER SIZE 3–4mm wide.
FLOWERING TIME April–July.
LEAVES Alternate, linear to lance-shaped.
FRUIT Fleshy, red berry, 5–7mm long.
DISTRIBUTION Throughout the region.
SIMILAR SPECIES O. quadripartita of Iberia, which is taller, with 3–4 parted flowers.

Roman Nettle

Urtica pilulifera (Urticaceae)

This tall and conspicuous nettle is covered with stinging hair on the leaves, stems, and even on the flowers. Male and female flowers are usually borne in the same leaf axils but in separate inflorescences: the female flowers form large spherical clusters on short stalks; the tiny male flowers grow in slender branching spikes. The oval leaves are often distinctively toothed.

PROLIFERATES *on damp waste ground, particularly where rich in nutrients, such as rubbish dumps and near houses.*

coarsely-toothed leaves

flowers in leaf-axils

globular female flower cluster

tough, stringy stems

ANNUAL

PLANT HEIGHT 40–100cm.
FLOWER SIZE About 1cm wide.
FLOWERING TIME February–May.
LEAVES Oval or heart-shaped, toothed.
FRUIT Globular cluster of achenes.
DISTRIBUTION Throughout the region.
SIMILAR SPECIES U. membranacea has long male racemes above, short female ones below.

Pellitory-of-the-Wall

Parietaria diffusa (Urticaceae)

This non-stinging member of the nettle family is a common sight on the old walls of Mediterranean villages. It grows in a rather untidy manner, spreading and branching at the base before sending up erect flowering shoots. Covered with short hair, the stems often have a reddish tinge. It has separate male and female flowers, both on the same plant, but they are inconspicuous and little more than green or reddish globular clusters attached to the leaf axils. The leaves are simple, with a glossy upper surface, though the plant is often covered in roadside dust.

OCCURS *as clumps or tufts on old walls or rocks, and in damp, shady places. Will grow in sunshine provided there is some moisture for the roots.*

PERENNIAL

fringed leaves

glossy leaf surface

small, globular flowers

NOTE

The leaves and young shoots are edible, and the plant has been valued for centuries for its diuretic action and restorative effect on the kidneys. However, its pollen is one of the most virulent to affect hay fever sufferers.

PLANT HEIGHT *Up to 40cm.*
FLOWER SIZE *3–5mm wide.*
FLOWERING TIME *April–October.*
LEAVES *Elliptical, blunt-pointed, with tiny hairs on the margin.*
FRUIT *Tiny black achenes.*
DISTRIBUTION *Throughout most of Europe.*
SIMILAR SPECIES *P. officinalis, of the Western Mediterranean, which is less branching, with larger leaves, and prefers dry, open places.*

Round-leaved Birthwort

Aristolochia rotunda (Aristolochiaceae)

Birthworts are instantly recognizable by their intriguing, trumpet-shaped flowers with a globular ovary at the base, looking rather like organ-pipes. In this species, each flower is borne from the leaf-axils on zig-zagging stems, with a greenish yellow, striped tube and chocolate brown flap which partially covers the mouth. The leaves are heart-shaped but rounded, with lobes at the base that often overlap.

GROWS *in spreading patches in damp, slightly shady places such as woodland clearings, olive groves, under hedges, and alongside ditches.*

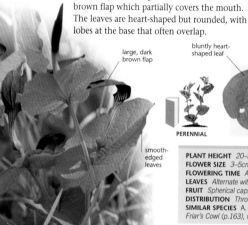

large, dark brown flap

smooth-edged leaves

bluntly heart-shaped leaf

PERENNIAL

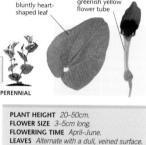

greenish yellow flower tube

PLANT HEIGHT	20–50cm.
FLOWER SIZE	3–5cm long.
FLOWERING TIME	April–June.
LEAVES	Alternate with a dull, veined surface.
FRUIT	Spherical capsule 1–2cm wide.
DISTRIBUTION	Throughout except N. Africa.
SIMILAR SPECIES	A. pistolochia (below); Friar's Cowl (p.163), which has glossy leaves.

Aristolochia pistolochia

Aristolochia pistolochia (Aristolochiaceae)

Similar in many ways to Round-leaved Birthwort (above), this species is often leafier and more robust, and grows in drier, more open places. The flowers have a reddish brown tube, which is a paler shade of the flap colour. The leaves are distinctly arrow-shaped, rather grey-green, with a crisply wavy margin, and rear lobes that never overlap.

greyish leaf

OCCURS *in dry, rocky, and scrubby places, mountain scree, dry olive groves, and gravelly roadsides.*

arrow-shaped leaves

reddish flower-tube

PERENNIAL

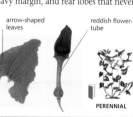

PLANT HEIGHT	20–60cm.
FLOWER SIZE	Up to 5cm long.
FLOWERING TIME	March–July.
LEAVES	Alternate, with wavy edges.
FRUIT	Rounded capsule 2–3cm long.
DISTRIBUTION	Throughout W. Mediterranean.
SIMILAR SPECIES	A. altissima, which is a climbing plant with hanging, U-shaped flowers.

Sea Purslane

Halimione portulacoides (Chenopodiaceae)

GROWS *over large areas of mud in salt marshes, or around the tidemark and edges of coastal pools and channels.*

This common salt marsh plant forms very extensive colonies. It has woody stems at the base, which produce a mass of fleshy leaves. The leaves are mealy on the surface, giving the whole plant a grey or silvery appearance. The ascending stalks hold clusters of tiny, yellowish flowers in late summer.

grey-green leaf surface

branching flower stalks

thick, fleshy leaf

small flower clusters

PERENNIAL

PLANT HEIGHT 20–60cm.
FLOWER SIZE 2–3mm wide.
FLOWERING TIME July–October.
LEAVES Opposite, oblong, untoothed, thick, fleshy, and silvery-mealy.
FRUIT Single-seeded achene.
DISTRIBUTION Throughout the region.
SIMILAR SPECIES None.

Glasswort

Salicornia europaea (Chenopodiaceae)

PROLIFERATES *in drifts on estuaries, coastal mudflats, and salt marshes.*

A familiar sight in estuaries, Glasswort appears as huge blue-green to red drifts of succulent, upward-pointing fingers protruding from the mud at low tide. The whole plant is edible, although it can be rather woody when mature. The stems are jointed, and the leaves are reduced to scales fused to the stem. The flowers are insignificantly tiny, with two barely visible stamens, on fleshy, branched spikes.

ANNUAL

ascending branches

scale-like leaves fused to stem

stems often red-tinged

fleshy, jointed stems

PLANT HEIGHT 10–30cm.
FLOWER SIZE Spike 1–5cm long.
FLOWERING TIME August–September.
LEAVES Triangular scales fused to stem.
FRUIT Tiny achene.
DISTRIBUTION Throughout the region.
SIMILAR SPECIES Annual Seablite (Suaeda maritima), which has narrow grey-green leaves.

Prickly Saltwort

Salsola kali (Chenopodiaceae)

Although unusual for a plant that is out of reach of grazing animals, Prickly Saltwort is recognizable by the sharp spine on the tip of each leaf. This plant is succulent, much branched, and bluish green. The tiny flowers, hidden at the base of the fleshy leaves, may have a pinkish tinge.

OCCURS *on sandy coastal beaches, or in shingle, often close to the tide line.*

flowers at base of upper leaves

narrow leaves

ANNUAL

5-parted flower

ridged stems

PLANT HEIGHT *20–80cm.*
FLOWER SIZE *2–3mm wide.*
FLOWERING TIME *July–October.*
LEAVES *Alternate, linear to oval, spine-tipped.*
FRUIT *Achene covered by flower parts.*
DISTRIBUTION *Throughout Mediterranean and Atlantic coasts.*
SIMILAR SPECIES *Saltwort (S. soda) is taller.*

Stinking Hellebore

Helleborus foetidus (Ranunculaceae)

This unpleasant smelling plant is distinctive for its bell-like green flowers, which hang in clusters in spring. The large sepals are bright yellow-green and rimmed with purple. The deep green leaves are palmately lobed, with up to 12 finger-like lobes. This plant is poisonous.

FOUND *in the light shade of open woodland and scrub, on stony, chalky soil; also grown in gardens.*

palmate leaves

bell-like flowers

deep green leaves

PERENNIAL

purple sepal rim

narrow leaf lobes

PLANT HEIGHT *40–80cm.*
FLOWER SIZE *1–3cm wide.*
FLOWERING TIME *January–April.*
LEAVES *Alternate, with slightly toothed lobes.*
FRUIT *Cluster of three many-seeded follicles.*
DISTRIBUTION *Throughout W. Mediterranean.*
SIMILAR SPECIES *Green Hellebore (H. viridis), which has saucer-shaped flowers.*

Large Mediterranean Spurge

Euphorbia characias (Euphorbiaceae)

One of the most imposing and eye-catching spurges of the region, this plant has upright, rather woody stems that bear tall columns of bright flowerheads in spring and summer. The stems are clothed in a dense foliage of grey-green, lance-shaped leaves, which often droop down like a raffia skirt. Each flower has distinctive dark brown, almost circular nectar glands at the base; from Italy eastwards however, the subspecies *wulfenii* has yellow glands, and grows much taller. Its striking appearance has made it a popular garden plant.

FORMS *clumps in rocky places such as roadsides, dry open ground, cliffs, or among the scrub of garigue and maquis.*

PERENNIAL

dense flowerheads

yellow-green bracts surround flowers

grey-green leaves, paler beneath

hanging ovary

brown nectar glands

NOTE

The stems of Euphorbia *species exude a thick, milky latex when cut, which is toxic and highly irritant on the skin, causing a light-sensitive reaction and severe inflammation.*

PLANT HEIGHT *0.8–1.8m.*
FLOWER SIZE *1.5–2cm wide including bracts.*
FLOWERING TIME *January–July.*
LEAVES *Alternate, lance-shaped and crowded, particularly at the top.*
FRUIT *Hairy green capsule, 6mm wide.*
DISTRIBUTION *Throughout the region.*
SIMILAR SPECIES *Whorled Spurge (E. biumbellata), which is shorter with flat-topped umbels of bright yellow bracts and narrower leaves.*

Tree Spurge

Euphorbia dendroides (Euphorbiaceae)

In spring, this shrub is covered in bright yellow bracts that surround the flowers growing at the tips of the new season's growth. By summer, however, the leaves, bracts, and flowers are shed, leaving bare branches, in preparation for the dry period ahead. At the base of the plant the thick, woody stems merge to form a short, stout trunk.

FOUND *on dry rocky hillsides, roadsides, and cliffs near the sea; often forms loose colonies.*

narrow green leaves in whorls

PERENNIAL

bright yellow bracts

flowers clusters at shoot tips

PLANT HEIGHT *Up to 2m.*
FLOWER SIZE *1.5–2cm, including bracts.*
FLOWERING TIME *April–June.*
LEAVES *Linear, at tips of branches.*
FRUIT *Rounded grey capsule, 6mm long.*
DISTRIBUTION *Throughout the region.*
SIMILAR SPECIES *The large size and tree-like growth is unique in the W. Mediterranean.*

Cypress Spurge

Euphorbia cyparissias (Boraginaceae)

This erect, clump-forming plant looks like a miniature fir tree with its narrow, linear leaves. Borne on slender, hairless stems, the small, lateral flower umbels are encircled by pale yellow-green bracts, which often turn a fiery red in summer. The flower is made up of kidney-shaped glands, surrounded by tiny horns.

OCCURS *in grassy and rocky habitats, garigue, roadsides, olive groves, scrub and waste places, often on limestone.*

yellow-green bracts

9–18 flowers in umbel

PERENNIAL

soft, needle-like leaves

red bracts

PLANT HEIGHT *20–50cm.*
FLOWER SIZE *0.8–1.5cm wide, with bracts.*
FLOWERING TIME *April–July.*
LEAVES *Alternate, linear, and dense.*
FRUIT *Three-lobed capsule.*
DISTRIBUTION *Throughout the region.*
SIMILAR SPECIES *Ground Pine (Ajuga chamaepitys), which has very similar leaves.*

Euphorbia serrata

Euphorbia serrata (Euphorbiaceae)

OCCURS along field margins, rocky places, scrub, garigue, abandoned fields, and embankments.

There are many *Euphorbia* species in the region which show a great diversity in form. This species makes an obvious clump of upright stems, distinguished by the more or less oval leaves which have a finely serrated margin. The bracts beneath the umbels of flowers are similar to the leaves, though somewhat rounder.

grey-green stems

serrated leaf margin

PERENNIAL

umbels of yellow-green flowers

complex flower-shape

PLANT HEIGHT *40–70cm.*
FLOWER SIZE *1–2cm wide with bracts.*
FLOWERING TIME *April–June.*
LEAVES *Oval with a finely toothed margin.*
FRUIT *Capsule, 3–5mm wide.*
DISTRIBUTION *Throughout the region.*
SIMILAR SPECIES *E. nicaeensis, which has narrow leaves without a toothed margin.*

Euphorbia spinosa

Euphorbia spinosa (Euphorbiaceae)

This species may safely be identified at a distance due to its habit of forming distinct, rounded hummocks. The lower branches are often woody and bare, hidden from view by the profusion of small, blue-green elliptical leaves growing from the weak, spiny upper stems, which terminate in small yellow-green flower clusters.

GROWS in mounds on cliffs, rock-faces, hillsides, garigue, and in the montains or the lowlands.

PERENNIAL

yellow-green bracts

rounded hummock

many-branched shrub

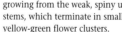

PLANT HEIGHT *Up to 40cm.*
FLOWER SIZE *1–2cm including bracts.*
FLOWERING TIME *April–June.*
LEAVES *Elliptical, untoothed, up to 2cm long, bright green or blue-green.*
FRUIT *Capsule, with warts, up to 4mm long.*
DISTRIBUTION *S. France, Italy, and Sicily.*
SIMILAR SPECIES *None.*

Sea Spurge

Euphorbia paralias (Euphorbiaceae)

This widespread inhabitant of sandy beaches has hairless, erect stems. Sea Spurge is branched only at the base to produce a few upright stems which carry dense ranks of oblong or elliptic leaves, all held horizontally like fins on a radiator. The whole plant is rather blue-green in appearance, especially when young. The flowers are produced from upper leaf axils.

APPEARS *on rocky and sandy coastal habitats and dunes; usually in small colonies.*

PERENNIAL

yellow-green flowers

umbels with rays

green bracts cup small flowers

PLANT HEIGHT *30–70cm.*
FLOWER SIZE *2–3.5cm wide.*
FLOWERING TIME *May–September.*
LEAVES *Oblong or oval, up to 3cm long.*
FRUIT *Granular capsule, 3–5mm wide.*
DISTRIBUTION *Throughout the region.*
SIMILAR SPECIES *E. pithyusa of S. France and Italy, which has narrow leaves.*

Purple Spurge

Euphorbia peplis (Euphorbiaceae)

This highly distinctive, mat-forming spurge of coastal habitats has succulent, hairless stems, which usually branch into four from the base, and then subsequently branch again. The stems are a bright orange-red colour, contrasting with the darker, asymmetrical blue-green leaves, which take on a purplish tinge towards the stem tips and flowers.

FORMS *small mats or carpets on sandy or shingly seashores, above the high water mark.*

ANNUAL

asymmetrical leaves at base

tiny, dark red flowers

orange-red succulent stems

PLANT HEIGHT *5–10cm.*
FLOWER SIZE *2–3mm wide.*
FLOWERING TIME *May–September.*
LEAVES *Opposite, oblong, blue-green.*
FRUIT *Smooth capsule up to 5mm wide.*
DISTRIBUTION *Throughout the region.*
SIMILAR SPECIES *E. maculata, which has leaves with a dark blotch in the centre.*

Mediterranean Buckthorn

Rhamnus alaternus (Rhamnaceae)

FORMS *thickets in maquis, garigue, and in open, coniferous woodland; usually on limestone.*

Mediterranean Buckthorn is a common evergreen shrub, typical of maquis and garigue vegetation in the region. Its leaves are stiff and leathery with a very glossy upper surface. They are generally spear-shaped though sometimes with a rounded base or sometimes with tiny teeth on the margin. The pale yellow male and female flowers are borne on separate plants, but are tiny, appearing early in the year. The plant is more noticeable in fruit, when it may be covered in abundant red berries, which eventually ripen to black.

PERENNIAL

spear-shaped leaf

berries in leaf-axils

glossy upper surface

unripe red fruit

NOTE

This plant is frost hardy and survives well in colder climates where it is sometimes used for hedging, though it has become a serious weed in New Zealand where it has been introduced.

PLANT HEIGHT *1–5m.*
FLOWER SIZE *2–3mm wide.*
FLOWERING TIME *February–April.*
LEAVES *Spear-shaped, glossy above, sometimes toothed.*
FRUIT *Hard red berry ripening black, 4–6mm long.*
DISTRIBUTION *Throughout the region.*
SIMILAR SPECIES *Rhamnus lycioides of Spain and the Balearic Islands, which has dense, almost linear leaves.*

Grapevine

Vitis vinifera (Vitaceae)

This familiar and economically important plant has been cultivated in the region for thousands of years. Many of the cultivated varieties are the result of hybrids with other *Vitis* species from North America and elsewhere, to give them greater resistance to disease, particularly the aphid Phylloxera. The plant occurs commonly as a result of naturalization or as a relict of former cultivation. It may be recognized by its branched tendrils, and five- and seven-lobed, coarsely-toothed leaves. The green or purplish flowers are tiny and occur in dense panicles.

PLANTED *as a crop but also found in abandoned fields and waste land; wild form is found in damp, wooded areas.*

flowers and fruits in branched clusters

PERENNIAL

5–7-lobed leaf

immature fruits

fruit ripens green, red, or purple

NOTE

The skin of grapes contain resveratrol, which helps combat coronary heart disease. It is more prevalent in red wine than in white, as the skins are used in the fermentation process.

PLANT HEIGHT Usually 1–2m, but may grow to 30m.
FLOWER SIZE 1–2mm wide.
FLOWERING TIME April–June.
LEAVES Palmately lobed, toothed, with opposing tendrils.
FRUIT Juicy berry, 0.8–3cm long, green, red, or purple.
DISTRIBUTION Throughout the region.
SIMILAR SPECIES The wild form, subsp. sylvestris, which has male and female flowers on separate plants and 6mm black fruit.

Oleaster

Elaeagnus angustifolia (Eleagnaceae)

OCCURS *in hedgerows, roadsides, rocky slopes, or near rivers; frequently planted near the coast.*

Although very similar at first sight to a willow, this broadly conical to spreading tree has spiny shoots covered in silver scales. The lance-shaped leaves may be dark green or whitish with hair above, but are intensely silvery below. Clusters of small, fragrant yellow flowers form in the leaf axils. These eventually form a yellow to reddish, egg-shaped fruit, which are edible, though not tasty.

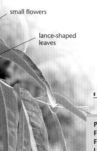

small flowers

lance-shaped leaves

untoothed leaves

PERENNIAL

PLANT HEIGHT *Up to 8m.*
FLOWER SIZE *0.8–1cm long.*
FLOWERING TIME *May–June.*
LEAVES *Up to 8cm long, silvery below.*
FRUIT *Berry-like, 1.5–2.5cm long.*
DISTRIBUTION *Throughout, except Portugal.*
SIMILAR SPECIES *Mediterranean Willow (Salix pedicellata) has non-silvery leaves and catkins.*

Spurge Laurel

Daphne laureola (Thymelaeaceae)

GROWS *in shady places, woodlands, and dry, chalky soil; also in hedgerows.*

This is a slightly spreading or small shrub, which takes on a rather weedy appearance with only one, woody stem when growing in deep shade. In better light, it becomes more bushy, and may easily be mistaken for a small rhododendron bush. Its leathery leaves are glossy green and the inconspicuous, four-petalled green flowers are found hanging within the upper leaves.

tubular flowers

leathery leaves

clusters of green flowers

oval black berries

PERENNIAL

PLANT HEIGHT *0.5–1.2m.*
FLOWER SIZE *0.8–1.2cm long.*
FLOWERING TIME *January–April.*
LEAVES *Alternate, lance-shaped.*
FRUIT *Oval berry.*
DISTRIBUTION *Throughout the region.*
SIMILAR SPECIES *D. gnidium (p.30), which has creamy white flowers and is less branched.*

Thymelaea sanamunda

Thymelaea sanamunda (Thymelaeaceae)

This dwarf shrub has the showiest flowers of a largely inconspicuous genus. It forms a tuft of green stems which grow each year from a woody base, covered with short, ascending leaves. The flowers are formed in small lateral clusters, each flower with a slender tube splaying out to four short, pointed lobes. At a distance, it resembles a young *Genista* species.

FORMS *tufts in dry, rocky places and garigue or scrub; sometimes associates with Genista hispanica.*

greenish yellow flower

upswept leaves

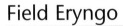

PERENNIAL

elliptical leaf

four pointed lobes

PLANT HEIGHT *Up to 50cm.*
FLOWER SIZE *7–9mm long.*
FLOWERING TIME *May–June.*
LEAVES *Elliptical or lance-shaped, pointed.*
FRUIT *Dry, hairless achene.*
DISTRIBUTION *C. and E. Spain and S. France.*
SIMILAR SPECIES *T. dioica of mountain regions, has fleshier leaves on woody stems.*

Field Eryngo

Eryngium campestre (Apiaceae)

This very prickly, spiny plant is thistle-like, but the insignificant flowerheads show that it is actually a member of the carrot family. The tiny flowers are buried within a mass of green bracts, forming a greenish white domed head. The three-lobed, leathery leaves are stiff and spiny on much-branched stems, the lower ones further divided.

GROWS *in dry, grassy habitats and rocky places, garigue, near the coast or inland.*

PERENNIAL

prickly leaf margin

long, spiny bracts

dense, thistle-like flowerhead

tiny white flowers

stout stems

PLANT HEIGHT *40–75cm.*
FLOWER SIZE *1–1.5cm wide flowerhead.*
FLOWERING TIME *July–August.*
LEAVES *Alternate, lower leaves divided further.*
FRUIT *Two-parted mericarp with scales.*
DISTRIBUTION *Throughout the region.*
SIMILAR SPECIES *Blue Eryngo (E. amethystinum), which has blue flowers.*

Branched Plantain

Plantago arenaria (Plantaginaceae)

OCCURS in dry open habitats such as waste ground, roadsides, and field margins, on sandy soil.

Also known as *Plantago psyllium*, this common plant has a considerable reputation for its seeds, which absorb large quantities of water and swell to many times their original volume, forming a gelatinous mass which is used widely as a laxative. The flowers are clustered together on branched stems, like an untidy candelabra, with tangles of almost linear leaves.

white or brown anthers

branched, hairy stems

bracts of unequal size

ANNUAL

PLANT HEIGHT *15–20cm.*
FLOWER SIZE *Clusters 0.6–1cm wide.*
FLOWERING TIME *April–June.*
LEAVES *Opposite pairs or whorled, almost linear with a central groove.*
FRUIT *Capsule containing oblong seeds.*
DISTRIBUTION *Throughout the region.*
SIMILAR SPECIES *P. afra, which is sticky.*

Buck's-horn Plantain

Plantago coronopus (Plantaginaceae)

This plant has a rosette of leaves which are kept very close to the ground, so they both conserve moisture and are able to withstand trampling from passing feet. Basal and narrow, each leaf has regularly spaced pairs of long teeth or pointed lobes. The flowers are borne in long, cylindrical spikes on long stems, which curve upwards to form a crown.

GROWS on sandy soil on beaches or close to the coast, and sometimes in dry fields.

neatly-lobed leaves

upright flower-stems

PERENNIAL/ BIENNIAL

long flower spike

flat rosette of leaves

PLANT HEIGHT *20cm.*
FLOWER SIZE *3mm long.*
FLOWERING TIME *March–October.*
LEAVES *Up to 20cm long, fringed with hair.*
FRUIT *Capsule containing three to six seeds.*
DISTRIBUTION *Throughout the region.*
SIMILAR SPECIES *P. macrorhiza, which is branched at the base.*

Butcher's Broom

Ruscus aculeatus (Ruscaceae)

The leaf-like structures of this extraordinarily spiky, evergreen plant are in fact flattened extensions of the stem called cladodes. The small green flowers appear directly on the surface of the cladodes and each has three green petals and three sepals, the male flowers with purple anthers. Successfully pollinated female flowers form a bright red berry, which persists on the plant for some time.

OCCURS *in woodland, scrub, hedgerows, even in deep shade; and in rocky places by the sea.*

PERENNIAL

tough, spine-tipped cladodes

bright red berry

3-petalled flowers

PLANT HEIGHT *25–80cm.*
FLOWER SIZE *3–5mm wide.*
FLOWERING TIME *January–April.*
LEAVES *Alternate, elliptical, dark green.*
FRUIT *Berry, 1–1.5cm wide, borne singly.*
DISTRIBUTION *Throughout much of Europe.*
SIMILAR SPECIES *Spanish Butcher's Broom*
(R. hypophyllum), *which has larger cladodes.*

finely grooved stem

Smilax

Smilax aspera (Smilacaceae)

This sprawling, climbing plant is deceptively prickly, for the twining stems are armed with tiny hooks. The leaves are distinctively heart-shaped and easily recognized; those at the tip of the stems are narrower. Hanging clusters of fragrant, creamy flowers are produced in autumn, followed by berries which ripen from red to black.

CLIMBS *over hedges and fences or sprawls over the ground and other vegetation in woods and maquis.*

strongly-veined leaves

tough stems with hooks

broad basal leaf

glossy red berries

PERENNIAL

PLANT HEIGHT *Up to 10m, usually less.*
FLOWER SIZE *3–5mm.*
FLOWERING TIME *August–November.*
LEAVES *Alternate, with rounded basal lobes, glossy green above, with tiny teeth.*
FRUIT *2–4mm wide, in clusters of up to 30.*
DISTRIBUTION *Throughout the Mediterranean.*
SIMILAR SPECIES *None in the region.*

Asparagus acutifolius

Asparagus acutifolius (Liliaceae)

Asparaguses have straggly stems and numerous tiny leaves which give them a feathery appearance. In this species, however, they are borne at right-angles to the main stem which gives them a slightly spiky feel. Tiny tubular flowers are produced along the branches, (with female flowers on separate plants), followed by large berries which mature from green to black.

OCCURS in woodland thickets, maquis, garigue, rocky habitats, and hedgerows; often in shade.

tapering branches

needle-like leaves

PERENNIAL

flowering stems

unripe berries

PLANT HEIGHT *Up to 2m but mostly less.*
FLOWER SIZE *4mm long.*
FLOWERING TIME *April–June.*
LEAVES *8mm long, in clusters of 10–30.*
FRUIT *5–8mm wide, round, green berry.*
DISTRIBUTION *Throughout the region.*
SIMILAR SPECIES *Common Asparagus (A. officinalis), which has a red berry.*

Snake's-head Iris

Hermodactylus tuberosus (Iridaceae)

This small member of the iris family grows from a tuber rather than a rhizome, and produces narrow, four-angled leaves taller than the flowering stem. The sweetly-scented flowers are formed singly, with three greenish yellow standard petals protecting the erect, petal-like styles, and three velvety brown fall petals which droop downwards. Occasionally, all yellow flowers are produced.

FOUND on rocky and grassy hillsides, garigue, roadsides, scrubby places, and waysides.

yellow standard petals

velvety brown fall petal

PERENNIAL

4-angled, grass-like leaves

PLANT HEIGHT *20–40cm.*
FLOWER SIZE *4–5cm long.*
FLOWERING TIME *February–April.*
LEAVES *2–3mm wide, square in cross-section.*
FRUIT *Three-parted capsule.*
DISTRIBUTION *S.E. France eastwards.*
SIMILAR SPECIES *This is the only species in its genus.*

Giant Reed

Arundo donax (Poaceae)

This enormous grass is a common sight in the region, and is often mistaken for bamboo or sugar cane. It produces dense thickets of very leafy, unbranched stems. The stems do not flower until their second year, by which time they become brown and woody. The tall plumes of flowers are greenish purple at first, becoming yellow as they mature, and often persisting for many months. When fully grown, the flat, alternate leaves arch over gracefully under their own weight. The leaves and stems have several uses such as making baskets, mats, screens, musical instruments, roofing, as well as manufacturing paper.

GROWS *on marshy ground, field margins, drainage ditches, and near the coast; sometimes planted inland as a windbreak.*

PERENNIAL

persistent fruiting head

erect leaves

flat leaves

woody flowering stem

NOTE

The plant's prodigious growth rate has led to research on its biomass as a source of energy production, which would be carbon-neutral and therefore combat global warming.

PLANT HEIGHT *Up to 6m.*
FLOWER SIZE *Panicle to 60cm long.*
FLOWERING TIME *August–December.*
LEAVES *Alternate, overlapping, and 5cm wide at the base.*
FRUIT *Seed with a short awn.*
DISTRIBUTION *Throughout the Mediterranean.*
SIMILAR SPECIES *Other large grasses in the region, which do not grow as tall.*

Hare's Tail

Lagurus ovatus (Poaceae)

OCCURS *in dry, stony, or sandy places, frequently by the sea but also found inland.*

This grass is easily recognized by its silvery or golden, egg-shaped flowerheads that bob to and fro in the breeze. The head is made up of tightly packed individual spikelets, each with a silky awn – a long filament-like projection, that forms a soft "fur" around the entire flowerhead. Seeds are produced only by the upper spikelets.

ANNUAL

egg-shaped flowerhead

very thin stems

silvery-white flowerhead

PLANT HEIGHT *10–50cm.*
FLOWER SIZE *Flowerheads up to 2cm long.*
FLOWERING TIME *April–June.*
LEAVES *Soft and downy, up to 1cm wide.*
FRUIT *Seed in upper part of flowerhead only.*
DISTRIBUTION *Throughout the region.*
SIMILAR SPECIES *Rough Dog's Tail (Cynosurus echinatus), which has a rougher flowerhead.*

Large Quaking Grass

Briza maxima (Poaceae)

GROWS *on dry hillslopes, roadsides, and cultivated, fallow, or waste land.*

It is the "fish-tail"-like spikelets with 3–10 pairs of overlapping scales that make this is one of the most distinctive Mediterranean grasses. They hang down under their own weight and tremble or quiver in the breeze. This erect and slender plant has narrow and hairless leaves. The dried flowerheads are often used in flower arrangements.

ANNUAL

1–12 flowerheads on each stem

slender stems

flowerhead with overlapping scales

PLANT HEIGHT *20–60cm.*
FLOWER SIZE *Flowerhead up to 2.5cm long.*
FLOWERING TIME *April–June.*
LEAVES *2–4mm wide and up to 20cm long.*
FRUIT *Flat on one side, round on the other.*
DISTRIBUTION *Throughout the region.*
SIMILAR SPECIES *Quaking Grass (Briza media), which has much smaller flowerheads.*

Italian Lords-and-Ladies

Arum italicum (Araceae)

This imposing species may be easily recognized by its large leaves alone, which first appear in the autumn. They are arrow-shaped and mottled with conspicuous white veins or blotches against a glossy green surface. The true flowers are hidden at the base of the yellow, cigar-shaped spadix, which is enclosed by a large cowl-like spathe.

FOUND *in moist, shaded sites such as woods, hedgerows, and scrubby or rocky places.*

greenish yellow spathe

club-like spadix

variable, arrow-shaped leaves

PERENNIAL

cluster of berries

PLANT HEIGHT *25–50cm.*
FLOWER SIZE *Spathe 15–30cm long.*
FLOWERING TIME *April–May.*
LEAVES *Up to 35cm long.*
FRUIT *10–15cm-long cluster of berries.*
DISTRIBUTION *Throughout the region.*
SIMILAR SPECIES *Arum maculatum, which has dark leaf blotches and a purple spadix.*

Friar's Cowl

Arisarum vulgare (Araceae)

This common and rather short arum-like plant is best seen in the winter months or early spring. Often found in patches, it produces a short spathe or cowl, marked with greenish yellow and purple stripes, that is usually bent over forwards. The small greenish or purple spadix often protrudes from the mouth.

FORMS *patches in shaded or semi-shaded areas in open woodland, field margins, and grassy places.*

glossy green leaves

hooded spathe

protruding spadix

green and purple stripes

PERENNIAL

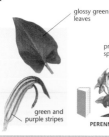

PLANT HEIGHT *20–40cm.*
FLOWER SIZE *Spathe 4–5cm long.*
FLOWERING TIME *October–May.*
LEAVES *Heart-shaped, up to 10cm long.*
FRUIT *Greenish berry.*
DISTRIBUTION *Throughout the region.*
SIMILAR SPECIES *Round-leaved Birthwort (p.147), which has rounded leaves.*

Lizard Orchid

Himantoglossum hircinum (Orchidaceae)

GROWS *in grassy places such as scrub, meadows, woodland clearings, road verges, and sand dunes; also found near hedgerows. May form small, loose colonies.*

An impressive plant, Lizard Orchid can grow to be the largest orchid in Europe. When in bud, the flowering spike resembles an enormous asparagus tip. The oblong lower leaves are unspotted and grey-green, and may be partially withered by flowering time. The flowers have green petals and sepals, which form a small hood, and a short downturned spur and long, narrow ribbon. The lower lip of the flower is extraordinary, uncoiling like a watch-spring to form a long, twisted, purple-spotted ribbon, on each side of which is a brownish "arm". This is sometimes likened to a long-tailed lizard.

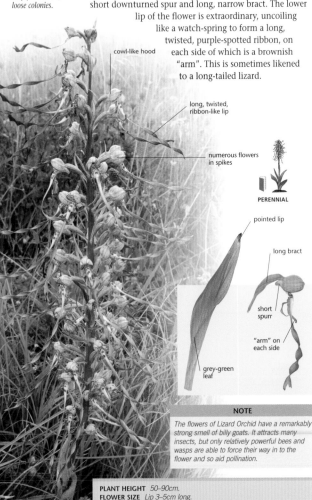

cowl-like hood

long, twisted, ribbon-like lip

numerous flowers in spikes

PERENNIAL

pointed lip

long bract

short spurr

"arm" on each side

grey-green leaf

NOTE

The flowers of Lizard Orchid have a remarkably strong smell of billy goats. It attracts many insects, but only relatively powerful bees and wasps are able to force their way in to the flower and so aid pollination.

PLANT HEIGHT 50–90cm.
FLOWER SIZE Lip 3–5cm long.
FLOWERING TIME June–July.
LEAVES Alternate; upper leaves smaller and narrower.
FRUIT Three-parted capsule, containing many seeds.
DISTRIBUTION Throughout, but absent from most of the islands.
SIMILAR SPECIES H. calcaratum of the E. Mediterranean has longer arms and a more deeply forked "tail".

Mirror Orchid

Ophrys speculum (Orchidaceae)

This is one of the darkest of the *Ophrys* species of orchids, but the shiny blue speculum often catches the light so this diminutive plant may shine out brightly. The three narrow sepals are green, suffused with brown and red, the central one of which forms a small hood. The two upper petals are very small and dark purple. The lower lip is clearly three-lobed and rather bulbous, with a large, heart-shaped speculum and margin of long, brown or black hair. The flowers are pollinated by the male wasp *Campsoscolia ciliata*.

FORMS *colonies, sometimes extensive, in maquis, garigue, olive groves, open woodland, and grassy places.*

domed hood

leaves sheath the stem

elliptical leaves

large blue speculum

2–10 flowers in a spike

margin of long hair

PERENNIAL

brownish green petals

PLANT HEIGHT *10–25cm.*
FLOWER SIZE *Lower lip 1–1.3cm long.*
FLOWERING TIME *March–May.*
LEAVES *Oblong-elliptical, stem leaves narrower.*
FRUIT *Capsule containing numerous tiny seeds.*
DISTRIBUTION *Throughout the region.*
SIMILAR SPECIES *Subspecies* lusitanica *of Portugal, which has a narrower lip fringed with yellow hair, and is taller.*

NOTE

The name Ophrys comes from Greek for "eyebrow" and refers to the hairy margin on the lip, particularly prevalent in this species. Speculum means mirror, referring to the shiny patch on these orchids.

Sombre Bee Orchid

Ophrys fusca (Orchidaceae)

OCCURS *in maquis, garigue, grassy or rocky places, open woodland, and olive groves.*

One of the most common bee orchids in the region, the Sombre Bee Orchid is a robust plant. The centremost of the three fairly large, green sepals often curves over to from a hood, but the true upper petals are reduced to almost linear appendages. The flowers are held almost horizontally, and as the name suggests, the lower lip is dark brown, with an often rather matt, two-lobed speculum.

broad basal leaf

upright linear petal

PERENNIAL

sepal curving over flower

dull pattern on lower lip

PLANT HEIGHT *10–30cm.*
FLOWER SIZE *Lower lip 1–1.5cm long.*
FLOWERING TIME *February–May.*
LEAVES *Broadly elliptic, 4–6, mostly basal.*
FRUIT *Capsule containing many tiny seeds.*
DISTRIBUTION *Throughout the region.*
SIMILAR SPECIES O. iricolor, *which has a longer lip (1.5–2.2cm) and a blue speculum.*

Bumblebee Orchid

Ophrys bombyliflora (Orchidaceae)

FOUND *among grass in olive groves, maquis, garigue, scrub, and other grassy and stony habitats.*

It takes sharp eyes to spot this species – the smallest and least noticeable bee orchid in the region. It has rounded green sepals, and two tiny triangular green petals, which are darker at the base. The lower lip has two pointed, lateral lobes with hairy bosses, and is velvety black or very dark brown, with an often indistinct speculum.

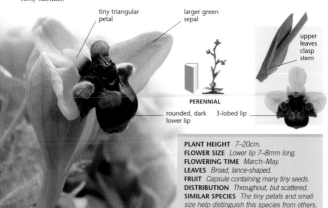

tiny triangular petal

larger green sepal

upper leaves clasp stem

PERENNIAL

rounded, dark lower lip

3-lobed lip

PLANT HEIGHT *7–20cm.*
FLOWER SIZE *Lower lip 7–8mm long.*
FLOWERING TIME *March–May.*
LEAVES *Broad, lance-shaped.*
FRUIT *Capsule containing many tiny seeds.*
DISTRIBUTION *Throughout, but scattered.*
SIMILAR SPECIES *The tiny petals and small size help distinguish this species from others.*

Early Spider Orchid

Ophrys sphegodes (Orchidaceae)

With many subspecies recognized across the Mediterranean, Early Spider Orchid is a highly variable plant. To make identification more difficult, it often hybridizes with other similar species. In the Western Mediterranean however, fairly constant characters to look for are green sepals, that are sometimes flushed with red, and a blue speculum that is shaped like an H, or the Greek letter π (pi). The dark brown lower lip may have two lobes at the base or be more rounded. The two upper petals are generally lance-shaped, often with a wavy edge, and are green or flushed red.

GROWS *in grassy ground, meadows, roadsides, maquis, garigue or rocky habitats, generally in fairly sunny conditions.*

green sepals

π-shaped speculum

PERENNIAL

furry brown lower lip

sheathing stem leaf

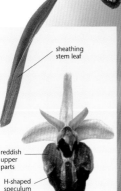

reddish upper parts

H-shaped speculum

NOTE

The tiny seeds of orchid species depend on a symbiotic relationship with fungi in the soil to enable them to grow. In the early stages, the orchid embryo digests the fungal tissue until it is large enough to form roots of its own.

PLANT HEIGHT *10–40cm*
FLOWER SIZE *Lower lip 1–1.2cm long.*
FLOWERING TIME *March–May.*
LEAVES *Basal leaves oval, stem leaves lance-shaped and pointed.*
FRUIT *Capsule containing many tiny seeds.*
DISTRIBUTION *Throughout the region.*
SIMILAR SPECIES *Most likely to be confused with other species in the Eastern Mediterranean, such as in Greece.*

Yellow

Flowers with yellow petals, such as the Spanish Broom below, seem to be particularly attractive to pollinating insects, including flies, beetles, butterflies, and bees. Studies have shown that many bees are able to detect ultraviolet light, and that yellow flowers are among those that reflect it. Shrubby members of the pea family (Fabaceae) and many members of the daisy family (Asteraceae), frequently have yellow flowers.

YELLOW CHAMOMILE

SHRUBBY HARE'S EAR

CHONDRILLA

YELLOW STAR-THISTLE

Birthwort

Aristolochia clematitiis (Aristolochiaceae)

Birthwort is a rather attractive plant, with its large, rounded leaves and erect "organ-pipes" of yellow flowers clustered at the leaf-axils. The flowers carry a foetid smell of rotting flesh however, which attracts flies deep into the hairy mouth of the flower, where they may become trapped for a while in order to effect pollination. The leaves have short stalks with inset veins above and raised veins below. The flowers have a greenish yellow tube opening into a wide mouth partially covered by a flap, and a rounded swelling at the base.

FORMS *small colonies in damp, partially shaded places such as the base of old walls or alongside ditches.*

slightly folded leaf blades

PERENNIAL

inset veins above

greenish yellow throat

egg-shaped fruit capsule

NOTE

Birthwort stimulates the uterus and was once used to induce childbirth, but it is now considered too dangerous. It also has anti-cancer properties but causes damage to the kidneys, and is too toxic for use.

PLANT HEIGHT Up to 1m.
FLOWER SIZE 2–3cm long.
FLOWERING TIME May–July.
LEAVES Alternate, rounded and heart-shaped, strongly veined.
FRUIT Round or egg-shaped capsule, 2–5cm long.
DISTRIBUTION Throughout the region.
SIMILAR SPECIES The clustered yellow flowers are unlike any other species in the region.

Cytinus hypocistis

Cytinus hypocystis (Rafflesiaceae)

PARASITIZES *the roots of* Cistus *species wherever they grow, usually on maquis and garigue.*

This curious, low-growing plant only occurs beneath the bushes of white-flowered *Cistus* species (see pp.31–32). It is entirely parasitic upon the roots of those plants and so has no green leaves of its own. The bright yellow flowers grow at ground level in clusters of five to ten and are surrounded by red-tipped scales.

PERENNIAL

reddish scales

4 spreading lobes

female flowers on the outside

male flowers on the inside

PLANT HEIGHT *3–7cm.*
FLOWER SIZE *1.2cm wide.*
FLOWERING TIME *April–June.*
LEAVES *Small, reddish scales.*
FRUIT *Pulpy berry.*
DISTRIBUTION *Throughout the region.*
SIMILAR SPECIES *C. rubra, which is crimson and white.*

Ranunculus gramineus

Ranunculus gramineus (Ranunculaceae)

OCCURS *in dry, rocky, and grassy hillsides and garigue; most often in mountain areas at altitude.*

There are many buttercup species in the Mediterranean region, though this is one of the easiest to identify due to its very narrow, grass-like leaves. Most of the blue-green leaves arise directly from the base, though some smaller ones branch from the stem. The usually solitary flowers are typical of buttercups, with yellow petals and numerous stamens.

solitary flower

5 bright yellow petals

long stalk

PERENNIAL

grass-like leaf

bluish-green leaves

PLANT HEIGHT *20–50cm.*
FLOWER SIZE *About 2cm wide.*
FLOWERING TIME *April–June.*
LEAVES *Linear, mostly basal, blue-green.*
FRUIT *Cluster of hooked achenes.*
DISTRIBUTION *Throughout the region.*
SIMILAR SPECIES *None with linear leaves; R. bullatus, which has a rosette of oval leaves.*

Yellow Horned Poppy

Glaucium flavum (Papaveraceae)

This distinctive and colourful beach poppy is recognized by its fleshy, grey-green leaves, which are pinnately divided into coarse, toothed segments with an undulating and slightly hairy surface. The large, bright yellow flowers have four tissue-like petals which overlap to form a cup, and the unusual fruit is an elongated, narrow capsule.

GROWS on shingle or sandy beaches, dunes, sea-cliffs, and very occasionally on waste ground inland.

grey-green leaves

BIENNIAL/PERENNIAL

overlapping petals

long, slender capsule

large yellow flowers

PLANT HEIGHT 50–90cm.
FLOWER SIZE 6–9cm wide.
FLOWERING TIME April–August.
LEAVES Pinnately divided, wavy, and toothed.
FRUIT Elongated capsule to 30cm long.
DISTRIBUTION Throughout W. Europe coasts.
SIMILAR SPECIES Red Horned Poppy (p.63), which has yellow or orange flowers.

Hypecoum imberbe

Hypecoum imberbe (Papaveraceae)

Though this unusual member of the poppy family is rather buttercup-like with its bright yellow flowers, these have two pairs of unequal, lobed petals so from above they appear oblong rather than circular. The leaves are pinnately-lobed into feathery, linear segments, as are the bracts. The seed pod is slender and curved.

INHABITS sandy and gravelly places, though not on the coast, such as fields, olive groves, and cultivated land.

3-lobed outer petals

stamens in short column

ANNUAL

small inner petals

leaves with feathery lobes

PLANT HEIGHT Up to 20cm.
FLOWER SIZE 1–1.5cm wide.
FLOWERING TIME March–May.
LEAVES Pinnate with linear segments.
FRUIT Slender capsule 4–6cm long.
DISTRIBUTION Throughout the region.
SIMILAR SPECIES H. procumbens, which has smaller flowers and segmented pods.

Woad

Isatis tinctoria (Brassicaceae)

OCCURS *on roadsides, embankments, waste ground, grassy meadows, and dry, rocky places up to an altitude of 2000m.*

BIENNIAL

One of the more robust members of the cress family in the Mediterranean region, Woad is easy to recognize. It produces tall, stout stems which generally begin to branch only in the upper half; the lower stems are covered with neat, overlapping ranks of greyish green leaves which clasp the stem with arrowhead-like lobes. The slender top branches produce a mass of frothy yellow flowers in domed heads, and each individual flower has four petals. By late spring, the characteristic fruit begin to appear as rows of pendant teardrop-shaped siliculas that hang from the arching stems, green at first and then ripening to brown by late summer.

spear-shaped

oblong fruit

clasping stem-leaf

brown when ripe

yellow flowers

branching upper stems

NOTE

Woad has been cultivated since ancient times for the blue dye obtained from its leaves. It has now been largely replaced by synthetic dyes, except for certain specialized uses.

PLANT HEIGHT *0.6–1.2m.*
FLOWER SIZE *About 4mm wide.*
FLOWERING TIME *May–July.*
LEAVES *Untoothed, grey-green; stem leaves stalkless, basal leaves stalked.*
FRUIT *Pendant brown, teardrop-shaped silicula.*
DISTRIBUTION *Throughout from N.E. Spain eastwards.*
SIMILAR SPECIES *Charlock (Sinapis arvensis), which has lobed leaves and a long, thin siliqua.*

Buckler Mustard

Biscutella laevigata (Brassicaceae)

This would be an undistinguished member of the cress family were it not for the extraordinary fruit. They are two almost translucent green discs or siliculas joined together rather like a pair of spectacles, and produced in abundance on the slender branching stems. It is the foodplant for, and is often attended by the Moroccan Orange-tip butterfly (*Anthocharis belia*).

GROWS *on dry rocky or stony places, abandoned fields, woodland clearings, and on limestone soil.*

flowers in small clusters

4-petalled yellow flowers

PERENNIAL

coarse, toothed stem-leaf

spectacle-like fruit

PLANT HEIGHT *20–50cm.*
FLOWER SIZE *0.6–1cm wide.*
FLOWERING TIME *March–June.*
LEAVES *Hairy and lance-shaped.*
FRUIT *Two discs, 4–7mm wide, joined together.*
DISTRIBUTION *Portugal, Spain, France, Italy.*
SIMILAR SPECIES *B. didyma, which is an annual and is found from Italy eastwards.*

Wallflower

Erysimum cheiri (Brassicaceae)

Native to the Eastern Mediterranean, Wallflower is widely used as a garden plant and has become established in many parts of Europe. It has a remarkably thick, woody stock that produce numerous upswept, lance-shaped leaves. The four-petalled flowers are highly fragrant, and range in colour from a warm yellow to orange and golden brown, often with dark-coloured sepals. Escapes from garden varieties sometimes occur, which may be purple or white.

CLINGS *to cliffs, old walls, and rocks, often close to the sea, usually on limestone.*

golden yellow flowers

4-petalled flowers

narrow, hairy leaves

PERENNIAL

long, slender seedpod

PLANT HEIGHT *30–60cm.*
FLOWER SIZE *2–2.5cm wide.*
FLOWERING TIME *March–June.*
LEAVES *Alternate, hairy, and lance-shaped.*
FRUIT *Siliqua, 7.5cm long.*
DISTRIBUTION *Throughout the region.*
SIMILAR SPECIES *Allyssoides sinuata of the Adriatic coast, which has smaller flowers.*

Rocket

Eruca vesicaria (Brassicaceae)

THRIVES *on disturbed soil, cultivated or waste ground, roadsides, or sandy areas.*

ANNUAL

Rocket is a leafy plant with rather lax stems so it tends to sprawl on the ground, though it sometimes grows taller. The leaves are pinnately lobed, with a large terminal lobe. The flowers have four widely-separated petals which are creamy with distinct violet veins. The fruit is torpedo shaped with a sharp beak.

fruit with sharp beak

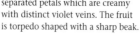

large terminal leaflet

large, cross-shaped flowers

purple veined petals

PLANT HEIGHT *20–80cm.*
FLOWER SIZE *1.8–3cm wide.*
FLOWERING TIME *February–June.*
LEAVES *Pinnately-lobed, large terminal leaflet.*
FRUIT *Siliqua, 1.2–2.5cm long.*
DISTRIBUTION *Throughout the region.*
SIMILAR SPECIES *E. sativa, which is almost identical and often included in this species.*

Wild Radish

Raphanus raphanistrum (Brassicaceae)

GROWS *on arable land, field margins, wastelands, roadsides, and on sand or shingle along the coast.*

Similar to Rocket (above), this plant has faintly-veined white or pale yellow flowers. The lobes of the leaves are much more rounded, especially in the large terminal leaflet. The chief distinguishing and characteristic feature, however, is the fruit, which although similarly shaped, divides into spherical segments as it matures, like a row of beads.

joined fruit with sharp beak

rounded leaf lobes

slender, immature fruit

ANNUAL/ PERENNIAL

yellow or white flowers

PLANT HEIGHT *20–50cm.*
FLOWER SIZE *1.5–3cm wide.*
FLOWERING TIME *March–July.*
LEAVES *Pinnately divided with round lobes.*
FRUIT *Siliqua, 3–7cm long, beaded.*
DISTRIBUTION *Throughout the region.*
SIMILAR SPECIES *Subspecies maritimus, which has thicker fruit and leaves in a rosette.*

Wild Mignonette

Reseda lutea (Resedaceae)

The attractive yellow flowers of this plant have short stalks and deeply notched petals, giving them a "fluffy" look, accentuated by its branched, bushy habit. The rough, dark green leaves have a wavy margin and fold around the midrib. The fruit is an elongated, open-ended capsule.

OCCURS on roadsides, embankments, field margins, and dry grassland, usually on limestone soil.

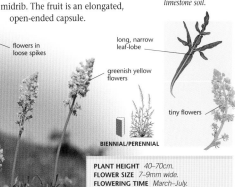

flowers in loose spikes

long, narrow leaf-lobe

greenish yellow flowers

tiny flowers

BIENNIAL/PERENNIAL

PLANT HEIGHT 40–70cm.
FLOWER SIZE 7–9mm wide.
FLOWERING TIME March–July.
LEAVES Pinnately divided into long, thin lobes.
FRUIT Open-ended capsule, 0.7–1.2cm long.
DISTRIBUTION Throughout the region.
SIMILAR SPECIES White Mignonette (p.22), which has white flowers and more leaf-lobes.

Sedum sediforme

Sedum sediforme (Crassulaceae)

This species of stonecrop produces several short, leafy but non-flowering stems as well as long, fleshy flowering stems that become woody at the base. The thick, waxy leaves are lance-shaped and flat on one side, but often fall off by flowering time. The greenish yellow, star-shaped flowers have many yellow stamens, and are produced in heads that uncurl to become almost flat-topped.

FOUND on roadsides, embankments, cliffs, and other dry places, on the coast or inland.

5–8 petals

PERENNIAL

flowerheads uncurl as they open

numerous yellow anthers

thick, fleshy leaf

PLANT HEIGHT 20–60cm.
FLOWER SIZE 0.8–1.4cm wide.
FLOWERING TIME May–July.
LEAVES Succulent, pointed, 1–1.5cm long.
FRUIT Upright follicles, contains many seeds.
DISTRIBUTION Throughout the region.
SIMILAR SPECIES Many other Sedum species, which are often shorter, occur in the region.

Swamp Wattle

Acacia retinodes (Fabaceae)

PLANTED *in parks, gardens, hedges, and along roadsides, but also naturalized by sandy tracks and in garigue.*

There are several *Acacia* species introduced into the Mediterranean region, mostly from Australia. They are characterized by their globular "fluffy" flower clusters, actually composed of many peaflowers like a clover but with conspicuous stamens. The linear or lance-shaped "leaves" are actually phyllodes – an enlarged midrib that functions as a leaf, and is held erect on the stem. The pale yellow flowerheads are about 4–6mm wide and borne in stalked clusters of five to ten. The fruit is a slender hanging pod.

lemon yellow flowers

flattened pod

cluster of flowerheads

erect leaves

PERENNIAL

NOTE

Acacia seeds are highly nutritious and contain almost equal amounts of protein, carbohydrate, and fat. The starch is absorbed by the gut particularly slowly, thereby regulating blood sugar.

PLANT HEIGHT *Up to 10m but often less.*
FLOWER SIZE *Flowerhead 4–6mm wide.*
FLOWERING TIME *February–April.*
LEAVES *Greyish, 5–15cm long.*
FRUIT *Slender, flattened pod, 6–12cm long.*
DISTRIBUTION *Throughout the region.*
SIMILAR SPECIES *Blue-leaved Wattle (A. cyanophila), which has longer, pendent leaves and larger flowerheads.*

Hairy Thorny Broom

Calycotome villosa (Fabaceae)

This is one of several yellow-flowered, shrubby members of the pea family growing in the region. *Calycotome* species are distinguished by their calyx, part of which splits off like a cap when the flower opens. This species also has small, trifoliate leaves and long, sharp thorns. The young stems and the greyish fruit pod are covered with silky hair. The pod has a thickened ridge along its length.

OCCURS *in rocky hillsides, scrub, cleared woodland, and maquis or garigue.*

yellow peaflowers

PERENNIAL

flowers in small clusters

split calyx tip

thickened ridges

PLANT HEIGHT *Up to 3m.*
FLOWER SIZE *1.2–1.8cm long.*
FLOWERING TIME *February–June.*
LEAVES *Small, trifoliate, with oval leaflets.*
FRUIT *Grey-haired pod, 2.5–4cm long.*
DISTRIBUTION *Throughout the region.*
SIMILAR SPECIES *Thorny Broom (C. spinosa), which is less hairy and has solitary flowers.*

Cytisus villosus

Cytisus villosus (Fabaceae)

This is a spineless broom species with five-angled stems and trifoliate leaves. The yellow peaflowers droop profusely in groups of two or three, all along the length of the upper stems. The standard petal is folded and bent back upon itself, and has red streaks at the base on its upper surface.

GROWS *in maquis, scrub, open woods, and along tracks and paths; avoids limestone soil.*

trifoliate leaves

sharply folded upper petal

hairless, flattened pod

PERENNIAL

flowers in leaf axils

PLANT HEIGHT *1–2m.*
FLOWER SIZE *1.5–1.8cm long.*
FLOWERING TIME *March–May.*
LEAVES *Oval leaflets, 1.5–2cm long.*
FRUIT *Slightly curved pod, 2–4.5cm long.*
DISTRIBUTION *Throughout the region.*
SIMILAR SPECIES *Tree Medick (p.183), which has tightly coiled seed pods.*

Spanish Broom

Spartium junceum (Fabaceae)

OCCURS *as single bushes or forms large colonies on roadsides, scrub, waste ground, maquis, and garigue, particularly on limestone soil.*

PERENNIAL

This common shrub renders swathes of the Mediterranean countryside bright yellow throughout the spring and early summer, though odd plants may continue to flower until August. It is a tall, robust plant, seemingly shrouded in large, sweet-scented flowers, made even more visible by the almost total absence of leaves. The leaves themselves are reduced to simple, lance-shaped projections sparsely scattered along the supple, smooth stems, which are green and so perform some of the functions normally carried out by leaves. By late summer, the tips of the stems carry numerous flattened, brown seed pods.

large, erect
standard petal

supple
green stems

almost stalkless
flowers

NOTE

The tough but flexible stems are used for making brooms and basket-weaving. They also yield a strong fibre, used to make thread, coarse fabrics, paper, or for stuffing cushions.

flattened
seed pod

simple
lance-
shaped
leaves

PLANT HEIGHT *Up to 3m.*
FLOWER SIZE *2.5cm wide.*
FLOWERING TIME *April–June.*
LEAVES *Opposite, 1–3cm long, scattered on almost leafless stems.*
FRUIT *Flattened pod 5–8cm long containing 10–18 seeds.*
DISTRIBUTION *Throughout the region.*
SIMILAR SPECIES *Broom (Cytisus scoparius), which is shorter with small, trifoliate leaves.*

Spanish Gorse

Genista hispanica (Fabaceae)

This is a very short but attractive shrub when in flower. It's soft appearance belies a thorny interior. The young growth on the upper half of the plant is bright green, flexible, and covered with numerous lance-shaped leaves and clusters of bright yellow flowers. The older growth beneath is much darker green with sharp spines.

OCCURS *as small, low colonies in rocky habitats, woodland clearings, and maquis.*

clusters of 3–8 flowers

PERENNIAL

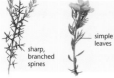

simple leaves

hairy leaves and stems

sharp, branched spines

PLANT HEIGHT *Up to 50cm.*
FLOWER SIZE *6–8mm long.*
FLOWERING TIME *April–June.*
LEAVES *Alternate, bright green, 4–8mm long.*
FRUIT *Flattened pod with a hooked beak.*
DISTRIBUTION *E. Spain and France.*
SIMILAR SPECIES *G. hirsuta of S. Spain and Portugal, which has unbranched spines.*

Genista cinerea

Genista cinerea (Fabaceae)

There are many Broom-like species in the Mediterranean, many of which are thorny to deter browsing animals, but this is a spineless example. The long, erect or arching stems are ribbed and covered with very fine hair to give them a greyish appearance. The very small, simple leaves are either single or in groups of three, and the flowers are usually in pairs.

GROWS *in loose colonies in scrub, on waste ground, woodland clearings, and rocky, open places, mostly on limestone soil.*

greyish, ribbed stems

simple leaves

flowers in pairs

typical pea-flower

PERENNIAL

PLANT HEIGHT *Up to 2m.*
FLOWER SIZE *1–1.2cm long.*
FLOWERING TIME *April–June.*
LEAVES *Alternate and lance-shaped.*
FRUIT *Flattened pod 1.5–1.8cm long.*
DISTRIBUTION *W. Mediterranean, N. Africa.*
SIMILAR SPECIES *G. scorpius, which is similar but more branched and very spiny.*

Bladder Senna

Colutea arborescens (Fabaceae)

This small tree or shrub is very distinctive with its curiously inflated bladder-like seed pods, which become reddish brown and more inflated as they ripen. They may be so numerous that they appear to colour the whole tree red in late summer. Typically pea shaped, the flowers grow in stalked clusters of three to eight. The leaves are divided into neat ranks of 7–13 oval leaflets, each of which often has a small notch at the tip.

FOUND on rocky and grassy hillsides, woods, and garigue; usually on limestone though frequently grown in gardens.

PERENNIAL

NOTE

The plant bears a slight resemblance to the much smaller shrub Senna (Cassia sp.), and the leaves share some of its laxative properties, but they are considerably milder in their action.

pinnately-divided leaves

flowers in clusters of 3–8

oval leaflets

broad standard petal

narrow keel

ripe, inflated pod

PLANT HEIGHT Up to 3m.
FLOWER SIZE 1.6–2cm long.
FLOWERING TIME May–August.
LEAVES Pinnate with four to six pairs of oval leaflets.
FRUIT Papery, inflated pod, reddish brown, 5–7cm long, and persisting into the winter.
DISTRIBUTION Throughout the region.
SIMILAR SPECIES None.

Large Yellow Rest-harrow

Ononis natrix (Fabaceae)

This small shrubby plant is covered with sticky hair and has a profusion of yellow peaflowers at the stem tips. The standard petal is often distinctly red-veined on the outside. The leaves have three oval or narrow leaflets, which are usually toothed. This plant is highly variable, with a range of flower sizes.

OCCURS *in sandy, rocky, or bushy places, waste ground, and garigue; in shade or in the open.*

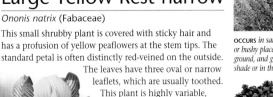

red-veined flowers

PERENNIAL

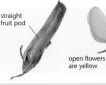

straight fruit pod

open flowers are yellow

PLANT HEIGHT 20–60cm.
FLOWER SIZE 0.6–2cm.
FLOWERING TIME *April–July.*
LEAVES *Trifoliate; oval, toothed leaflets.*
FRUIT *Straight pod up to 2.5cm long.*
DISTRIBUTION *Throughout the region.*
SIMILAR SPECIES *O. pusilla, which is less woody and has flowers with red veins.*

Hairy Yellow Vetch

Vicia hybrida (Fabaceae)

This rather delicate plant has slender stems and uses its branched tendrils to hold on to other vegetation for support. The leaves are divided into three to eight pairs of narrow oblong leaflets, often with a notch at the tip. The flowers are solitary in the leaf axils, and of a pale, insipid yellow color, so the plant is not easily noticed.

PREFERS *slightly shaded places, woodland edges, cultivated ground, and waysides; avoids very dry areas.*

calyx with pointed teeth

ANNUAL

branched tendrils

oblong, notched leaflets

pale yellow flower

PLANT HEIGHT 20–60cm.
FLOWER SIZE 1.8–3cm long.
FLOWERING TIME *March–June.*
LEAVES *Pinnate, three to eight pairs of oblong leaflets.*
FRUIT *Brown hairy pod, 2.5–4cm long.*
DISTRIBUTION *Throughout the region.*
SIMILAR SPECIES *None.*

Yellow Vetchling

Lathyrus aphaca (Fabaceae)

OCCURS *on roadsides, cultivated or waste ground, open pine woods and rocky places, in sheltered sites.*

This rather delicate climbing plant is notable for its curiously-shaped and greatly enlarged stipules, each like a rounded arrowhead. The stipules are always held upright, in pairs clasping the stem like two hands. The true leaves are actually the thread-like tendrils that cling on to other vegetation for support. The small yellow peaflowers are usually borne singly on long flower stalks, and they produce a pod containing up to eight seeds.

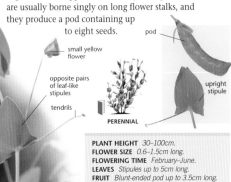

small yellow flower

opposite pairs of leaf-like stipules

tendrils

pod

upright stipule

PERENNIAL

PLANT HEIGHT *30–100cm.*
FLOWER SIZE *0.6–1.5cm long.*
FLOWERING TIME *February–June.*
LEAVES *Stipules up to 5cm long.*
FRUIT *Blunt-ended pod up to 3.5cm long.*
DISTRIBUTION *Throughout the region.*
SIMILAR SPECIES *The stipules make this plant unique.*

Small Melilot

Melilotus indica (Fabaceae)

INHABITS *cultivated and waste places, alongside ditches, and roadsides, preferring damp, sandy soil.*

This common plant of waysides is similar in many ways to White Melilot (p.26) but much shorter. The straggly stems produce leaves divided into three leaflets with toothed margins, and only tiny, needle-like stipules at their base. The tiny yellow flowers, only about 3mm long, are produced in dense but untidy racemes.

leaves divided into three

dense flowerhead

oval to lance-shaped leaflet

needle-like stipule

PERENNIAL

flowers droop downwards

PLANT HEIGHT *20–50cm.*
FLOWER SIZE *2–3mm long.*
FLOWERING TIME *April–June.*
LEAVES *Divided into three toothed leaflets.*
FRUIT *Tiny spherical pods.*
DISTRIBUTION *Throughout the region.*
SIMILAR SPECIES *M. italicus, which has longer flowers (6–9mm).*

Tree Medick

Medicago arborea (Fabaceae)

A fairly large, leafy shrub which originates from the Eastern Mediterranean, Tree Medick is now widespread through cultivation. There is huge variety in the shape and form of the fruit in members of the pea family, and this is especially true in *Medicago* species. The pods are frequently ornamented with spines or teeth and are coiled tightly into a disc, often with a hole remaining right through the middle. The young stems are green and softly hairy. The leaves are divided into three heart-shaped leaflets that are hairy below and this gives them a greyish appearance. The yellow flowers are borne in untidy clusters at the stem tips.

FOUND *in dry rocky habitats or cliffs, especially close to the sea, or planted in gardens and on roadsides.*

PERENNIAL

leaves often folded

orange-yellow flowers

NOTE

In the Eastern Mediterranean, the plant is cultivated for its young shoots and leaves, which are often eaten in salads. However, they become rather bitter and unpleasant if allowed to mature.

developing seed pod

3-lobed leaves

leaves greyish below

ripe, coiled seed pod

PLANT HEIGHT *1–2.5m.*
FLOWER SIZE *Up to 1.5cm long.*
FLOWERING TIME *February–August.*
LEAVES *Trifoliate with leaflets folded upwards.*
FRUIT *Coiled pod, 1.2–1.5cm wide, with a hole in the centre.*
DISTRIBUTION *Throughout the region.*
SIMILAR SPECIES *Cytisus villosus (p.177), which has more numerous, brighter yellow flowers and straight seed pods.*

Sea Medick

Medicago marina (Fabaceae)

This is a low creeping plant covered entirely with densely woolly foliage. The grey-felted leaves are divided into three leaflets and are stalked. They alternate regularly to produce a herringbone effect. The tiny egg-yolk yellow flowers are produced in small clusters of 5–12 at the ends of the stems, and go on to develop woolly, coiled pods, which often have small spines on their margins.

CREEPS *over sand on beaches and dunes; this plant is exclusively associated with coastal habitats.*

PERENNIAL

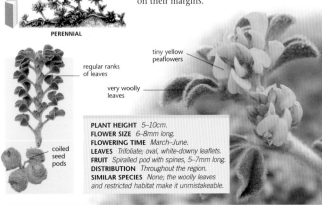

tiny yellow peaflowers

regular ranks of leaves

very woolly leaves

coiled seed pods

PLANT HEIGHT *5–10cm.*
FLOWER SIZE *6–8mm long.*
FLOWERING TIME *March–June.*
LEAVES *Trifoliate; oval, white-downy leaflets.*
FRUIT *Spiralled pod with spines, 5–7mm long.*
DISTRIBUTION *Throughout the region.*
SIMILAR SPECIES *None; the woolly leaves and restricted habitat make it unmistakeable.*

Large Disc Medick

Medicago orbicularis (Fabaceae)

This is an untidy, sprawling plant that leaves its large, spiral seed pods scattered over the ground. The roughly oval leaves are divided into three leaflets, each with a toothed margin towards the tip. The tiny yellow flowers are generally solitary and produced from the leaf axils.

GROWS *in waste and cultivated ground, olive groves, sandy or stony places, and fallow land.*

oval leaflet toothed at tip

PERENNIAL

trifoliate leaves

tiny yellow flowers

spiralled pod

PLANT HEIGHT *20–80cm.*
FLOWER SIZE *2–4mm long.*
FLOWERING TIME *April–June.*
LEAVES *Three oval leaflets.*
FRUIT *Circular disc, 1–2cm wide.*
DISTRIBUTION *Throughout the region.*
SIMILAR SPECIES *M. scutellata, which has larger flowers and pods with 4–8 spirals.*

Common Bird's-foot Trefoil

Lotus corniculatus (Fabaceae)

This common member of the pea family produces erect stems topped with fan-shaped clusters of brightly coloured yellow or orange peaflowers with orange streaks, which are red-tipped in bud. The fruit cluster is also a fan of long, narrow pods, somewhat resembling a bird's foot. The stalkless leaves are five-lobed.

THRIVES in grassy fields, pastures, scrub, and also along roadsides and embankments.

cleft standard petal

yellow to orange flowers

PERENNIAL

oval leaflets

PLANT HEIGHT *10–30cm.*
FLOWER SIZE *1–1.6cm long.*
FLOWERING TIME *April–July.*
LEAVES *Five-parted with untoothed leaflets.*
FRUIT *Cylindrical pod, 1.5–3cm long.*
DISTRIBUTION *Throughout the region.*
SIMILAR SPECIES *L. uliginosus, which is taller, hollow-stemmed, and prefers damper sites.*

Dragon's Teeth

Tetragonolobus maritimus (Fabaceae)

Although similar to *Lotus* species, *Tetragonolobus* may be differentiated by having three, not five, leaflets and curiously four-sided pods. Dragon's Teeth has upright stems and widely-spaced leaves. The solitary pale yellow flowers are borne on long stalks, and have a red-streaked calyx with a three-lobed bract at the base. The pod has four longitudinal ribs.

INHABITS damp, grassy places, waste ground, and banks; often along the margins of ditches or streams.

red-streaked calyx

solitary flower on long stalk

3-lobed bract

long pod

PERENNIAL

three leaflets

PLANT HEIGHT *10–30cm.*
FLOWER SIZE *2.5–3cm long.*
FLOWERING TIME *May–July.*
LEAVES *Three oval or wedge-shaped leaflets.*
FRUIT *Four-winged pod, 3–5cm long.*
DISTRIBUTION *Throughout N. Mediterranean.*
SIMILAR SPECIES *Lotus edulis, which has five leaflets and an inflated, slightly curved pod.*

Bladder Vetch

Tripodion tetraphyllum (Fabaceae)

OCCURS *on waste or cultivated land, road- and tracksides, and garigue. Prefers bare soil with little competition.*

This small, ground-hugging plant has a large, rounded terminal leaflet, other leaflets being much smaller. The small peaflowers have a large creamy standard petal, yellow wings, and a long calyx which inflates greatly in fruit to produce an egg-shaped bladder, which reddens as it matures.

inflated calyx

upright flower cluster

ANNUAL

large, rounded terminal leaflet

standard paler than wings

PLANT HEIGHT *5–30cm.*
FLOWER SIZE *0.8–1.2cm long.*
FLOWERING TIME *March–June.*
LEAVES *Divided into four or five leaflets.*
FRUIT *Inflated pod, red tinge on darker veins.*
DISTRIBUTION *Throughout, except for the Balearic Islands.*
SIMILAR SPECIES *None.*

Kidney Vetch

Anthyllis vulneraria (Fabaceae)

INHABITS *grassy fields, roadsides, garigue, and stony places, preferring limestone soil.*

This extremely variable species comes in many colour forms, often associated with a particular region. The flowers may be cream, pink, red, purple, or yellow and are borne from a tight cluster of hairy sepals above a ruff of bracts. The leaves are divided into ladder-like leaflets, though the lowest leaves may have only a single, large leaflet. The fruit is a pod, hidden in the calyx.

upper stem leaf

PERENNIAL

variable colours for individual flowers

many colour forms exist

ruff of narrow bracts

PLANT HEIGHT *Up to 40cm.*
FLOWER SIZE *1.2–1.5cm long.*
FLOWERING TIME *March–July.*
LEAVES *Divided into ladder-like leaflets.*
FRUIT *Pod with one or two seeds.*
DISTRIBUTION *Throughout the region.*
SIMILAR SPECIES *Subspecies* praepropera, *which has dark red or purple flowers.*

Coronilla valentina

Coronilla valentina (Fabaceae)

This attractive and decorative shrub is a popular garden plant, even in northern Europe, where it may flower as early as January and provide some cheerful winter colour. The leaves are divided into 2–6 pairs of oval leaflets, often blue-grey below, with a rounded or notched tip. The bright yellow flowers are borne in ring-like heads of 4–12 blooms, helping to immediately distinguish *Coronilla* species from the superficial brooms such as *Cytisus* or *Genista* species. The long, segmented pods droop in clusters.

GROWS *among scrub or on cliffs, rocks, and on stony ground; frequently seen in gardens or in parks.*

PERENNIAL

2–6 pairs of leaflets

yellow "crown" of flowers

cluster of ripe pods

flowerheads on long stalks

NOTE

Coronilla, meaning little crown, refers to the cluster of flowers in a ring. The plants are also known as Scorpion Vetches, as the jointed seed pods are reminiscent of a scorpion's tail.

similar-sized leaflets

PLANT HEIGHT *Up to 1.5m.*
FLOWER SIZE *0.8–1.2cm long.*
FLOWERING TIME *February–June, sometimes earlier.*
LEAVES *Pinnately divided with dark green oval leaflets.*
FRUIT *Segmented pod, 2–5cm long.*
DISTRIBUTION *Found from S.E. France eastwards.*
SIMILAR SPECIES *Coronilla emerus, of the W. Mediterranean, which has fewer flowers in each cluster.*

Rush-like Scorpion Vetch

Coronilla juncea (Fabaceae)

This semi-woody shrub has an upright habit with only a few small leaves spaced widely on the stems, and have tiny, fleshy leaflets. The stems are grey-green, erect, cylindrical and rush-like, bearing their "crowns" of yellow flowers at the tips of slender branches.

GROWS *in open, dry, rocky areas such as cliffs and garigue, usually on limestone.*

ring of yellow flowers

branched upper stems

small, oblong leaves

PERENNIAL

slender, segmented pods

PLANT HEIGHT	*40–100cm.*
FLOWER SIZE	*1.2cm long.*
FLOWERING TIME	*March–June.*
LEAVES	*1–2.5cm long.*
FRUIT	*Cluster of hanging, jointed pods, 2–5cm long.*
DISTRIBUTION	*Throughout the region.*
SIMILAR SPECIES	*None.*

Hippocrepis unisiliquosa

Hippocrepis unisiliquosa (Fabaceae)

This small, ground-hugging plant is much more likely to be noticed for its distinctive fruit rather than its flowers. The fruit form long, slightly curved pods, divided into seven or more segments with horseshoe-shaped indentations between each segment. The flowers are tiny and are borne singly or in pairs.

FOUND *on bare soil of fields, hillsides, waste or cultivated ground, or in damp, sandy places.*

ANNUAL

indented pod

pinnate leaves

flowers usually solitary

stems radiate outwards

PLANT HEIGHT	*5–20cm.*
FLOWER SIZE	*4–7mm long.*
FLOWERING TIME	*March–June.*
LEAVES	*Alternate, 3–7 pairs of oblong leaflets.*
FRUIT	*1.5–4cm long pods.*
DISTRIBUTION	*Throughout the region.*
SIMILAR SPECIES	*H. multisiliquosa, which has fruit pods curved almost into a complete circle.*

Bermuda Buttercup

Oxalis pes-caprae (Oxalidaceae)

Of South African origin, this species has become a widespread weed in the Mediterranean region, turning large areas completely yellow in early spring. The flowers have five petals in a shallow trumpet shape, and are clustered on a long stalk. The leaves comprise of three heart-shaped, folding leaflets, often speckled black.

FORMS *extensive carpets in cultivated land, particularly olive groves, vineyards, and plantations, especially in damp soil.*

brilliant yellow flower

5-petalled flowers (sometimes double petalled)

black-speckled leaves

cluster of flowers

PERENNIAL

PLANT HEIGHT *10–40cm.*
FLOWER SIZE *3–4cm wide.*
FLOWERING TIME *December–May.*
LEAVES *Three-parted, heart-shaped leaflets.*
FRUIT *Fruit is rare, plant spreads by bulbils.*
DISTRIBUTION *Throughout the region.*
SIMILAR SPECIES *Oxalis corniculata, which is much smaller with flowers 1–1.5cm wide.*

Upright Yellow Flax

Linum strictum (Linaceae)

This small yellow flax can easily go unnoticed as it tends to be swamped by other vegetation, and the flowers often fall by midday. The slender stems branch either at the top or near the base, with the five-petalled flowers crowded together at the stem tips, although young plants may be unbranched. The leaves are mostly alternate, and form a simple lance-shape with a sharp point.

OCCURS *in dry, open places, rocky hillslopes, vineyards, or sandy ground near the coast.*

ANNUAL

5 yellow petals

flowers clustered at stem tips

narrow green sepals

solitary flowers on young growth

PLANT HEIGHT *10–40cm.*
FLOWER SIZE *0.8–1.2cm wide.*
FLOWERING TIME *May–July.*
LEAVES *Narrow, lance-shaped.*
FRUIT *Rounded capsule, 3mm long.*
DISTRIBUTION *Throughout the region.*
SIMILAR SPECIES *Linum trigynum, which has smaller flowers, 4–7mm wide.*

Fringed Rue

Ruta chalapensis (Rutaceae)

OCCURS in dry, rocky habitats and scrub, garigue, and roadsides. It is often found in mountain areas.

PERENNIAL

This is a rather curious small, evergreen shrub with a smoky, greyish appearance. It has several stiff, erect stems, some of them woody, which bear the extraordinary flowers. They may have four or five spoon-shaped yellow petals, each of which is fringed with long, wispy yellow hair, and has a long stamen running along the length of it so that the anther protrudes beyond each petal. The leaves are twice-divided into narrow, delicate grey lobes, and have a strong foetid or chemical smell when crushed, which has been likened to wet fur.

pinnately divided leaves

developing capsule in centre of flower

petals fringed with long hair

4–5 petals

NOTE

This plant and the related Rue (Ruta graveolens) were used for many ailments, though the sap can cause blistering of the skin in sunlight. The essential oil is still used in perfumery.

PLANT HEIGHT *30–80cm.*
FLOWER SIZE *1.4–1.8cm wide.*
FLOWERING TIME *April–July.*
LEAVES *Bipinnate, grey-green with delicate leaflets.*
FRUIT *Capsule with pointed lobes.*
DISTRIBUTION *Throughout the region.*
SIMILAR SPECIES *Rue (R. graveolens), which has toothed but not hairy petals, often grown in gardens.*

Perforate St John's-wort

Hypericum perforatum (Clusiaceae)

There are many similar St John's-worts, but this one may be identified by its round stems, which have two opposite ridges or wings that are more easily felt than seen. The plant has an upright, branched habit. Its oval, unstalked leaves are peppered with tiny, translucent dots, which are visible only when the leaf is held up to the light. They also have a few tiny black glands on the underside, as do the margins of the petals. The flowers are yellow, with five petals and numerous stamens, and are borne in clusters. The fruit is a capsule, containing many seeds.

OCCURS *singly or in loose clumps in woodland margins, hedgerows, grassy places, on roadsides and banks, in open or semi-shaded places.*

flowers in terminal clusters

many stamens

PERENNIAL

leaf margins dotted black below

translucent dots

5 petals

NOTE

St John's-wort has become popular in recent years as a remedy for nervous depression, as well as other medicinal uses. It should, however, be used with caution and under medical advice, and never by pregnant women.

PLANT HEIGHT *40–80cm.*
FLOWER SIZE *1.8–2.2cm wide.*
FLOWERING TIME *May–July.*
LEAVES *Opposite, oval, with translucent dots.*
FRUIT *Small, many-seeded capsule.*
DISTRIBUTION *Throughout the region.*
SIMILAR SPECIES *H. perfoliatum, also common throughout, which has leaves with wide bases that clasp the stem.*

Spotted Rock-rose

Tuberaria guttata (Cistaceae)

OCCURS in maquis, garigue, sandy or grassy places, open woodlands, and along waysides, near the sea and in the mountains.

This is a rather delicate annual plant, often with unbranched stems. The leaves are mostly in a rosette, more or less oval and sometimes hairy; the stem leaves are narrower. The five-petalled yellow flowers have a dark purplish spot towards the base, which is extremely variable in size, and very occasionally may be absent altogether.

exceptionally large spots

dark-spotted petals

hairy stem

ANNUAL

PLANT HEIGHT *10–30cm.*
FLOWER SIZE *1–2cm wide.*
FLOWERING TIME *March–June.*
LEAVES *Elliptical to oval in shape.*
FRUIT *Three-parted capsule.*
DISTRIBUTION *Throughout the region.*
SIMILAR SPECIES Halimium halimifolium *is a large shrub with dark-spotted yellow flowers.*

Fumana ericoides

Fumana ericoides (Cistaceae)

FORMS small, open bushes in maquis or garigue, dry stony places, road, and track sides, on limestone soil.

Fumana species may be told apart from the very similar *Helianthemum* species by their alternate, rather than opposite, stem leaves. This plant is a much-branched, dwarf shrub with a woody base. The leaves are linear and evenly spaced along the stems. The yellow flowers have striped sepals of unequal sizes.

sepals coil around bud

PERENNIAL

numerous yellow stamens

3 large and 2 small sepals

linear leaves

PLANT HEIGHT *Up to 20cm.*
FLOWER SIZE *1–1.6cm wide.*
FLOWERING TIME *March–June.*
LEAVES *Linear, alternate, without stipules.*
FRUIT *Three-parted capsule.*
DISTRIBUTION *Throughout the region.*
SIMILAR SPECIES Common Rock-rose (Helianthemum nummularium) *has opposite leaves.*

Squirting Cucumber

Ecballium elaterium (Cucurbitaceae)

Unlike other members of the gourd family, this spreading plant has no tendrils. The bristly, hairy leaves are triangular or arrow-shaped and have crisply-wavy margins. Male and female flowers occur on the same plant: the male flowers have yellow anthers, while the female have green ovaries and remain open longer into the afternoon than the males. Squirting Cucumber is notable for its remarkable fruit, which explode violently due to the build-up of pressure inside, scattering their seeds over a considerable distance in a jet of sticky fluid.

SPRAWLS over waste ground, roadsides, sandy or stony places, beaches, car parks, and other bare places.

wavy leaf margin

male flower with yellow anthers

arrow-shaped leaf

green unripe fruit

PERENNIAL

PLANT HEIGHT 20–40cm.
FLOWER SIZE 1.6–2cm wide.
FLOWERING TIME *March–September.*
LEAVES *Roughly triangular with very wavy margin.*
FRUIT *Oblong like a small cucumber, 4–5cm long, turning yellowish when ripe.*
DISTRIBUTION *Throughout the region.*
SIMILAR SPECIES *None.*

NOTE

The juice from the fruit is highly toxic, but was prepared commercially for use as a laxative. However, its effect is violent and is now considered too dangerous to use.

Prickly Pear

Opuntia maxima (Cactaceae)

There are several Prickly Pear species in the Mediterranean, all introduced from the Americas, chiefly for their edible fruits and usefulness as a hedging plant. The paddle-like structures are actually flattened stems, constricted at narrow joints, the true leaves are tiny and soon fall. Small brown apertures all over the surface of the stems, called areoles, produce up to four very thin and sharp spines.

OCCURS on garden walls and terraces, but also naturalized on cliffs, dry places, and rocky slopes.

numerous stamens

PERENNIAL

club-shaped fruit

flowers on stem margins

spines protrude from areoles

PLANT HEIGHT *1–3m.*
FLOWER SIZE *5–10cm wide.*
FLOWERING TIME *April–July.*
LEAVES *Leaves absent, stems to 40cm long.*
FRUIT *Red, club-shaped, to 9cm long.*
DISTRIBUTION *Throughout the region.*
SIMILAR SPECIES *Several species which are difficult to separate.*

Alexanders

Smyrnium olusatrum (Apiaceae)

One of the earliest members of the carrot family to flower, this is a robust, clump-forming, very leafy plant. The leaves are divided into three groups of three flat leaflets, the upper ones arranged opposite on the stem and often yellowish in colour. The five-petalled yellow or greenish yellow flowers are borne in tight, domed umbels without bracts.

OCCURS as clumps or patches on damp ground, often by the sea, along estuaries and coastal cliffs.

broad, flat leaflets

tiny yellow flowers

PERENNIAL

rounded flower umbels

succulent stems

PLANT HEIGHT *0.8–1.5m.*
FLOWER SIZE *Umbels 4–8cm wide.*
FLOWERING TIME *February–May.*
LEAVES *Alternate at base, opposite at top.*
FRUIT *Oval mericarp, black when ripe.*
DISTRIBUTION *Throughout the region.*
SIMILAR SPECIES *Perfoliate Alexanders (S. perfoliatum) has upper leaves clasping the stem.*

Rock Samphire

Crithmum maritimum (Apiaceae)

Like many seaside plants, Rock Samphire has thickened, succulent leaves to conserve moisture in its arid environment, and can withstand frequent wetting by salt spray. The stems and leaves have an upswept appearance and branch to form tight, rounded clumps or mounds; they smell of polish when crushed. The tight, fairly rounded umbels are made up of small, creamy white flowers which form oval, corky fruit.

OCCURS *on coastal rocks, sea-cliffs, sand, and shingle, always very close to the sea.*

PERENNIAL

finger-like leaves

greenish yellow umbels

tiny flowers

PLANT HEIGHT *20–50cm.*
FLOWER SIZE *Umbels 3–6cm wide.*
FLOWERING TIME *June–August.*
LEAVES *Alternate, triangular, divided into cylindrical, fleshy, upward-pointing segments.*
FRUIT *Oval mericarp, purple when ripe.*
DISTRIBUTION *Throughout the region.*
SIMILAR SPECIES *None in the region.*

Shrubby Hare's Ear

Bupleurum fruticosum (Apiaceae)

Unlike most members of the carrot family, Hare's Ears have undivided leaves. This is a particularly large and imposing species, with leathery, evergreen leaves not unlike those of a Eucalyptus tree. The flowerheads are produced in abundance, each umbel forming an almost perfect hemisphere. It is often grown as a garden plant, and is tolerant of maritime exposure.

FORMS *substantial clumps or hedges in rocky places, garigue, roadsides, and waste places, or close to the sea, on limestone.*

leathery leaves

domed flowerheads

umbels with up to 25 rays

umbels in bud appear green

PERENNIAL

PLANT HEIGHT *Up to 2.5m.*
FLOWER SIZE *Umbels up to 10cm wide.*
FLOWERING TIME *April–September.*
LEAVES *Alternate and evenly spaced.*
FRUIT *Egg-shaped mericarp, 8mm long.*
DISTRIBUTION *Throughout, except the Balearic Islands.*
SIMILAR SPECIES *B. gibraltericum, of Spain.*

Fennel

Foeniculum vulgare (Apiaceae)

This common and statuesque member of the carrot family has very fine, hair-like, aromatic leaves with inflated leaf bases. The broad, loose umbels of flowers are bright yellow-green, remaining yellowish when in fruit. The tough, ridged stems are shiny and hollow with a blue-green sheen.

GROWS *singly or in patches, on roadsides, in rocky places, and wasteland; usually on limestone soil and often near the coast.*

hair-like leaves

fruiting head

many-branched umbels

oblong fruit

PERENNIAL

PLANT HEIGHT *1.5–2.2cm.*
FLOWER SIZE *Umbels 4–8cm wide.*
FLOWERING TIME *April–September.*
LEAVES *Finely divided, blue-green.*
FRUIT *Oblong, ridged mericarp, 4–8mm long, sweet and aromatic.*
DISTRIBUTION *Throughout the region.*
SIMILAR SPECIES *Giant Fennel (below).*

Giant Fennel

Ferula communis (Apiaceae)

In its full glory, this robust plant is unmistakeable. It produces a large tuft of fan-like basal leaves, each divided into several linear, flat segments, and with the aroma of celery. The massive flower stems can be as much as 10cm thick, and support numerous rounded umbels of bright yellow flowers.

OCCURS *on dry hillsides and cliffs, grassy and waste places, roadsides, and along ditch edges.*

PERENNIAL

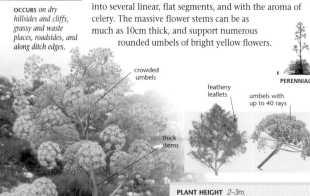

crowded umbels

feathery leaflets

umbels with up to 40 rays

thick stems

PLANT HEIGHT *2–3m.*
FLOWER SIZE *Umbels 10–15cm wide.*
FLOWERING TIME *March–June.*
LEAVES *Pinnate, bright green lobes.*
FRUIT *Elliptical, flattened mericarp, 1.2–1.5cm long, with thin wings and ribs.*
DISTRIBUTION *Throughout the region.*
SIMILAR SPECIES *Fennel (above).*

Olive

Olea europaea (Oleaceae)

This is almost certainly the most important plant in the Mediterranean; indeed botanically the region may be defined by the occurrence of olives. Groves of cultivated olives are usually heavily pruned trees with twisted trunks, and lance-shaped leaves that are grey-green above and silvery below. The flowers are small and yellowish white, borne in erect clusters. The familiar fruit ripen from green to black. Wild ancestors of the olive may still be found in old woodlands and can be distinguished by their spiny stems and smaller leaves and fruit. The Olive tree may grow up to 15m in height.

CULTIVATED in groves throughout, but sometimes naturalizes on waste ground. Grows wild in maquis and old woodlands.

leaves darker above

narrow, lance-shaped leaf

fruit 1–2.5cm long

leaf silvery white below

unripe green fruit

NOTE

For edibility, the fruit are cured in brine, oil, or salt. To extract oil, the seeds are pressed cold to produce "Extra Virgin" quality. Oil extracted by heating the seeds results in a greater yield but lower quality.

PLANT HEIGHT *Up to 15m, much less if cultivated.*
FLOWER SIZE *4–5mm wide.*
FLOWERING TIME *May–June.*
LEAVES *Leathery, 2–8cm long.*
FRUIT *Fleshy, with hard stone, green, ripening brown or blue-black.*
DISTRIBUTION *Throughout the region.*
SIMILAR SPECIES *None.*

PERENNIAL

Shrubby Jasmine

Jasminum fruticans (Oleaceae)

FOUND *growing among other vegetation or against trees, rocks, and walls in open woodland and scrub.*

A delicate, evergreen or semi-evergreen shrub, this plant is often half-hidden from view by other vegetation. It's small, trifoliate leaves with oval leaflets are scattered sparsely along the slender green, ridged stems. The bright yellow flowers grow in small clusters. They are few in number and do not have the fragrance of garden jasmines. The fruit is a small brown or black berry.

flowers in small clusters

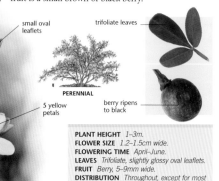

small oval leaflets

trifoliate leaves

PERENNIAL

5 yellow petals

berry ripens to black

PLANT HEIGHT *1–3m.*
FLOWER SIZE *1.2–1.5cm wide.*
FLOWERING TIME *April–June.*
LEAVES *Trifoliate, slightly glossy oval leaflets.*
FRUIT *Berry, 5–9mm wide.*
DISTRIBUTION *Throughout, except for most of the islands.*
SIMILAR SPECIES *None.*

Honeywort

Cerinthe major (Boraginaceae)

OCCURS *on roadsides, field margins, grassy or stony places, cultivated and waste land, and vineyards.*

One of the few yellow-flowered species in the borage family, Honeywort has an upright habit and distinctive leaves. The blue-green leaves are often dappled with white swellings and clasp the stem. The overlapping, leafy bracts are tinged with purple and crowd the drooping, tubular yellow flowers, which are often purple at the base.

overlapping purplish bracts

white-spotted leaves

tubular yellow flowers

ANNUAL

white ring

PLANT HEIGHT *20–60cm.*
FLOWER SIZE *1.5–3cm long.*
FLOWERING TIME *March–June.*
LEAVES *Oval, blue-green spotted with white.*
FRUIT *Two pairs of shiny black nutlets.*
DISTRIBUTION *Throughout the region.*
SIMILAR SPECIES *Var. purpurascens, which has completely purple bracts and flowers.*

Phlomis lychnitis

Phlomis lychnitis (Lamiaceae)

This small but attractive, somewhat shrubby plant has softly hairy stems and long, paired leaves which are grey and silky below. The leaf margins usually have rounded teeth. The yellow flowers are in whorls with soft-haired bracts below each whorl, so the buds appear to grow out of tufts of silk. Each flower is two-lipped, the upper lip forming a hood but not longer than the broad lower lip.

GROWS in clumps in garigue or other dry rocky and grassy places; particularly on limestone soil.

PERENNIAL

narrow linear leaves

soft, hairy bracts

upper lip forms hood

flowers in whorls

PLANT HEIGHT 2–60cm.
FLOWER SIZE 2.5cm long.
FLOWERING TIME May–July.
LEAVES Opposite, linear, hairy below.
FRUIT Four nutlets within the calyx.
DISTRIBUTION Portugal, Spain, and S. France.
SIMILAR SPECIES Jerusalem Sage (P. fruticosa), which is bigger with oval leaves.

Yellow Woundwort

Stachys recta (Lamiaceae)

This is a variable and slightly aromatic plant with erect, often curved stems. The oblong or lance-shaped leaves are hairy and finely toothed, in opposite pairs, and found mostly on the lower part of the stems. Borne in whorls and opening from sepals with very pointed teeth, the pale yellow flowers each have a widely-separated upper and lower lip marked with faint crimson dots.

INHABITS dry, rocky, and waste places, stony paths and tracks, garigue and maquis; usually on limestone.

PERENNIAL

wide open flower mouth

finely-toothed leaf

faint red marks

PLANT HEIGHT 20–80cm.
FLOWER SIZE 1.5–2cm long.
FLOWERING TIME May–July.
LEAVES Opposite, oblong, finely toothed.
FRUIT Four nutlets within the calyx.
DISTRIBUTION Throughout the region.
SIMILAR SPECIES Sideritis hirsuta, which has leafier stems and densely whorled flowers.

Verbascum sinuatum

Verbascum sinuatum (Scrophulariaceae)

This is one of the most common *Verbascum* species in the region. A statuesque plant, it may be recognized by its robust stem with regular, curving branches, producing a candelabra effect. It bears numerous flowers in several small and isolated clusters; each flower with five slightly unequal, bright yellow petals, and stamens that have long, purple hair on the brush-like filaments. The leaves are densely covered with woolly hair both above and below. Those at the base are in a distinctive rosette and have strongly undulated margins.

OCCURS in sandy, rocky places, roadsides, grassy fields, waste ground, and sometimes in coastal habitats.

BIENNIAL

isolated clusters of flowers

NOTE

The leaves of this plant and the related Verbascum thapsus have soothing and expectorant properties, and are used to treat rasping coughs. They were also used in herbal tobacco.

curved side branches

flowers bloom sporadically

wavy-margined basal leaf

violet-haired filaments

PLANT HEIGHT 0.5–1.50m.
FLOWER SIZE 2–3cm wide.
FLOWERING TIME April–July.
LEAVES Oblong, with grey woolly hair and very wavy margin.
FRUIT Rounded capsule containing numerous seeds.
DISTRIBUTION Throughout the region.
SIMILAR SPECIES Verbascum chaixii of N.E. Spain, France, and Italy, which has leaves that are less lobed and wavy.

Large Snapdragon

Antirrhinum latifolium (Scrophulariaceae)

This snapdragon often has numerous branches, which produce abundant pale yellow flowers. Each flower is two-lipped with a pronounced, slightly darker "palate"– a raised fold that seals the flower against small insects that might steal the nectar without pollinating them. The whole plant is often densely covered with hair.

FOUND *on rocky ground, against old walls and cliffs, close to old buildings, or on cultivated ground.*

lance-shaped leaves

pale yellow petal tube

deep yellow palate

erect flower-clusters

PERENNIAL

PLANT HEIGHT *0.6–1m.*
FLOWER SIZE *3.5–4.5cm long.*
FLOWERING TIME *April–August.*
LEAVES *Lance-shaped, untoothed, dark green.*
FRUIT *Oval, hairy capsule.*
DISTRIBUTION *N. Spain, S. France, and Italy.*
SIMILAR SPECIES *Snapdragon (p.90), which often has yellow flowers, but is hairless.*

White Henbane

Hyoscyamus albus (Solanaceae)

All parts of this member of the potato family are extremely poisonous. It is a clump-forming plant covered with sticky hair, and often produces erect stems with regular ranks of leaves on either side. The flowers have five creamy yellow petals and a dark purple throat, though sometimes this is absent. The fruit capsule is supported by the conspicuous, hairy calyx, which has five flared teeth.

INHABITS *waste ground, rubbish dumps, old walls, around human habitation and farm buildings.*

purple throat (sometimes absent)

greenish yellow flowers

flowers in one-sided clusters

ANNUAL/PERENNIAL

PLANT HEIGHT *30–90cm.*
FLOWER SIZE *2–3cm long.*
FLOWERING TIME *February–September.*
LEAVES *Oval with jagged edge, hairy.*
FRUIT *Capsule within a toothed calyx.*
DISTRIBUTION *Throughout the region.*
SIMILAR SPECIES *Henbane (H. niger), which has pale yellow flowers with brown veins.*

Evax pygmaea

Evax pygmaea (Asteraceae)

Also known as *Filago pygmaea*, this is a stemless, understated member of the daisy family that may easily go unnoticed. It forms several rosettes of oblong or spoon-shaped leaves. In the centre of each rosette nestles a greenish yellow flowerhead of minute tubular florets and pointed bracts, often surrounded by smaller flowerheads.

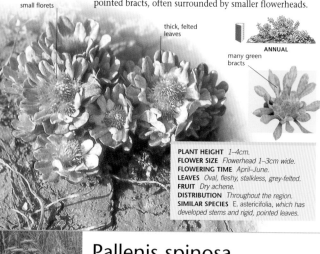

small florets

thick, felted leaves

ANNUAL

many green bracts

PLANT HEIGHT *1–4cm.*
FLOWER SIZE *Flowerhead 1–3cm wide.*
FLOWERING TIME *April–June.*
LEAVES *Oval, fleshy, stalkless, grey-felted.*
FRUIT *Dry achene.*
DISTRIBUTION *Throughout the region.*
SIMILAR SPECIES *E. astericifolia, which has developed stems and rigid, pointed leaves.*

Pallenis spinosa

Pallenis spinosa (Asteraceae)

This plant has side branches that often grow longer than the central ones, and woody-based stems. It has a few narrow stem leaves but most of its leaves are basal and spoon-shaped. The bright yellow flowers have both disc and ray florets and are surrounded by a ruff of 5–8 narrow, long, leafy green bracts which have sharp spine-tips.

spine-tipped bract

spoon-shaped basal leaf

outer ray florets

central disc florets

ANNUAL/BIENNIAL

PLANT HEIGHT *15–50cm.*
FLOWER SIZE *1.8–2.5cm wide.*
FLOWERING TIME *April–July.*
LEAVES *Mostly basal, softly hairy, untoothed.*
FRUIT *Small achene with silky hair.*
DISTRIBUTION *Throughout the region.*
SIMILAR SPECIES *Fleabane (Pulicaria dysenterica), which does not have spines.*

Helichrysum stoechas

Helichrysum stoechas (Asteraceae)

A common dwarf shrub, *Helichrysum stoechas* is well adapted to the driest conditions of the region. It produces a mound of hairy, upright stems covered with linear, white-felted leaves that have inrolled margins to conserve moisture, and which have a strong curry-like smell. The flowerheads consisting of many bright yellow tubular florets grow in rounded clusters, each surrounded by semi-transparent, papery bracts.

FORMS *mounds on dry, sandy or rocky ground, garigue, open maquis, and sand dunes; often near the sea.*

PERENNIAL

narrow leaves

yellow tubular florets

papery bracts

clusters of flowerheads

persisting dead brown flowers

NOTE

The "everlasting" properties of the flowers are much in demand for dried flower arrangements. An essential oil is also extracted from the strong-smelling leaves for use in aromatherapy.

PLANT HEIGHT *20–50cm.*
FLOWER SIZE *Flower clusters 1.5–3cm wide.*
FLOWERING TIME *April–July.*
LEAVES *Narrow, 2–3cm long, with inrolled margins.*
FRUIT *Small achene.*
DISTRIBUTION *Throughout the region.*
SIMILAR SPECIES *H. italicum, which is less mound-forming and has a more upright habit.*

Golden Samphire

Inula crithmoides (Asteraceae)

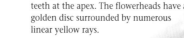

GROWS *on rocky coasts and on salt marshes, occasionally inland, particularly in E. Spain.*

This is an attractive and late-flowering member of the daisy family that branches mainly from the base producing a number of erect, leafy stems. The fleshy leaves are almost linear, but broaden towards their tips, often with three teeth at the apex. The flowerheads have a golden disc surrounded by numerous linear yellow rays.

PERENNIAL

golden yellow central disc

ascending leaves

flowers in loose clusters

PLANT HEIGHT *Up to 1m.*
FLOWER SIZE *2.5–3cm wide.*
FLOWERING TIME *July–October.*
LEAVES *Linear or lance-shaped, fleshy.*
FRUIT *Achene with a tuft of white hair.*
DISTRIBUTION *Throughout the region.*
SIMILAR SPECIES *Dittrichia viscosa, is sticky with a resinous smell and has broader leaves.*

Cocklebur

Xanthium strumarium (Asteraceae)

FOUND *in damp, disturbed places, particularly alongside streams and rivers; originally from North America.*

This unusual plant is best recognized by its characteristic leaves rather than the flowers, which are small and inconspicuous and are borne in groups of a single sex. The leaves are long-stalked and broadly triangular with a bristly surface. The small male flowers sit above the female ones, which go on to develop into an egg-shaped fruiting head covered in tough, hooked spines.

triangular leaf

leaf with bristly surface

PERENNIAL

hooked bristles on fruit

developing green fruit

PLANT HEIGHT *20–100cm.*
FLOWER SIZE *5–6mm wide.*
FLOWERING TIME *June–September.*
LEAVES *Oval-triangular, slightly toothed.*
FRUIT *Egg-shaped, spiny, 1.5–2.5cm long.*
DISTRIBUTION *Throughout the region.*
SIMILAR SPECIES *Spiny Cocklebur (X. spinosum) has spines at base of leaf-stalks.*

Cotton Lavender

Santolina chamaecyparissus (Asteraceae)

This clump-forming shrub is strongly aromatic and often grown in gardens. The upright stems have numerous silvery grey, linear leaves, each with attractively toothed or lobed margins. The button-like flowerheads are always above a leafless section at the very tops of the stems, and consist of bright yellow or cream-colored disc florets, surrounded by grey, cottony bracts.

FORMS *large clumps in dry, rocky habitats in mountains or lowlands; planted on roadsides.*

PERENNIAL

small hairy bracts

yellow disc florets

flowers at stem tips

PLANT HEIGHT *20–70cm.*
FLOWER SIZE *Flowerheads 0.6–1cm wide.*
FLOWERING TIME *June–September.*
LEAVES *Linear, silvery, toothed margins.*
FRUIT *Oblong, hairless achene.*
DISTRIBUTION *Throughout the region.*
SIMILAR SPECIES *Cottonweed (Otanthus maritimus), which has branching flowerheads.*

Yellow Chamomile

Anthemis tinctoria (Asteraceae)

There are many *Anthemis* species in the region, most of them with yellow discs and white ray florets, but this common species has all-yellow flowers. It is generally a rather untidy plant with many branches, and may be identified by its leaves; these are divided into very finely-toothed leaflets, which are dark green above but woolly with white hair below.

GROWS *on cultivated and wasteland, roadsides, scrub, and dry places near the sea.*

finely divided leaflets

solitary flowerheads

all-yellow flowers

PERENNIAL

disc florets

PLANT HEIGHT *30–60cm.*
FLOWER SIZE *2.5–4cm wide.*
FLOWERING TIME *May–August.*
LEAVES *Pinnate, narrow-toothed.*
FRUIT *Spiky, hairless schene.*
DISTRIBUTION *From France eastwards.*
SIMILAR SPECIES *A. maritima, which is a coastal plant with white ray florets.*

Yellow Milfoil

Achillea tomentosa (Asteraceae)

This plant has many spreading non-flowering shoots with characteristic leaves. Almost rounded in cross-section, the leaves are divided into numerous, tiny segments, almost like a short-bristled brush. They are often covered in cottony hair when young. The flowerheads are on long, hairy stalks, with bright yellow disc- and short-rayed florets.

GROWS *in dry, grassy habitats and open scrub, or in bare, stony places and banks; up to 1,200m.*

all-yellow flowers

flat-topped clusters

PERENNIAL

downy, bristly leaf

PLANT HEIGHT *15–30cm.*
FLOWER SIZE *Flowerhead 5–8mm wide.*
FLOWERING TIME *May–July.*
LEAVES *Narrow, with pimply surface and downy hair.*
FRUIT *Flattened, hairless achene.*
DISTRIBUTION *Spain, S. France, and Italy.*
SIMILAR SPECIES *None.*

Field Marigold

Calendula arvensis (Asteraceae)

In spite of its bright colour, this is an small, erect plant is inconspicuous with simple, sometimes toothed, lance-shaped leaves. The flowers have a small disc in the centre and fairly broad, strap-shaped ray florets on the outside. The fruit is a collection of large, curved, spiny achenes clustered like orange segments.

OCCURS *on disturbed ground of roadsides, cultivated fields, waste ground, and olive groves.*

ANNUAL

central small disc

simple stem leaves

broad ray florets

spiny, curved achene

PLANT HEIGHT *15–25cm.*
FLOWER SIZE *1–2cm wide.*
FLOWERING TIME *March–October.*
LEAVES *Alternate, lance-shaped, dark green.*
FRUIT *Curved, knobbly, or spiny achene.*
DISTRIBUTION *Throughout the region.*
SIMILAR SPECIES *Pot Marigold (C. officinalis) has larger, bright orange flowers.*

Silver Ragwort

Senecio cineraria (Asteraceae)

There are several *Senecio* species in the region, but with its attractive silver foliage this particular plant is perhaps the easiest to identify, though it is sometimes regarded as a near-identical subspecies of *Senecio bicolor*. The stems are thickly covered with white, felt-like hair. The leaves are dark green above, but silvery with hair below, and their narrow lobes are often curled upwards so the whole plant appears to be silvery grey. The golden yellow flowers are in domed and stalked clusters.

INHABITS *sandy or rocky places on the coast; also grown in gardens where various cultivars exist.*

PERENNIAL

yellow disc and ray florets

leaves often curled

erect flowering stems

flowers in rounded clusters

NOTE

The juice from the leaves of Silver Ragwort has been used to treat conjunctivitis, but one should be cautious as it contains alkaloids that are highly toxic to the liver.

PLANT HEIGHT *30–60cm.*
FLOWER SIZE *Flowerhead 1.2–1.5cm wide.*
FLOWERING TIME *May–August.*
LEAVES *Very narrow lobed, silvery below.*
FRUIT *Achene with a tuft of hair.*
DISTRIBUTION *Throughout the region.*
SIMILAR SPECIES *S. gallicus, which is a smaller, more delicate plant with grey-green leaves and green or red stems.*

Yellow Star-thistle

Centaurea solstitialis (Asteraceae)

OCCURS *in dry fields, garigue, stony ground, roadsides, olive groves, grassy habitats, and embankments.*

This slender, branching thistle often provides a splash of colour when most of the other vegetation has turned brown and dry. The small, bright yellow florets sit above a rounded head of woolly bracts that end in a long, straw-coloured spine. The upper leaves are narrow and untoothed, while the lower are lance-shaped and pinnately lobed.

brilliant yellow ray florets

pinnately lobed basal leaves

solitary flowerheads

long, sharp spines

BIENNIAL

PLANT HEIGHT *30–80cm.*
FLOWER SIZE *Flowerheads 1.2–1.8cm wide.*
FLOWERING TIME *June–September.*
LEAVES *Upper lance-shaped; lower lobed.*
FRUIT *Achene with long hair.*
DISTRIBUTION *Throughout the region.*
SIMILAR SPECIES *Red Star-thistle (p.98), which has similar spines but red florets.*

Carthamus lanatus

Carthamus lanatus (Asteraceae)

FOUND *on fallow and waste ground, cultivated land, vineyards, and olive groves.*

This is a rather weedy-looking plant with straw-coloured stems that branch towards the top. The stem leaves are lobed or toothed with spiny margins, and the whole plant is covered with white, woolly hair. The flowerheads are solitary, producing just a small tuft of yellow florets with a cluster of spiny bracts below.

narrow tuft of florets

lobed or toothed leaves

pale yellow flowers

spiny bracts

ANNUAL

PLANT HEIGHT *30–70cm.*
FLOWER SIZE *2–3cm long.*
FLOWERING TIME *June–August.*
LEAVES *Pinnate with spiny lobes, numerous.*
FRUIT *Dark brown achene.*
DISTRIBUTION *Throughout the region.*
SIMILAR SPECIES *C. arborescens of S. Spain, which is much taller with a woody base.*

downy stem

Urospermum

Urospermum dalechampii (Asteraceae)

The attractive, pale yellow flowerheads of this plant are
a common sight along roadsides in the Mediterranean
region. They have numerous strap-shaped ray florets,
sulphur yellow at the base and paler towards the tip, and
very often – though not always, a black central spot. The
hollow stems thicken towards the top to join the plump
involucre, which has broad, downy bracts, often with
dark violet margins. The stems are covered with fine,
downy hair and bear smaller, stalkless leaves. The lance-
shaped leaves are pinnately divided with triangular lobes,
and often wavy margined. The dark achene has a long
pappus of feathery brown hair.

FORMS *small colonies in
grassy ground, field
edges, wasteland, olive
groves, and cultivated
and fallow ground.*

PERENNIAL

lobed
basal leaf

wavy
margins

central black
spot

numerous
ray florets

strap-shaped
florets finely
toothed at tips

deeper yellow
towards centre

NOTE

Urospermum *comes
from the Greek word
meaning "tailed
seed" referring to the
"beak" or filament
that connects the
achene to the
pappus of hair; this
is more noticeable in
U. picroides.*

PLANT HEIGHT *25–40cm.*
FLOWER SIZE *3.5–5cm wide.*
FLOWERING TIME *April–August.*
LEAVES *Lower leaves pinnately lobed, upper unlobed.*
FRUIT *Achene with a long beak and brown hair.*
DISTRIBUTION *Throughout the region.*
SIMILAR SPECIES *U. picroides, which has long, pointed bracts with
long, white bristles, and achenes with white hair.*

Spanish Oyster Plant

Scolymus hispanicus (Asteraceae)

Well adapted to the arid conditions of sandy soil, Spanish Oyster Plant always looks fresh and green, and is covered in abundant flowers even in midsummer when other plants are scorched and brown. It has irregularly branching stems with numerous spiny, thistle-like leaves, which merge with spiny wings that run down the stem. The bright orange-yellow, stalkless flowerheads – each made up of conspicuous ray florets – are produced in the leaf axils, with several in flower on each stem.

OCCURS *on sandy soil of waste and fallow ground, roadsides, olive groves, and along the coast; always in the open.*

BIENNIAL/PERENNIAL

NOTE

The sweet-tasting, fleshy root of this plant may be eaten, raw or cooked, as a vegetable, though the root is not particularly large. It may also be dried, roasted, and ground, and used like coffee.

spiny green shoots

leaves up to 8cm long

strap-shaped ray florets

spiny wings on stem

PLANT HEIGHT *30–100cm.*
FLOWER SIZE *2–3cm wide.*
FLOWERING TIME *June–September.*
LEAVES *Alternate, narrow, and very spiny, especially towards the top.*
FRUIT *Achene with short bristles.*
DISTRIBUTION *Throughout the region.*
SIMILAR SPECIES *S. grandiflorus, which is smaller but with larger flowers and very hairy bracts.*

Scorzonera hirsuta

Scorzonera hirsuta (Asteraceae)

This plant belongs to a group known as Viper's Grasses, which, unusually for dandelion-like plants, have narrow, unlobed leaves. In *Scorzonera hirsuta*, almost all the leaves are arranged at the lower half of the stem, and are almost linear, tapering to a fine point, and covered with wispy grey hair. The flowers are made up of yellow strap-shaped ray florets that have toothed edges.

INHABITS *grassy and rocky habitats, roadsides, and embankments; usually on undisturbed sites.*

tapering leaf

ray florets yellow below

PERENNIAL

usually unbranched stem

linear leaves towards base

PLANT HEIGHT *20–30cm.*
FLOWER SIZE *2–3cm wide.*
FLOWERING TIME *April–June.*
LEAVES *Linear, with wispy grey hair.*
FRUIT *Achene with long, dense hair.*
DISTRIBUTION *N.E. Spain, S. France, Italy, and Sicily.*
SIMILAR SPECIES *Black Salsify (S. hispanica).*

Chondrilla

Chondrilla juncea (Asteraceae)

By the time the flowers appear on this plant, almost all the leaves have died down, so that the plant seems little more than a jumble of very narrow, branching grey-green stems (the name *juncea* means "rush-like"). The stalkless flowers, which are produced only sparingly and have just a few ray florets, arise directly from odd points along the stem. The leaves are variable in shape.

THRIVES *in sandy or stony ground, garigue, hillslopes, and other dry, open places.*

narrow, straight bracts

8–12 ray-florets

stalkless stem leaves

PERENNIAL

grey-green stems

PLANT HEIGHT *40–100cm.*
FLOWER SIZE *0.9–1cm wide.*
FLOWERING TIME *June–September.*
LEAVES *Lower leaves: oblong and lobed; upper leaves: small, linear, stalkless.*
FRUIT *Achene with a long pappus of hair.*
DISTRIBUTION *Throughout the region.*
SIMILAR SPECIES *None.*

Wild Tulip

Tulipa sylvestris (Liliaceae)

This is the most widespread tulip in the region. Its usually solitary flowers have yellow pointed tepals which are often flushed with green or red on the outside. Like other tulips, the overall shape of the flower is determined by the weather. In dull or cool conditions, the tepals form a narrow bullet shape, but in still and hot weather they open out wide to form a six-pointed star. The leaves are very narrow, channelled, and slightly blue-green in colour.

FORMS *colonies in fields, scrub, open woodlands, hillsides, and mountain meadows; often cultivated.*

PERENNIAL

pointed tepals

tepals often flushed red (or green)

flower closed in cool weather

narrow, linear leaf

slightly recurved tepals

NOTE

This species rarely sets fruit and often spreads by underground stolons that form new bulbs some distance away. It is believed to have been derived from the ssp. australis, which fruits freely.

PLANT HEIGHT 15–40cm.
FLOWER SIZE 4–7cm long.
FLOWERING TIME *April–May.*
LEAVES *Linear, basal, and channelled.*
FRUIT *Capsule, but rarely produced.*
DISTRIBUTION *Throughout the region.*
SIMILAR SPECIES *Subspecies* australis, *which has flowers only 2–3.5cm long and a more pronounced red flush.*

Century Plant

Agave americana (Agavaceae)

This native of Mexico has a rosette of very large, fleshy, grey-green or variegated leaves with spine-tipped margins. The flowers are not produced until the plant is at least 10 years old, when a 7m stem is formed. This has 20 to 30 horizontal branches, each supporting large clusters of tubular yellow flowers. The plant dies after flowering.

OCCURS *on steep, rocky cliffs near the coast, though often planted on garden terraces.*

stiff, erect leaves

spiny-toothed margins

PERENNIAL

PLANT HEIGHT Up to 2m, or 7m in flower.
FLOWER SIZE 7–9cm long.
FLOWERING TIME June–August.
LEAVES Up to 2m long, spiny-margined.
FRUIT Three-sided capsule.
DISTRIBUTION Throughout the region.
SIMILAR SPECIES Yucca (Yucca gloriosa) has narrower leaves and pendent creamy flowers.

Sternbergia

Sternbergia lutea (Amaryllidaceae)

This autumn-flowering species looks similar to a crocus but has six (not three) stamens, and a short scape or stalk below the flower. It produces a tuft of green leaves up to 1.5cm wide at the same time as it flowers. The flower has six equal, golden yellow tepals emerging from a green spathe.

GROWS *in stony or grassy places, scrub, pastures; often in hills and low mountains.*

golden yellow tepals

PERENNIAL

6 stamens

dark green leaves

PLANT HEIGHT 10–25cm.
FLOWER SIZE 4–5cm long.
FLOWERING TIME September–October.
LEAVES Linear, 0.7–1.5cm wide.
FRUIT Berry-like capsule with three parts.
DISTRIBUTION Throughout the region.
SIMILAR SPECIES S. colchiciflora has smaller flowers appearing after the leaves have died.

Common Jonquil

Narcissus jonquilla (Amaryllidaceae)

This daffodil has a remarkably sweet scent. It has been cultivated to form many varieties, and is much used in the perfume industry. The bright yellow flowers are produced in clusters of two to five, and each has an exceptionally long, cylindrical tube between the yellow tepals and green ovary.

FORMS *clumps in damp meadows and other damp, grassy habitats; frequently grown in gardens.*

shallow corona

leaves 2–4mm wide

spreading tepals

narrow, chanelled leaf

papery spathe

PERENNIAL

PLANT HEIGHT *Up to 20cm.*
FLOWER SIZE *2.2–3.2cm wide.*
FLOWERING TIME *March–May.*
LEAVES *Narrow-linear, grooved, dark green.*
FRUIT *Three-parted capsule.*
DISTRIBUTION *Spain, France, and Italy.*
SIMILAR SPECIES *N. requienii, which has solitary or paired flowers with little fragrance.*

Hoop-petticoat Daffodil

Narcissus bulbocodium (Amaryllidaceae)

This small but very distinctive daffodil has a golden yellow, relatively long, cone-shaped corona, surrounded by very narrow, pointed tepals that curve backwards, and which are often flushed green on the outside. The flowers are solitary on the stems, and the leaves are extremely narrow and grass-like.

OCCURS *as extensive colonies in mountain pastures, rocky ground, and sandy hillsides, often at altitudes exceeding 1,000m.*

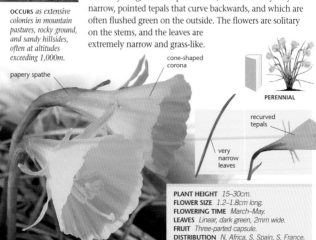

papery spathe

cone-shaped corona

PERENNIAL

recurved tepals

very narrow leaves

PLANT HEIGHT *15–30cm.*
FLOWER SIZE *1.2–1.8cm long.*
FLOWERING TIME *March–May.*
LEAVES *Linear, dark green, 2mm wide.*
FRUIT *Three-parted capsule.*
DISTRIBUTION *N. Africa, S. Spain, S. France.*
SIMILAR SPECIES *White Hoop Petticoat Daffodil (N. cantabricus) has white flowers.*

Provence Orchid

Orchis provincialis (Orchidaceae)

This attractive orchid is notable for its yellow flowers, an uncommon colour within the *Orchis* genus. The flowers are in clusters of up to 20, though in the subspecies *pauciflora*, in the east of the region, there may be as few as three to seven. The lower lip is only slightly lobed and often folded backwards, usually with small red or orange spots, and there is a long upwardly-curving spur at the back. Mostly basal, the leaves are dark glossy green, spotted or blotched with purple-brown.

OCCURS *in maquis, garigue, open woodland, scrub, grassy places, and hillslopes, often forming colonies.*

greenish yellow flowers

folded lower lip

PERENNIAL

NOTE

This and several other European orchids produce a faint scent of vanilla from their flowers. The culinary vanilla pod is the seed capsule of a tropical species of orchid Vanilla planifolia.

lance-shaped leaf

spur

dark brown spots

spots on lower lip

PLANT HEIGHT *15–35cm.*
FLOWER SIZE *Lower lip 0.8–1.2cm long.*
FLOWERING TIME *March–May.*
LEAVES *Basal in a rosette, lance-shaped to oblong, with dark spots.*
FRUIT *Capsule containing many tiny seeds.*
DISTRIBUTION *Throughout, except the Balearic Islands.*
SIMILAR SPECIES *Dacylorhiza romana and D. sambucina, both of which have yellow-flowered forms but unspotted leaves.*

Yellow Bee Orchid

Ophrys lutea (Orchidaceae)

Yellow Bee Orchid is a variable plant, but is still easily recognized as no other *Ophrys* species has such a clear yellow lip. Each flower, which usually faces upwards, has three green sepals, and two small yellowish green, roughly triangular petals. The flower lip is brown with a glossy speculum and a broad, yellow, three-lobed margin, with a notch in the central lobe. However, a form in Greece, subspecies *melena*, has a blackish lip with only the narrowest yellow margin. The lower lip produces sex pheromones that attract male *Andrena* bees, which in attempting to mate with the flower effect pollination.

GROWS *in scattered clumps in garigue, rocky, and grassy places, pine woodland, and open scrub; common on road verges.*

small green petals

flowers face upwards

PERENNIAL

narrow-margined form

3-lobed yellow margin

NOTE

Orchid flowers turn through 180 degrees as the petals start to unfurl, as can be seen by the twisted ovary at the flower's base. So, technically, all orchid flowers are upside-down.

PLANT HEIGHT *10–30cm.*
FLOWER SIZE *Lower lip 1.2–1.8cm long.*
FLOWERING TIME *March–May.*
LEAVES *Oval to broadly elliptical, mostly basal.*
FRUIT *Capsule containing many tiny seeds.*
DISTRIBUTION *From S. France eastwards.*
SIMILAR SPECIES *Sawfly Orchid (p.112), which occasionally has green sepals and a hairy yellowish lip margin.*

Glossary

Many of the terms defined here are illustrated in the general introduction (pp. 8—13). For anatomical terms see also pp. 8—9. Words in *italics* are defined elsewhere in the glossary.

ACHENE A dry, one-seeded, non-splitting fruit, often with a *pappus*.

AXIL The angle between two structures, such as the leaf and stem or the midrib and a small vein.

BOSS A rounded projection on a petal.

BRACT A leaf-like organ at the base of a flower stalk.

BRACTEOLE A small leaf-like organ at the base of secondary branches of the flower stalk.

BULBIL A small, bulb-like organ that breaks off to form a new plant.

CLADODE A modified stem that looks like a leaf.

CLEISTOGAMOUS Used to describe self-pollinating flowers, whose petals and sepals never open.

CYME A flower cluster with lateral branches, each ending in a flower.

DISC FLORET In the Daisy family, a flower in the central part of the *flowerhead*, whose petals are fused into a tube.

DRUPE A fleshy fruit whose seeds are surrounded by a tough coat.

DRUPELET One of several small *drupes* joined together.

EPICALYX A ring of sepal-like organs just below the true sepals (calyx).

ESCAPE A non-native plant, commonly cultivated and now established in the wild.

FALL PETAL In the Iris family, one of three outer petals that droop down.

FAMILY A classification unit, grouping one or more closely related *genera*.

FLORET One of a group of small or individual flowers usually clustered together to form a *flowerhead*.

FLOWERHEAD A cluster of *florets*.

GARIGUE An uncultivated, often rocky habitat of dwarf shrubs and low plants, brought about by past grazing.

GENUS (pl. genera) A unit of classification grouping together one or several closely related *species*.

KEEL PETAL The lower, fused petals of a *peaflower*, folded and curved like the keel of a boat.

LIP A protruding petal, as in members of the Orchid and Mint families.

MAQUIS A thicket formation of shrubs.

MERICARP A one-seeded portion of a fruit formed by splitting from the rest.

NATURALIZED A non-native plant, introduced into a region, and now forming self-sustaining populations.

NECTARY A nectar-secreting gland.

PANICLE A branched flower cluster, with stalked flowers.

PAPPUS A tuft of hair on *achenes* or other fruits, which aids wind dispersal.

PEAFLOWER A flower, usually from the Pea family, with sepals fused into a short tube, and with a usually erect upper petal, two *wing petals*, and two *keel petals*.

RACEME An unbranched flower cluster where each flower is clearly stalked.

RAY/RAY FLORET The outer, distinctively flattened flower of a daisy-type *flowerhead*.

RECURVED Curved backwards or splayed out.

RHIZOME A (usually underground) thickened stem which serves as a food storage organ.

RUNNER A stem which creeps along the ground, forming roots at intervals and eventually separate plants.

SAPROPHYTE A plant which feeds on rotting vegetation in the soil.

SCAPE A leafless stem bearing flowers.

SILICULA A fruit of the Cabbage family, less than three-times as long as broad, and often rounded.

SILIQUA A fruit of the Cabbage family, long and linear or pod-like.

SIMPLE Describes leaves not divided into leaflets.

SPADIX A fleshy *spike* with many unstalked flowers.

SPATHE The large, hooded *bract* that encloses a *spadix*.

SPECIES A classification unit defining a group of similar individuals that breed true in the wild.

SPECULUM A shiny, shield-like patch on the petals of some orchids.

SPIKE An unbranched flower cluster, with unstalked flowers.

SPUR A hollow, cylindrical or pouched structure projecting from a flower, usually containing nectar.

STANDARD PETAL The upright, upper petal of a *peaflower*, often larger than the others.

STEMLESS Describes a plant without an obvious stem; the flower stalk arising directly from the ground.

STIGMA The part of the flower that receives pollen.

STIGMA-RAY A *stigma* that forms a star with radiating branches.

STIPULE A leaf-like organ at the base of a leaf stalk.

STYLE The part of the female reproductive organ that joins the ovary to the *stigma*.

SUBSHRUB A small perennial with some stems that become woody.

TEPAL Petals and sepals that cannot be distinguished.

TRIFOLIATE A leaf made up of three distinct leaflets.

UMBEL A flat-topped or domed flower cluster with all the stems originating at the same place.

WING PETAL The lateral petals of many flowers, particularly orchids and *peaflowers*.

Index

Acknowledgments

THE AUTHOR would like to thank his wife, Christine, for her constant support.

PICTURE CREDITS
Picture librarian: Richard Dabb, Claire Bowers.

Abbreviations key: a = above, b = bottom, c = centre, f = far, l = left, t = top, r = right.

The publishers would like to thank the following for their kind permission to reproduce the photographs:

Benton, Ted: 66 cbl.
Dorn, Wendelin: 115 tr.
Fletcher, Neil: 5 ca; 16 cb, tl; 18 tl, cla, clf, br; 19 tr, cla, crb, br; 20 tl, cb; 21 tl, cb; 22 tl, cra, clb, bl; 23 tl, cb; 24 clb, br; 25 tr, crb; 26 tl, cb; 27 tl, cb; 28 tl, cla, br; 29 tr, cb; 30 tl, cra; 31 tl, cb; 32 tl, cla, clb, br; 33 tr, cla; 34 tl, cra, clb, bl; 37 tl, crb; 38 tl, cb; 39 tl, cb; 40 tl, clb; 41 tl, cb; 42 tl; 44 tl, cla, clb; 46 tl, cb; 47 tr, cla; 48 tl, cra; 49 tr, crb, bl; 50 tl, cla, clb; 52 tr, cbl; 53 tr, cbl; 54 tl, cb; 56 tl, cra; 57 tr, cra, crb, cb; 58 cbl; 59 tr, cla, crb;61 tr, cb; 62 tl, clb, br; 63 tr, cla; 64 tl, cb; 65 tr, cb; 66 tl, cra; 67 tr, cb; 69 tr, cla, crb, br; 70 tl, cla, clb, br; 71 tr, cb; 72 tl, clb; 73 tr, cla, crb, br; 74, clb; 75 tr, cla, crb, br; 77 tr, cla, crb, br; 78 tr, cb; 79 tr, cr, crb, bl; 80 clb, br; 81 tr, ca; 82 fl, clb; 83 tr, ca; 84 tl, cb; 85, tr, cla, crb, br; 86 tl, cl, clb, br; 87 crb, br; 88 tl, cb; 89 crb; 90 tl, cla, clb, br; 91 tr, ca; 92 tl, cbl; 93 tr; cra; 94 tl, cb; 95 tr, cla, crb, br; 96 tl, cb; 97 tr, cb; 98 tl, cla, clb, br; 99 tr, cb; 100 tl, cla, clb, br; 101 tl, cb; 102 clb, br; 104 tl, cl, clb; 105 tr, crb; 106 tl, cb; 108 tr, cb; 108 tl, cb; 110 tl; 111 tr, cb; 112 tl, cra, clb; 114 tl, cla, clb, br; 115 cla, crb; 116 tl, cb; 117 tr, cb; 118 tl, cb; 119 tr, cra, crb, br; 120 tl, cb; 121 tr, cla, crb, br; 122 tl, cla; 123 tr, cb; 124 clb, bl; 125 tr, cb; 126 tl, cb; 127 tr, cla, crb; 128 tl, cb; 129 tr, cb; 130 tl, cb; 131 tr, cb; 132 tl, cla, clb; 133 crb, br; 134 tl, clb, br; 135 tr, crb, br; 136 tl, cra, clb; 137 tr, cb; 138 tl, cra, clb, bl; 139 tr, cb; 140 tl, ca, clb, br; 141 tr; 142 tl, cbl; 143, tr, cla; 145 tr, cla, crb; 146 tl, cbl; 147 tr, cla, crb, br; 148 tl, cla, clb, bl; 149 tr; 150 tl, cbl; 151 tr, cra, crb; 152 tl, cla, clb, br; 153 tr, cla; 154 tl, cbl; 155 tr, cb; 156 tl, cla, clb, br; 157 br; 158 tl, cla, clb, br; 159 tr, cra, crb, bl; 160 tl, cra, clb; 161 tl, cb; 162 tl, cla; 163 crb; 164 tl, cbl; 166 tl; 167 tr, cb; 169 tr, cb; 171 tr, cla; 172 tl, cb; 173 tr, cla, crb, bc; 174 tl, clb, br; 175 tr, cla, crb, br; 176 tl, cb; 177 tr, cla, crb, br; 178 tl, cb; 179 tr, cra, crb, bl; 180 tl, cbl; 181 tr, cla, crb, cb; 182, tl, cla, clb, br; 183 tr, cbl; 184 tl, cra, clb; 185 tr, cra, crb, bl; 186 tl, clb, br; 187 tr, cb; 188 tl, cla, clb; crb, br; 190 tl, cb; 191 tr, cb; 192 tl, cra, clb, bl; 193 tr, cb; 194 tl, cla, clb, br; 195 crb, br; 196 tl, cra; 197 tr, cb; 198 tl, cla; 199 tr, cla, crb, bcr; 200 tl, cbl; 202 clb, br; 103 tr, cb; 204 clb, bl; 205 tr, cra, crb, bl; 206 clb, br; 207 tr, cb; 208 tl, cla, clb, br; 209 tr, cb; 210 tl, cb; 211 tr, cra, crb, bl; 212 tl, cb; 213 tr, cra; 215 tr.
Gibson, Chris: 3 ca; 17 tr; 24 tl; 30 bl; 33 crb; 35 tr, cb; 36 cb; 37 cla, br; 40 cla, br; 42, cra; 43 tr, cb; 45 tr; 47 crb, bc; 50 br; 56 clb; 58 tl,

59 bcr; 60 tl, cbl; 66 clb; 68 tl, cal; 72 cal; 74 tl, cla, br; 76 tl; 80 tl; 89 tr, cla, cbr; 93 bl; 102 tl; 104 crb; 122 clb, br; 124 tl, cra; 133 cla; 145 cbr; 149 cla; br; 151 bl; 153 crb, br; 157 crb; 163 tr, cla; 164 tr, cb; 170 tl, cra, cbr; 171 crb, cb; 174 cla; 186 cla; 188 br; 195 tr, cla; 202 tl, cla; 206 cla.
Hall, Derek: 51 tr; 53 cra; 103 tr, cbr; 105 br; 110 ca; 170 clb; 189 tr, cla; 196 clb, bl; 201 crb; 204 tl; 215 ca.
Hughes, Barry: 15 cla, cra; 42 clb, bl; 44 cbl; 45 cbr; 49 cra; 53 bl; 56 br; 72 br; 112 bl; 115 cb; 127 cbr; 135 cla; 141 ca; 143 crb, br; 149 crb; 160 bl; 166 cra, clb, bl; 198 clb, br; 201 br; 204 cra; 214 tl, cra, clb, cb.
sophy.u-3mrs.fr/sophy.htm: 15 cla, tr; 24 cla; 30 clb; 33 bl; 51 ca; 63 crb, br; 68 clb, br; 93 crb; 109 tr; 133 tr; 134 cla; 136 cbl; 157 tr; cla; 184 cbl; 201 tr, cla; 206 tl, cla; 213 crb.
Vega, Daniel: 87 tr, cla.
Visetti, Giovanni: 109 cbr.

All other images © Dorling Kindersley